Genteel Pagan

Genteel Pagan

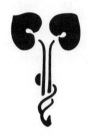

The Double Life of Charles Warren Stoddard

Roger Austen

EDITED BY JOHN W. CROWLEY

The University of Massachusetts Press

AMHERST

Copyright © 1991 by
The University of Massachusetts Press
All rights reserved
Printed in the United States of America
LC 91-8502
ISBN 0-87023-750-0
Designed by Jack Harrison
Set in Linotype Walbaum and Bernhard Modern (display)
by Keystone Typesetting, Inc.
Printed and bound by Thomson-Shore, Inc.

Library of Congress Cataloging-in-Publication Data
Austen, Roger.
    Genteel pagan : the double life of Charles Warren Stoddard / Roger
Austen ; edited by John W. Crowley.
        p.   cm.
    Includes bibliographical references (p.   ) and index.
    ISBN 0–87023–750–0 (alk. paper)
    1. Stoddard, Charles Warren, 1843–1909—Biography.
    2. Homosexuality and literature—United States—History—19th
century.
    3. Authors, American—19th century—Biography.
    I. Crowley, John William, 1945–   . II. Title.

    British Library Cataloguing in Publication data are available.

    Frontispiece: Charles Warren Stoddard in 1869, age twenty-six

All photographs are taken from Stoddard's Album, The Bancroft Library,
University of California, Berkeley.

Mark Twain's previously unpublished words quoted here are © 1991
by Edward J. Willi and Manufacturers Hanover Trust Company as
Trustees of the Mark Twain Foundation, which reserves all reproduction
or dramatization rights in every medium. Quotations are made
with the permission of the University of California Press and
Robert H. Hirst, General Editor of the Mark Twain Project.
Each citation is identified in the notes by an asterisk.

Contents

Abbreviations

Works by Charles Warren Stoddard that are cited frequently in the text are identified there by the following abbreviations:

CRP   "Confessions of a Reformed Poet." Draft of an unpublished autobiography. The Bancroft Library, University of California, Berkeley.

CSS   *Cruising the South Seas: Stories by Charles Warren Stoddard.* Edited by Winston Leyland. San Francisco: Gay Sunshine Press, 1987. (Reprints selections from *SSI* and *ITD.*)

CUC   *A Cruise Under the Crescent: From Suez to San Marco.* Chicago and New York: Rand, McNally, 1898.

D   Diary.*

EE   *Exits and Entrances: A Book of Essays and Sketches.* Boston: Lothrop, 1903.

FPHC   *For the Pleasure of His Company: An Affair of the Misty City: Thrice Told* (1903). San Francisco: Gay Sunshine Press, 1987.

IFP   *In the Footprints of the Padres.* San Francisco: A. M. Robertson, 1902.

IFPr   *In the Footprints of the Padres.* Revised edition. San Francisco: A. M. Robertson, 1911.

IH   "Island Heights." Unpublished notebook. The Bancroft Library, University of California, Berkeley.

ITD   *The Island of Tranquil Delights: A South Sea Idyl and Others.* Boston: Herbert B. Turner, 1904.

M   *Mashallah! A Flight into Egypt.* New York: Appleton, 1881.

SSI   *South-Sea Idyls.* Boston: J. R. Osgood, 1873.

TH   *A Troubled Heart and How It Was Comforted at Last.* Notre Dame, Indiana: *Ave Maria* Press, 1885.

*Stoddard's voluminous diaries were widely dispersed after his death in 1909, through the sale of his books and papers by Charles E. Goodspeed, the Boston dealer. They are now to be found, under a confusing array of titles, in several research libraries. When known, the locations of diaries from specific periods are indicated in the notes. I have been unable, however, to verify the location of a few passages that are quoted.—ED.

Editor's Preface

JOHN W. CROWLEY

At this rate, the most I can hope for, it seems, is posthumous publication.
—Roger Austen to John W. Crowley, 30 May 1979

I FIRST MET Roger Austen in January 1977, in his author's query to the *New York Times Book Review.* He was undertaking a biography of Charles Warren Stoddard and looking for leads to archival sources. Although I knew nothing at all about Austen—for instance, that he was about to publish *Playing the Game: The Homosexual Novel in America,* a pioneering work in what was to become "Gay Studies"—I did know about some Stoddard letters at the Massachusetts Historical Society. I had discovered them in 1969, in the course of researching my own biography of George Cabot Lodge, an author even more obscure than Stoddard.[1]

I well remembered Stoddard's letters to "Bay" Lodge: scrawled in purple ink on stationery headed "The Bungalow" in a hand that had defied my deciphering. Their friendship had prompted me to read Carl Stroven's "Life of Charles Warren Stoddard," an unpublished Duke dissertation completed in 1939, which hinted discreetly but did not elaborate on Stoddard's homosexuality. I could not imagine why Austen (or anyone else) would be bothering with Stoddard in 1977 unless it were to flesh out these hints. There was, I thought, no strictly literary reason to revive a writer whose prose was as purple as his ink: a product of "The Genteel Tradition" at its stupefying worst. I remained curious about Stoddard himself, however, and so I wrote to Austen about the papers in Boston.

We quickly moved to a first-name basis in an increasingly prolific and lively correspondence in which, among other things, Roger informed me about gay life in the nineteenth century and since, and I offered him advice and encouragement. His project was important, I believed (and still do), for its bearing on Victorian sexuality, a matter to which feminist scholars had first drawn my attention. Our letters crisscrossed the continent—between Syracuse and San Francisco, Spokane, and Los Angeles—until the end of 1983. Seven months later Roger consummated a desire for death with which I had, by then, become all too familiar.

Austen was nothing if not enthusiastic about the Stoddard book, confident he would surpass the modest success of his first one.[2] "*Playing the Game* now seems to me to be an embarrassment—too flip and glib, especially as I work on Stoddard in some depth," he wrote from San Francisco on 29 August 1978. Roger had immersed himself so deeply into Stoddard, in fact, that he felt like a medium of his subject's sensibility. "The nice thing about it," he said, "is that my moods so often coincide with Stoddard's that the bio will at least be a fairly perceptive re-creation of how he felt at any given time" (10 September 1978). Such intense identification, however, sometimes threatened Roger with emotional contagion. He later warned me not to make the same mistake with W. D. Howells in a biographical book I started in 1980.[3] "Don't get so far inside Howells that you can't get out again. Actually, I do think that this sort of happened to me in San Francisco, damn it all. After getting 'into' Stoddard and his letters and diaries and then, sort of under that general spell, putting everything down day after day from his fraidycat and warped and spoiled crybaby point of view, this perspective became somewhat engrained" (6 July 1980). What aroused Roger's disdain, but subtly appealed to him as well, was Stoddard's using "infantilism as a sort of armor," boasting of "his babyishness, as if it were an immediate explanation and defense of his inability to cope" (16 April 1979).

Neither a fraidycat nor a crybaby, Roger was nonetheless given to depression, against which his sardonic wit served as a tensile armor. Over the course of our friendship, I came to notice the oscillation of his moods between elation and despair. Circumstances often seemed to conspire in favor of the latter.

Soon after he finished it, Roger concluded that *Genteel Pagan: The*

Double Life of Charles Warren Stoddard would not only fail to outsell *Playing the Game*, but would also likely fail to be published at all. He had devoted two full years (1977–1978) to the biography, living in abstemious isolation while he did the extensive research and drafted nearly four hundred pages. Rejected by Harper & Row (on the basis of sample chapters) and by the Stanford University Press (after merely two days!), the book was gathering dust, early in 1979, on an agent's desk in New York. It was subsequently declined by Avon Books, by the University of Chicago Press, and (after unconscionable delay) by McGraw-Hill. Roger had predicted that the "problem" with *Genteel Pagan* would be "similar to that of *Playing the Game:* commercial presses will think it too esoteric, university presses will think it too popular in style if not in content" (16 April 1979). He was alternating between disappointment and exasperation at the time he deadpanned about "posthumous publication" for *Genteel Pagan* (30 May 1979), adding in a later letter: "At this point, I just want to get the fucking thing published, and expect to make zero money on it, so anything short of a vanity press would do" (6 July 1980).

I read the draft myself during the summer of 1979, which I spent in Seattle at the University of Washington. In order to shrink his expenses in accord with his dwindling savings, Roger had moved from California to live with his mother in Sunnyside, Washington, and I arranged to meet him face-to-face. At lunch on campus one day, he handed me the Stoddard typescript, which I eagerly read overnight and returned with my reactions. I could see a few problems in the book—it was diffuse and overwritten in spots—but the narrative was mainly clear and potentially compelling, and the new light cast on Stoddard and his times was unquestionably valuable. To Roger I stressed the book's virtues and assured him earnestly that publication was only a matter of time.

I was never to see him again—a tall and slender black-haired man in his forties (a year younger then than I am now), whose broad features were dominated by thick eyeglasses. Roger's hearing aid was attached to the black plastic frames. Despite a stapedectomy in 1971, he suffered from chronic tinnitus (ringing and buzzing in the ears); and I found it far more difficult to conduct our conversations in person than I had by mail. So did he, of course. I began to understand that his near deafness was a major reason for his loneliness. "More and more I feel like Emily Dickinson in Amherst," he had written from Sunnyside, "with only the bees and the bobolinks for company" (30 May 1979).

Much later—after his death, in fact—I gleaned a few basic facts about Roger Austen. A native of Washington, he was born (under another name, apparently)[4] on 25 September 1935—thus sharing his birthday, as I once pointed out to him, with William Faulkner. He grew up, like Charles Warren Stoddard, in a fundamentalist Christian household against which he rebelled. (Austen never mentioned his father to me, and he seldom alluded to his mother and sister, with whom his relationship was evidently strained.) After graduating from the University of Washington, he earned an M.A. from Seattle University, a Jesuit school, with a thesis on Tennessee Williams; and he subsequently taught English at the junior high and high school levels. After a year at the University of California, Irvine, Austen moved to San Francisco in the early 1970s in order to establish himself as a free-lance writer. His articles and reviews appeared in such places as the *Bay Guardian, San Francisco Theatre, California Living, San Francisco Review of Books*, and the *Advocate;* for a while he was even the host of a television talk show. Then, after serving as managing editor of the *Sentinel*, a gay paper, he wrote ad copy for Capwell's department store in Oakland. The income from this job supported his work on *Genteel Pagan* throughout 1977 and the following year, during which he wrote full-time, having quit Capwell's.

In the fall of 1980, when other options had been exhausted, I persuaded Roger to submit *Genteel Pagan* to the Syracuse University Press, where I could at least put in a partisan word, for what it might be worth. Along with a tepid reader's report, the typescript was returned late in November with detailed suggestions for revision. The door to later acceptance was left ajar, but Roger could never bring himself to do what he did not think was necessary.

The anonymous reader had been annoyed by what he (unlikely she) regarded as "excessively personal reflection on incidents and the character"—a personal note that arose from Roger's imaginative fusion with Stoddard, but also from his sense of himself as a self-appointed gay gadfly and provocateur. He was especially fond of those passages in which he had attempted—at the risk of transgressing the generic boundary between biography and fiction by his use of novelistic interior monologues—to bring his subject to life: "through a little bit of extrapolation, to paint the view in Stoddard's eyes." He worried that if such "personal reflection" were to be cut from *Genteel Pagan*, its vitality would be "snuffed out" (2 December 1980).

"I took it for granted, in reading the MS.," I replied, "that part of the point of the book was to suggest that there may be a distinctive gay aesthetic in American literature and elsewhere and that you were trying to liberate CWS from the distorting context of genteel American letters, in part by writing about him in a deliberately ungenteel and unacademic way." The reader, I speculated, had been resisting the self-conscious "feyness" (as I called it, for lack of a better word) of *Genteel Pagan*, "its very voice and manner." This was, I thought, "a political issue and nothing less" (9 December 1980).

Roger conveyed his relief that I at least had grasped "exactly what I am about" and had perceived "correctly, I think, the pointlessness of re-doing it in a dry, academic style from every point of view" (16 January 1981). Thus there were to be no revisions by Roger himself, although he acknowledged a need "to improve and streamline the Stoddard" (2 December 1980). A few months earlier, when he was reworking one chapter into an article for the *Journal of Homosexuality* (the editorial board of which he had been invited to join), he had become aware "of how awful it was and how sloppy much of that Stoddard ms. now seems to me to be" (20 August 1980). The next year he had a brainstorm, in the bathtub, about how to enliven the opening: by skipping over Stoddard's early years to his first trip to Hawaii in the late 1860s; that is, to focus immediately on the moment of his sexual initiation. "But rather than getting excited and bubbling up and racing on ahead in my mind, I just stopped there, too languid to bother thinking beyond that." The book now resembled "a huge baby elephant who will *not* fly, for 400 pages, try as I will" (16 January 1981). The following July, although he was gratified by Carl Stroven's praise for the draft,[5] Roger was still feeling languid: "At present, though, the status of future drafts remains, like so much else, unclarified."

"Like so much else" was a wry allusion to recent events in Roger's life. In May 1981, when he had sent Stroven a copy of *Genteel Pagan*, he had also mailed the original typescript to me for safekeeping. "Since I may well not continue to serve as babysitter of this project," he had explained ominously, "it has occurred to me that I should do something to see that all the research does not go down the drain." Roger had been pondering *The Life and Death of Yukio Mishima*, and he added: "Like Mishima, I do not much believe in old age anyway, and my objections, like his, are aesthetic" (15 May 1981). This was, as I dreadfully perceived, a suicide note.

The downward gyre in Roger's mood had been gradual. Despite the disheartening response to *Genteel Pagan*, he had launched yet another book in the summer of 1980. This was *Boomerang*, an account of the 1919 and 1920 scandal over homosexual activities at the United States Naval Training Station in Newport, Rhode Island, in which incident the young Franklin Delano Roosevelt, then Assistant Secretary of the Navy, and several other prominent figures had been caught up.[6] Roger had soon lost himself in research—he was ploughing through forty-seven hundred pages of documents he had obtained from the National Archives—and he was thrilled by the sheer drama of the affair. "Nothing has given me more pleasure than putting this thing together: it is like a melodramatic mystery story that writes itself, with cliffhanging endings for each chapter bubbling up from the material of their own accord" (24 July 1980). Here was promise for trade publication, which would reroute his career from the dead-end detour of *Genteel Pagan*. When Roger learned that another scholar was also exploring the Newport story, he was alarmed at first, lest he be scooped, and finished the book at breakneck speed.[7] At the end of the year, as he pitched *Boomerang* to Scott Meredith and several other agents in New York, Roger was soaring again. He could envision a movie spin-off from his best-seller.

No sale. Another dead end.

An even harder blow fell in February 1981, when Roger discovered that Gore Vidal, a writer he admired even as he rejected his line on homosexuality, had made a mockery of him. In *Views from a Window*, a collection of old interviews, snippets of Vidal's correspondence with Judy Halfpenny (Roger, for some reason, could not believe this name was real) were quoted. "At one point Ms. Halfpenny, in one of her alleged letters to Vidal, asks what he thinks of my 'depressing' book" (10 February 1981).

Roger explained that he had sent Vidal a copy of *Playing the Game* in 1977, with the hope he might review it. Vidal had responded privately instead, committing himself only to the equivocal exclamation, "What a Job!" and promising to take account of Roger in a piece he was writing for the *New York Review of Books*. But when the essay, "Sex Is Politics," finally appeared in *Playboy* (January 1979), it contained no mention of *Playing the Game*.

"Well, in his next alleged letter to Ms. Halfpenny," Roger continued, with a mock-legalistic punctiliousness that did not mask his dismay, "Vidal allegedly wrote that I was 'dull,' that I hadn't had 'much of a life,' living in the ghetto as I was forced to do, that he couldn't stomach fag-novels, that he had never heard of most of them I had mentioned, etc."[8] For Roger, this was "devastating," although he claimed to have "developed a protective scab over the wound which allows me to view everything with some detachment." Self-defensively, he attributed Vidal's remarks to his own wounded vanity at having been lumped with so many earlier writers of "fag-novels" in *Playing the Game* and thus robbed of his pride of place as a homosexual novelist—one who steadfastly denied, however, that there was any such thing. "Rather than appearing on page 1 of my book, he comes in at about page 200 . . . and this may have been eye-opening in a rather unpleasant way for him, although I should think that he might have been more amused than distressed" (10 February 1981).

Badly wounded as he was, Roger also had to wonder if Vidal was right in some respects. Certainly, his present life was "dull." He was feeling gloomy and restive in Sunnyside, a name that seemed grotesquely inapt, marooned there as he was, washed up, it seemed, by his writing disasters. Early in 1981, he was talking vaguely about getting a teaching job at a prep school in Florida or reapplying to the doctoral program in English at the University of California, Irvine, from which he had discontentedly dropped out some ten years before.

Then out of the blue came that uncannily lucid letter announcing some other, fatal, plans. Roger had reached what seemed to him a logical impasse. Increasing deafness and age had deranged his "former savoir faire in the bedroom" and effectively ended his sex life, so he explained, and his literary career, meant to afford him compensatory mental pleasure, had brought only more frustration:

> I am left with a rather bleak prospect: no one wants to go to bed with me or publish me, and I find this state of affairs "unacceptable," as outraged politicians use that word to convey haughty disdain. "The heart asks pleasure first," Emily Dickinson says in that poem of gradually decreasing demands, and I have been finding myself being pushed further and further down the ladder of the options in her poem.[9]

Living in Sunnyside as a prodigal son was unbearable—"I have felt as if I were growing into a permanent town misfit"—and life anywhere else was no longer appealing. So Roger had joined the Neptune Society, a death-with-dignity organization, in order to prearrange his cremation and the scattering of his ashes at sea. (Roger had a strong wish not to be buried.) First, however, he intended to enjoy a last holiday; and he promised he would be writing once more from some unspecified "balmy climes" (15 May 1981).

From one of "Sheraton's two magnificent hotels on the beach at Waikiki" (as the printed caption put it), a picture postcard arrived a few days later. Its message was probably intended as a macabre parody of tourist breeziness: "If I told you that I came here to trace CWS's footsteps, you would not believe me. Nor should you. I came here with a friend [a male prostitute hired in Los Angeles] to have an unabashed fling and, I say, let 19th Century Literature be forgotten" (30 May 1981). But the trip to Hawaii was a pointedly ironic reference to Stoddard, whose situation Roger had ruefully contrasted to his own at the end of the earlier suicide letter:

> Finally, without wanting to wallow in self pity, I might mention that in doing the Stoddard notes [the documentation he had finished before mailing me the book] I couldn't help compare myself with the great amount of lovingkindness and support that was showered on this poor man by the rich and the famous throughout so many years of his life. If only there were a [William Sturgis] Bigelow to invite ME to a Tuckernuck right now, for instance, or a Bay Lodge to smile at me across the dinner table. To some extent Vidal was correct in assessing that I had not had "much of a life" (though his objection was not pertinent in the context he was discussing) in comparison with grand gaudy gay characters who have lived, for a time, at least, in splendor. Dying well may be the Best Revenge, if one has little choice in the matter. (15 May 1981)

Receiving this letter and then the postcard—*Genteel Pagan*, sent fourth-class, was long delayed in transit!—gave me a jolt, to say the least. Roger had carefully orchestrated his movements and mailings so as to prevent anyone's stopping him. However distressed I might be, I was also helpless by his design. The paper trail was cold, and it did not lead to the fatal site—Santa Monica, as it turned out.

Except that the overdose did not work. Two nights in a row Roger vomited the pills and then desisted from a third attempt. "Surprise/ groannn: Yes, I am still here, in spite of it all," he wrote laconically. "I had thought these letters were at an end, but they seemed destined to go on forever" (18 June 1981). I hoped sincerely that this was true, but my relief was alloyed by wariness. After suffering through the days when I had only to suppose that Roger was dead—there had been no telling if I would ever know for certain—I felt somewhat abused. But our epistolary friendship survived along with Roger himself despite the psychic lesions in him and me.

I offered, with some private misgivings, to shelter him for a while, if he wished; but he preferred to stay with a friend in Rhode Island, closer to the scene of *Boomerang*, until he could recover his bearings. He promised to come for a weekend visit in August but never did. He read a lot that summer, taking perverse delight in John Kennedy Toole's post-humously published *A Confederacy of Dunces*. That Toole had killed himself in despair of his literary career made it all the easier for Roger to enter into the darkly comic madness of *Dunces:* "The thing that made reading the novel especially poignant for me, as you can guess, was what I saw going on in the author's mind as he wrote this thing out in an attempt to preserve his mental balance" (31 July 1981). Having re-gained his own balance for now, Roger reviewed his options for living and settled on graduate school, but only after an interim year of re-cuperation and money-making.

Living in Spokane with his sister, Roger found another ad-writing position with a local department store, The Crescent. The work was easy, he said, and relatively lucrative. "In writing copy I have to hold back, of course, since I cannot possibly indulge in the sort of sentence structure which is characteristic of my style. It is similar, I guess, to speaking a foreign language—you just shift into COPYWRITING and the garbage flows out effortlessly" (1 November 1981). Keeping closely to himself on the job, he enjoyed what he imagined to be the puzzle-ment of his coworkers about him.

As always, Roger read voraciously; he was developing an interest in D. H. Lawrence, who, he believed, was an unacknowledged homosex-ual whose evasions had been abetted by his heterosexual biographers. Although he was already, in effect, planning his dissertation, Roger was extremely anxious about graduate school. As an older student (now forty-six)—and a nearly deaf one—would he really fit in? He fretted about retaking the Graduate Record Exams and seesawed about the relative merits of Stanford, Berkeley, UCLA, and Irvine. At my sugges-tion, he added the University of Southern California to his list. I knew someone there who might, on my recommendation, go out of the way to help Roger gain admission and financial aid.

Meanwhile Roger was trying to settle the score with Gore Vidal, whose polemical piece on "Neo-Con Homophobia" had appeared in *The Nation*.[10] Mentioned in passing—in support of Vidal's contention that serious work on homosexuality is ignored in the United States whereas "all-out attacks on faggots are perennially fashionable in our better periodicals"—was *Playing the Game*, "(a remarkably detailed account of American writing on homosexuality)," no review of which Vidal had ever seen.[11]

That the man who had himself not reviewed *Playing the Game* and who had attacked Roger personally was now citing his book in an ostensibly friendly manner—this was too much. In a long letter to the editor, Roger vented his hostility, accusing Vidal of obscurantism in his views on homosexuality and hypocrisy in his treatment of books like *Playing the Game*: "Which are we to believe? The Vidal who suggests in *Views from a Window* that 'fag novels' and books about 'fag novels' are a tedious business and should not be encouraged? Or the Vidal who appears to be regretting in *The Nation* that these interesting books have remained unreviewed? Both? Neither?"

Vidal took Roger's questions seriously enough to reply to them at length, and he also apologized for his remark about Roger's "dullness": "He has quite enough to contend with in his lonely vocation without a stab, as it were, in the back by me." But Roger was not mollified. He claimed, in fact, that he had "chosen not to read Vidal's rebuttal" (15 February 1982). Emboldened by his appearance in *The Nation*, "which is pretty much enemy territory for me" (15 February 1982), Roger thought about writing (but never did) a letter to *The New Republic* denouncing FDR, whom he considered a liberal sacred cow in need of debunking, for his role in the Newport scandal.

As the day for admissions notification approached, Roger was favoring USC more and more over Stanford (which ultimately rejected him anyway). He saw graduate school not as a move toward an academic career—he cared nothing about that—but as a commitment to the intellectual life, which would fill the void left by his attenuated sexual life:

> I have more or less come to the conclusion that my days as a sexpot are over. I was not gracious in acquiescence, as you will remember from my pilltaking last year, and I am not altogether a good sport about it now, since I still loathe anti-climax of any sort, most particularly in terms of my life. But USC seems to give me some sort of viable alternative, something that will lend a little logic and dignity to my days. (16 March 1982)

Unfortunately, Roger's attending USC did not work out that way. A prophetic sign of trouble was the bureaucratic snarl that cast his acceptance temporarily into doubt. Then he failed to receive a fellowship. Although he was willing enough to be a teaching assistant instead,

Roger worried that his poor hearing would be an impediment in the classroom. Certainly, some of the courses he took were stimulating, and he performed well for the professors he thought were sympathetic to his work and his peculiarities. Still, having expected far more personal attention than came his way, he felt aggrieved and neglected; and his off-campus life in a squalid Los Angeles apartment was extremely depressing. Roger considered leaving USC after his first semester but then resigned himself to sticking out the year. Over the holidays, probably on Christmas itself, he reread *A Confederacy of Dunces* to soothe his "troubled psyche": "If only I could rise to Toole's capacity to smile at capricious Fortuna!" (26 December 1982).

In January, Roger's stability seemed again to be wobbly. He told me of semi-delirious dreams, induced by the medicine he was taking for a cold that had blocked what was left of his hearing:

> On top of which is the inversion of the winds and weather known here as the Santa Anas: the wind blows in from the desert and yet all is still and tremulous, about 85 degrees, and to my weak, sick eyes yesterday, as I sat eating my sandwich at noon, all appeared to be in a lurid, garish Technicolor, with everyone walking around in shorts and whole months appearing to me to have been lost in a weird sort of way, as if it were suddenly June. I felt zonked by the Contac and further zonked by the strange, surrealistic ebb and flow of people, so nonchalant and mindless, as they walked by in their shorts. It was not until on last night's news that I heard a Santa Ana was in effect that I felt a bit comforted, knowing that the strangeness was not all a figment of my imagination. (12 January 1983)

This mood passed as Roger buried himself in work, producing one long paper on Lawrence and another on Jack London for his spring courses. His letters about these projects, so full of life and intellectual engagement, lulled me into thinking he was coping well enough.

Then I received another of those picture postcards from a resort hotel, this time from Puerto Vallarta. "Interesting news is coming your way. All is delightful here in the penthouse" (14 June 1983). I knew what that meant, and I urgently called my friend at USC to alert him to Roger's intentions. I hoped that since he had tipped us off to his whereabouts, he might be found in time.

The shock of this suicidal drama was less profound for me, inured by earlier experience, than for a friend I had put in contact with Roger a couple of years before. They had established an independent epistolary relationship, and to this now mutual friend Roger sent not merely a postcard but a voluminous diary that charted his final days in harrowing detail. The diary was quite bizarre but so "composed" (in a literary sense) that the two of us were suspended between dread and suspicious disbelief. Only when I heard from Roger directly did I fully comprehend that this latest attempt to kill himself had not been an elaborate hoax, that Roger had been—and still was—deadly serious.

He had truly taken another overdose, laced with Chivas Regal. Having booked a penthouse room with a small pool, he had swallowed the drugs, sipped the scotch, and, after removing his hearing aid, slipped into the water, expecting to drown when the pills and whiskey knocked him out. He was rescued literally at the last minute by the Mexican police, who were summoned by an old friend who had agreed at first to assist Roger's suicide and then had blown the whistle. Roger never forgave him for this "treachery."

Afterwards he wrote to explain that he had wanted to spare *me* a farewell letter, "since what is there to be said a second time when it is so difficult to think of anything to say the first time round?" He had redrawn his will, he added, to name me his heir and literary executor. (From reading the diary, I was already aware of this decision, but far from at ease with it.) "The $ is simply a way of saying thanks, that the Stoddard ms reverts to you or to Syracuse, as you choose, and there is of course no connection between the $ and getting the ms published, for instance, by a vanity press or some such" (27 June 1983). He hated to think that all his research might go to waste; there were cartons of Stoddardiana that ought to be saved for some scholar's future reference.

Roger had obtained more pills, Dalmane and codeine, and he was going to take them after the Fourth of July, wishing not "to detract from the celebration of our nation's birthday next week." Like Mishima, his model, he believed he had a right to die in his own fashion, without the misguided interference of supposed friends:

> Mind you, it has been most difficult to these last few weeks begin again and try to carve and craft out yet one more finale, especially since I had put so much care in having everything work out to a "T" in Puerto Vallarta. Longing to escape empty days, I am forced now for awhile to slog through them in a tiresome and languid and dull way, thanks to those who have presumed to play God. Whose life is it, anyway? . . .
>
> It all boils down to what I define as life on acceptable terms. I have found life to be increasingly unacceptable since about 1977 or 1978. That is all that need be said. (27 June 1983)

But the letter went on and on. There was a postscript dated "July 4th" and another, handwritten and marked simply "Wednesday," that ended: "I am just basically impatient to get everything over with & hopeful that, this time, there is no snag." He was holding back this letter so that it would be sure to reach me too late for any intervention.

I heard nothing again until 5 August 1983: "I have now concluded that it is my destiny to live: I have no heart to make further attempts, as each one takes an enormous emotional toll, and the huge, almost unbearable chagrin which follows takes a further toll until I am reduced to jelly. Amazingly, I seem to have a strange, strong capacity to bounce back, at least to some degree." Buoyed by his turnabout, Roger vowed to return to USC and pursue his Lawrence project. There was even some hope now for *Genteel Pagan:* "Yesterday I had a long chat at [*sic*] the people of One institute, subsidized by a gay millionaire from New Orleans, and they are interested in reading the Stoddard and perhaps seeing it into print. So I am cheered" (12 August 1983).

Then, after a long silence, I received what was to be the last letter from Roger: "I've decided to sell all my books & return to Washington, and give up all further research and writing & reviewing on gay lit subjects, since it so obviously has not been worthwhile" (26 November 1983). In what was to be my final reply, I tried, as always, to be encouraging. "I hope that Washington will not prove to be worse than LA," I concluded, "and I hope also that you will let me know how you are doing" (11 December 1983).

I think I sensed at the time that he would not. Roger had been telling our mutual friend that he felt too embarrassed to write me any longer, having "failed" me by dropping out of USC after I had gone to so much trouble to get him accepted. I knew, however, that his admission had depended finally on the strength not of my recommendation but of his own merits; and it did not really matter to me if he stayed or left, as long as he lived.

I kept track of Roger now at second hand; I received occasional updates from our mutual friend, to whom he was still writing. Since returning to Washington, Roger had become purposefully inert: he did no reading or writing except an occasional letter; he spent most of his waking hours spinning the television dial, seeking the most inane programs he could find.

Early in August 1984, I was notified by a Seattle lawyer that Roger had died, leaving me his estate of roughly three thousand dollars. Later

I was able to determine that Roger had played out a variation on the Puerto Vallarta scenario. On 19 July 1984, he checked into a Seattle hotel; a few hours later he drowned in nearby Lake Sammamish. He was forty-eight. His ashes were scattered at sea. If he had written any farewell letters this time, I did not receive one. Indeed, it was never confirmed to me, by the lawyer or anyone else, that Roger's death was a suicide.

The distribution of his few assets was contested by Roger's family, and I felt no more desire to resist them than I did to be his "residuary beneficiary." From the start, my primary interest had been to foster Roger Austen's work, and so I waived claim to anything except the literary rights to *Playing the Game* (in case of a new edition some day) and to Roger's unpublished manuscripts, of which I already possessed *Genteel Pagan* and his seminar papers from USC.[12] The cartons of Stoddard research material failed to surface; all of Roger's papers had evidently been destroyed. As for *Boomerang*, which I never read, I ceded all rights, as Roger had once requested, to his friend in Rhode Island, to whom the original typescript had been sent before the first suicide attempt. Who knows if that book will ever appear.

I have no doubt, however, that Roger was sincere when he suggested that none of my "inheritance" need be dedicated to publishing *Genteel Pagan*. But I know he hoped I would do everything in my power to see it into print—and not through a vanity press. Soon after his death, I tried to place the book with a few university presses. None considered the unedited typescript to be publishable: the tone was unduly flippant, the narrative prolix; and a certain intellectual sophistication was lacking, in part because the book had been written before the scholarly explosion in gender studies. At the very least, heavy editing was needed, as well as an introduction that would place Austen's work in a current frame of reference.

What follows is a version of *Genteel Pagan* revised by me to such speci-fications. The typescript has been reduced to about two-thirds of its original length through the omission or compression of long block quo-tations, the pruning of digressions, and an overall tightening of the nar-rative. Roger's style has also been "refined" in two senses: both polished and also tonally altered in places to sound less flippant. I am an invete-rate reviser of my own prose, and I have not hesitated to revise Roger's when it seemed advantageous for economy or clarity. Thus, at least in some passages, I have acted as a ghostwriter, if not exactly as a coauthor.

Those "personal" passages that once seemed so integral to Roger's purposes now strike me as being awkward and unnecessary; some of them have been revised or deleted. The chapter divisions are mine because Roger never decided on any, although he knew they were necessary. In chapter 5, I have replaced the original discussion of *South-Sea Idyls* with Roger's later revisions.[13] Errors in fact and/or quotation have been corrected where they have been detected, and the documentation has been painstakingly reconstructed from Roger's handwritten (and incomplete) notes, to which I have added here and there.[14]

In general, I have edited this book with the same care and rigor I would bring to one of my own, but without forgetting that it is not mine. As I have made changes, that is, I have also tried to honor the basic integrity of the text. Whether Roger would have approved of my editing I do not know. I hope so. I also do not know if or how it mattered to Roger that I am not gay, although my editing of his book must inevitably—and in ways of which I am unaware—reflect that fact. In any case, *Genteel Pagan* remains Roger's book in substance.

As I review what I have said here about my relationship to Roger, so tightly centered on our correspondence, I realize how much about him remains unsaid because it is (still) unknown to me: mainly the expanse of his life and mind beyond his letters to me. His successful career in San Francisco during the 1970s, for instance, is a conspicuous blank in my account. Roger rarely mentioned his past, and I asked no questions. There are others, I think, who must have known him far better than I ever did. But maybe not. He was an intensely private man, and he had a way of alienating his friends—so some of them have testified. He may not, finally, have trusted anyone very far. I also recognize that I have portrayed Roger at his most self-destructive. But he was far from being a feckless "victim," and I hope I have managed to capture some of his feisty spirit.

During the time he was writing ad copy in Spokane, Roger once related his strategy for avoiding office politics: "Am taking off, since tizzies have erupted at work and I choose not to get caught up in them, as my hero Bartleby would not have" (15 February 1982). In my role as editor, I have sometimes fancied that I was playing Maxwell Perkins to Roger's Thomas Wolfe. As his friend, however, I have often wondered if I were doubling the nameless narrator of Melville's tale in his dealings with the ruthlessly recalcitrant scrivener. This thought does not give me comfort, for I know how this narrator is usually read, how I read him myself when I am teaching the story: as the target of Melville's fiercest irony, a self-serving hypocrite for all of his cautiously delimited "charity" toward Bartleby.

Ah, Roger! Ah, humanity? No, in thunder! Unlike Bartleby, Roger Austen was a scrivener who preferred to write; unlike Stoddard, he deserves to be remembered for his writings.

The more formal and scholarly introduction that follows is meant to adjust for what may now seem dated in Roger's approach. In recent years, under the aegis of poststructuralism, it has become a common-place to say that language is constitutive of "reality" (and to dislodge the ordinary meaning of words by fencing them in "scare quotes"). Within the booming field of gender studies, a historicizing trend has yielded several important accounts of the formation of modern notions of sexuality, elements of which were circulating in the nineteenth-century culture that Stoddard inhabited. This historical context is largely missing in *Genteel Pagan*, produced nearly fifteen years ago in the spirit of Stonewall rather than of Foucault.

Unlike recent scholars steeped in poststructuralism, Austen understood homosexuality as a congenital and transhistorical reality. Although he granted that the perceptions, if not the practices, of same-sexuality have shifted over time, taking a recognizably modern form at the turn of the twentieth century, Austen was concerned not with the discursive representation of "homosexuality," but with the detection of homosexuality in the lives and works of premodern literary figures. The impetus to his research was "Gay Pride": a desire to unstop the (closet) door, in a Whitmanian spirit, in order to release those men, such as Charles Warren Stoddard, whose homosexuality had necessarily been concealed, at least in their writing.

Austen's argument with Gore Vidal was that the latter allegedly refused to accept "certain facts": that "(1) there is such a thing as a totally undeviating and justifiably unapologetic homosexual, and that (2) there are such things as worthwhile stories and novels written by and about gay males that can be termed, for the sake of convenience and parallelism with other minority literature, homosexual fiction."[15] The notion here of parallelism marks the affinity of Austen's aims with those of contemporaneous feminist and black critics: the definition of an "aesthetic" inherent to the writings and life experience of a distinctive "minority" group.

"As the black aesthetic of the 1970s celebrated a black consciousness in literature," Elaine Showalter remarks, "so too the female aesthetic celebrated a uniquely female literary consciousness."[16] A counterpart to Ellen Moers's innovative feminist study, *Literary Women* (1976), *Playing the Game* also resembles Jonathan Katz's encyclopedic *Gay American History* (1976), of which Austen later made use. All three books belong to a documentary or archival mode of gender studies; they are works of recovery and recanonization, of a kind now (all too readily) discredited by adherents of poststructuralist theory for their reliance on an essentialized idea of gender in their advocacy of a female or gay aesthetic.

Genteel Pagan, like *Playing the Game*, is not theoretically "sophisticated." Roger Austen was not a scholar of an academic stripe, despite his years of graduate study. By temperament and background, he was a "man of letters," and he always wrote for a general audience. I suspect he would have had neither patience nor use for much recent gender theory, even had he lived to read it. Nevertheless Austen's life of Charles Warren Stoddard, which is among the fullest and frankest biographies of nineteenth-century American homosexuals to appear so far, will undoubtedly provide grist for a variety of theoretical mills.

In bringing *Genteel Pagan* into the light, I owe a debt to those who offered me advice for revision of Austen's unedited typescript (but who are not responsible for my editorial decisions): George Arms, Robert Emmet Long, Robert K. Martin, Douglas Mitchell, and Michael Paller. Carl G. Stroven, who had been so helpful to Roger Austen, kindly provided me with photographs of Stoddard. For general encouragement I am grateful to Hayden Carruth, Richard Hall, Susan Wolstenholme, and Thomas Yingling. The production of this book would have been impossible without the able assistance, at different stages, of Margie May and Eve Crandall.

The following archives have granted me permission to quote unpublished letters in their collections: the American Antiquarian Society; the George Arents Research Library for Special Collections at Syracuse University (Charles Warren Stoddard Collection); the Bancroft Library, University of California, Berkeley (Charles Warren Stoddard Papers, C-H 53); the Clifton Waller Barrett Library, University of Virginia (Charles Warren Stoddard Collection, #8533); the Beinecke Rare Book and Manuscript Library, Yale University (Collection of American Literature); Brown University Library; The Catholic University of America

Library; the Houghton Library, Harvard University; The Huntington Library, San Marino, California; the Lilly Library, Indiana University; the Massachusetts Historical Society; Robert Louis Stevenson House, State of California, Department of Parks and Recreation, Monterey District; the Rutherford B. Hayes Presidential Center, Fremont, Ohio; Department of Special Collections, the Stanford University Libraries; the University of Hawaii at Manoa Library; The Archives of the University of Notre Dame (Charles Warren Stoddard Collection; Reverend Daniel Hudson Collection); the University of San Francisco Library.

In a revised form, a brief section of chapter 5 is derived from Roger Austen's article, "Stoddard's Little Tricks in *South Sea Idyls*," *Journal of Homosexuality* 8 (Spring/Summer 1983). Permission to reuse this material has been granted by The Haworth Press. A brief section of chapter 10 appeared originally as the Introduction to *For the Pleasure of His Company* (San Francisco: Gay Sunshine Press, 1987).

Finally, I wish to thank Clark Dougan and Bruce G. Wilcox of the University of Massachusetts Press for supporting a project that other publishers were so reluctant to consider. In these days of rampant homophobia, within government and without, to publish *Genteel Pagan* is not only a vindication of Roger Austen; it is also a welcome demonstration of good principles.

Editor's Introduction

JOHN W. CROWLEY

Known in his day primarily as a "California humorist," literarily akin to Bret Harte and Mark Twain, Charles Warren Stoddard (1843–1909) would now seem to have less significance for his work than for his life. Author of genteel poetry and exotic travel sketches that had largely been forgotten by the time of his death, Stoddard was also a lover of men at the historical moment when "homosexuality" and "heterosexuality" were being constructed by the scientific and other discourses that have organized modern common sense about human sexuality.[1]

In reviewing two of Stoddard's books that have recently been reprinted, Thomas Yingling observes that "the difference between reading *For the Pleasure of His Company* [1903] and reading the Balzac that inspired Barthes's *S/Z* is that in the Stoddard novel, the codes of homosexuality are self-consciously employed as codes." The effect is "artificial but not artful," Yingling claims, because "it was perhaps impossible in 1903 to produce a well-formed text on a discursively de-formed topic." He goes on to suggest that the very artlessness of Stoddard's only novel, whose plot is so conspicuously incoherent, makes it a "representation of sexual displacement and of the inability of the homosexual to gain a socially-defined and -sanctioned identity." Likewise the psychological vapidity of its protagonist Paul Clitheroe, the "vacuum at the center of his character," is "the textual equivalent to the vacuum homosexuality was for the West at the turn of the century."[2] Men like Stoddard, however, had little choice but to fill this vacuum for themselves as best they could, borrowing from the codes available to say who and what they were.

Soon after the turn of the century, Stoddard, then in his late fifties and in poor health, was planning to return from Washington, D.C., where he had been fired from his professorship at the Catholic University of America, to California, where he had first made his reputation in the 1860s as "The Boy Poet of San Francisco" and had later gained recognition for his travel writings from Europe and the South Seas. For a while he attached himself to the artists' colony at Carmel, where the poet George Sterling caught his eye and inspired some typically (for Stoddard) effusive letters. Deeply devoted to "darling Wolf," as he called Jack London, Sterling was nevertheless nonplussed and repelled by Stoddard's ardor. His is a "case of inversion of sex," he confided to his mentor Ambrose Bierce, who reassured Sterling after Stoddard's death that "my objection to him was the same as yours—he was not content with the way that God had sexed him."[3]

Stoddard himself told London that "I am what I was when I was born."[4] To define what he was when he was born, he would not have used the pathologizing label of "inversion," as applied to him by Sterling out of apparent "homosexual panic."[5] Moreover, he had usually been quite content with the way God had sexed him. (He did believe in God; a convert to Roman Catholicism, he remained devout to the end.) When, late in life, Stoddard encountered "Xavier Mayne" 's *Imre*, the first explicitly "homosexual" novel published by an American (albeit privately and pseudonymously), he copied a sentence into his notebook: "The silences of intimacy stand for the most perfect mutuality."[6] Stoddard had come of age before the proliferation of terms—"invert," "Uranian," "intermediate type," and so on—meant to distinguish, usually invidiously, between men seeking the mutuality of other men and those preferring "heterosexual" intimacy. His representations of his own desire were part and parcel of the discourses (and silences) that preceded the medical paradigm of "homosexuality." In the late nineteenth century, as Peter Gay remarks, homosexuals derived certain advantages from the reticence, bordering on obliviousness, of bourgeois culture: "Homosexual lovers . . . were safer in the earlier days of tight-lipped equivocations than in the later days of clinical inquisitiveness."[7]

Consider, for instance, the reception of *South-Sea Idyls* (1873), in which Stoddard made fiction of his travels in Hawaii and Tahiti during the late 1860s. The Island adventures most significant to him were undoubtedly his sexual initiation and subsequent affairs with native youths. Several tales based on these experiences have been reprinted by the Gay Sunshine Press precisely by virtue of what the publisher calls their "veiled homoeroticism," which the modern reader, it is presumed, will have no difficulty in *unveiling*.[8] *South-Sea Idyls* abounds in hints that Stoddard's intercourse with the natives had been more than meets the eye in the letter of the text. Like the word "intercourse" itself, the sexual connotations of which were as latent in nineteenth-century usage as they are dominant now, Stoddard's prose barely conceals its erotic implications—by means, as Roger Austen suggests, of an obfuscatory narrative technique.[9]

Exactly how much of Stoddard's "veiled homoeroticism" was visible to nineteenth-century readers is not easily determinable. But neither in 1873 nor in 1892, when it was republished, was *South-Sea Idyls* seen (in reviews, at least) to contain anything untoward. Except in the *Nation*, which urbanely observed that the book could not be recommended for "an invigorating and purifying tone" because the South Seas "—as it used to be said of Paris—are not a good place for deacons,"[10] the critical consensus was that *South-Sea Idyls* was a delightful example of "California humor." W. D. Howells in the *Atlantic Monthly* welcomed it "as a real addition to the stock of refined pleasures, and a contribution to our literature without which it would be sensibly poorer."[11]

"Sensibly" might now be read as possibly referring to a homoerotic subtext in *South-Sea Idyls*, but that subtext had yet to be written with modern explicitness for either Howells or Stoddard. Howells understood Stoddard's narrative pose of "prodigality" as a comic convention: "It all strikes us as the drollery of a small number of good fellows who know each other familiarly, and feel that nothing they say will be lost or misunderstood in their circle."[12] That is, what Stoddard might have meant in such homoerotic tales as "Chumming with a Savage," which Howells later called a "harmless story,"[13] went without saying among good fellows, whose appreciation of "refined pleasures" did not preclude their liminal awareness of *un*refined ones. "Drollery" covered and contained a multitude of implications, including sexual ones, which remained "harmless" *because* they were not and needed not be expressed, and thus did not invite misunderstanding. Whatever may have happened between Stoddard and his native chums was not lost within the small circle of male familiarity, but neither was it found. Indeed it was not sought.

As I have argued elsewhere,[14] this discursive system, in which silence played a crucial part, allowed such literary friends as Howells and Mark Twain to take Stoddard as a fellow good fellow even as Stoddard's same-sex preferences were not lost upon them. They "knew" about Stoddard but in a way that does not correspond to modern knowing through medicalized categories; and although they tolerated Stoddard's "homosexuality" insofar as it remained discursively marginal, they also did not hesitate to depreciate him, usually by treating him as a hapless child. From such men Stoddard could not expect complete acceptance and understanding. For that he turned at first, like many others, to Walt Whitman.

As Eve Kosofsky Sedgwick notes, Whitman became a major site for the "self-formation of many members of that new Victorian class, the bourgeois homosexual." Photographs of the bard, gifts of his books, scraps of his handwriting, gossip about him, admiring references in print—all "seem to have functioned as badges of homosexual recognition, were the currency of a new community that saw itself as created in Whitman's image."[15] As Stoddard once wrote to Horace Traubel, "Do you know what life means to me? It means everything that Walt Whitman has ever said or sung . . . He breathed the breath of life into me."[16]

After young Stoddard discovered the "Calamus" poems during the 1860s, he pressed his own first book of verse on Whitman. When the poet did not respond, Stoddard persisted, writing to profess that he was the "stranger" whom Whitman had enjoined to "speak" to him. He claimed kinship by recounting his experiences with the Pacific Islanders: "I have done wonders in my intercourse with these natives. For the first time I act as my nature prompts me. It would not answer in America, as a general principle,—not even in California, where men are tolerably bold." Stoddard went on to describe a typical night of love with one or another young native: awakening with "his arm over my breast and around me." "You will easily imagine," he asserted, "how delightful I find this life. I read your Poems with a new spirit, to understand them as few may be able to." Stoddard closed with a request for a photograph.[17] Whitman obliged, adding in a note: "I cordially accept your appreciation, & reciprocate your friendship. . . . Those tender & primitive personal relations away off there in the Pacific islands, as described by you, touched me deeply."[18]

In 1870, when he was preparing to return to the Islands, Stoddard explained to Whitman that he needed to "get in amongst people who are not afraid of instincts and who scorn hypocrisy." Only "barbarism" had given him "the fullest joy of my life," and he begged the poet's blessing: "I could then go into the South Seas feeling sure of your friendship and I should try to live the real life there for your sake as well as my own."[19] "As to you," Whitman replied, "I do not of course object to your emotional & adhesive nature, & the outlet thereof, but warmly approve them." But then he gently reproved Stoddard for looking unnecessarily far afield for that outlet: "But do you know (perhaps you do,) how the hard, pungent, gritty, worldly experiences & qualities in American practical life, also serve? how they prevent extravagant sentimentalism? & how they are not without their own great value & even joy?"[20]

From Michael Lynch's excellent study, we know that Whitman had adapted the word "adhesiveness" from phrenology to his own purposes—to have "an exclusive reference to same-sex love."[21] Whether or not Stoddard grasped this special usage in Whitman's letter, he never adopted the term himself. He seems also to have missed the point of Whitman's contrast between "South-Sea Bubbles" (the title Bret Harte had encouraged Stoddard to use for *South-Sea Idyls*) and the hard, pungent, gritty, and worldly realities at home. In effect, Whitman was challenging Stoddard's understanding of the spirit of his poems. What Stoddard considered to be the "real life" of the Islands Whitman saw as exoticism that amounted to "extravagant sentimentalism."

Stoddard's notion of "barbarism" was not only sentimental; it was also thoroughly in keeping with the prevailing racialism and imperialism of the American Gilded Age.[22] When Bierce once twitted Stoddard for going to the Islands to have love affairs with "nigger" boys,[23] he was exposing in his own contempt the underside of Stoddard's "tender and primitive relations." The very imprecision of Bierce's racialism, in which Polynesians are assimilated into the undifferentiated category of "nigger," is indicative of an undiscriminating discrimination against all nonwhites—or, more exactly, against non–Anglo-Saxons.

Although reviewers often compared him to Melville, Stoddard lacked the radically subversive vision of his predecessor's South-Sea romances. If he deplored, as Melville did, the influence of Christian missionaries over the Islanders, still he exempted the Catholic ones from blame. Despite his prodigal pose, Stoddard never forgot that he was civilized at heart; his chumming with the savages, whom he tended to reduce to comic stereotypes, was a form of slumming with those beyond the normal (and normalizing) bourgeois ken. In seeking to escape sexual "hypocrisy," Stoddard did not question the cultural presuppositions that shaped his attraction to "barbarism"—such as the idea that nonwhite races were less afraid of "instincts" and thus naturally more promiscuous than Anglo-Saxons.

From his youth, Stoddard felt a special (but not exclusive) attraction to those darker than he, whether the Mexicans he encountered as a child in San Francisco, or the "mezzo-tinted" boy that became his school chum in upstate New York, or the olive-skinned Italian youths whose nude photographs were smuggled through customs by his friend Theodore Dwight for Stoddard's delectation. Dwight, who was working at the time as librarian to the State Department, offered a special enticement for Stoddard to visit him in Washington: "Coffee in thin porcelain shall be served to you at your bedside by the African Sphinx, James the black and speechless, called by some the 'Mind Reader.' "[24] The combination here of racial darkness with devoted service and knowing silence was the ideal for Stoddard in his Island lovers.

The preferred color was "not black . . . not even brown" but "olive-tinted"—and not just any "olive," but the "tenderest olive . . . that has a shade of gold in it."[25] Such was Kána-aná, Stoddard's companion in "Chumming with a Savage," with whom he played out a "Crusoe life":

> We had fitful spells of conversation upon some trivial theme, after long intervals of intense silence. We began to develop symptoms of imbecility. There was laughter at the least occurrence, though quite barren of humor; also, eating and drinking to pass the time; bathing to make one's self cool, after the heat and drowsiness of the day. . . . Again and again he would come with a delicious banana to the bed where I was lying, and insist upon my gorging myself, when I had but barely recovered from a late orgie of fruit, flesh, or fowl. He would mesmerize me into a most refreshing sleep with a prolonged and pleasing manipulation. It was a reminiscence of the baths of Stamboul not to be withstood. From this sleep I would presently be awakened by Kána-aná's performance upon a rude sort of harp, that gave out a weird and eccentric music. The mouth being applied to the instrument, words were pronounced in a guttural voice, while the fingers twanged the strings in measure. It was a flow of monotones, shaped into legends and lyrics. I liked it amazingly; all the better, perhaps, that it was as good as Greek to me, for I understood it as little as I understood the strange and persuasive silence of that beloved place, which seemed slowly but surely weaving a spell of enchantment about me. (*CSS* 41–42)

Essential to this enchantment is not only Kána-aná's assiduous attention to Stoddard's physical pleasure but also his linguistic otherness, which precludes the possibility of *non*trivial conversation and his articulation of anything more than a desire to please. Innocent of civilization and its call, the native is bewildered when Stoddard suddenly abandons him. Rushing in the nude after the departing canoe, he "ran after us like one gone daft, and plunged into the cold sea, calling my name over and over as he fought the breakers." Stoddard knows that "if he overtook us I should never be able to escape again" (*CSS* 44).

In the account of this poignant parting, the emphasis falls primarily on the narrator's, not the native's, loss. The narrative silence about Kána-aná's thoughts and feelings—he has no fictive inner life— matches the "persuasive silence" of the enchanting Islands. Too primitive for complex human emotions, it is implied, Kána-aná is also too docile to feel anger at being exploited; he is a Good Man Friday to the last. Back home, now playing the prodigal son rather than Robinson Crusoe, Stoddard has no appetite for the fatted calf: " 'I don't deserve it; for I'd give more this minute to see that dear little velvet-skinned, coffee-colored Kána-aná than anything else in the wide world—because he hates business, and so do I' " (*CSS* 44–45). As the prodigal who identifies himself with the natives, Stoddard can distance himself from the America of commercial enterprise without recognizing his own importation of "business" to the Islands in his assumption of Crusoe-like mastery over Kána-aná/Friday.

"I'd rather be a south sea islander sitting naked in the sun before my grass hut than be the Pope of Rome," Stoddard once quipped, defining the antipodes of fantasy between which he alternated for much of his life.[26] When he was not dreaming of a return to the South Seas, he was imagining himself in monastic habit—a fantasy captured in the portrait of Stoddard painted by Joseph Strong during the 1870s.[27] As Jackson Lears has shown, "the aesthetic legacy of medieval Catholicism charmed increasing numbers of nineteenth-century American Protestants." As it developed beside a "more general interest in premodern art and ritual," this movement toward the church "merged, at its periphery, with *fin-de-siècle* aestheticism."[28]

The draw of Catholicism was certainly aesthetic for Stoddard, who even as a boy found the mass, the music, and the colorful ecclesiastical trappings all the more attractive by contrast to the starkly evangelical religion of his family. "The beauty of its ritual, the mysticism of its creed, the consolation of its confessional, all appealed to him intensely."[29] But the church, which he formally joined in 1867, also afforded Stoddard another way, alternative to "barbarism," of allying himself with antimodern resistance to the business ethos of the Gilded Age. And insofar as Catholicism was more "feminized" even than high-church Protestantism, Stoddard's aestheticism (his artistic vocation) became congruous with the asceticism (the religious life) of those under stricter orders than he could ever have abided himself.

Meditating over the ruins of the Acropolis on his first trip to Greece, Stoddard wrote: "It is not unlikely that in the flight of the gods mankind lost his reverence for the purely beautiful; they took with them that finer faculty—the sentiment is called feminine to-day, it may be considered infantile tomorrow—for the want of which the world is now suffering sorely."[30] This linkage of religion, beauty, and the "feminine" and/or "infantile" was commonplace in Stoddard's time. The gendering of aestheticism, which accompanied the refashioning of Victorian gender codes during the later nineteenth century, effected the redefinition, as Lears remarks, of "the 'feminine' ideal of dependence":

> In the *fin-de-siècle* imagination, many of the "childlike" qualities associated with premodern character, and with the unconscious, were also linked with femininity: fantasy, spontaneity, aesthetic creativity. The premodern unconscious generated androgynous alternatives to bourgeois masculinity. Those options especially appealed to the men and women who were most restive under bourgeois definitions of gender identity, and who suffered most acutely from the fragmenting of selfhood.[31]

For a man like Stoddard, who had never fit the Wild-West mold of masculinity, the androgynous elements of Catholicism could be embraced without the ambivalence felt by men like Henry Adams, whose "vestigial commitments to male ego-ideals, to individual autonomy and conscious control" made him fear the power of the Virgin he simultaneously worshiped from a safe distance.[32] What was "feminine" about the church tallied with Stoddard's need for a model of "masculinity" that was nurturing rather than aggressive, domestic rather than entrepreneurial, genteel rather than strenuous; one, in short, that affirmed his ideal of spiritual beauty in brotherly love. It was in the name of Mother Church, for instance, that Father Damien became a missionary martyr among the lepers at Molokai. In Stoddard's eyes, Father Damien was a saint. But even the ordinary Catholic priests whom he befriended seemed to represent a sure and universal refuge for pilgrims, like Stoddard, constantly in need of spiritual care and manly affection. No wonder, as he wrote from Europe in 1874, he was tempted to "bury myself out of this world in the seclusion of one of these monasteries. I never pass one here but I keel a little over to that side."[33]

For those capable of vowing celibacy, Catholicism provided one solution to the problem of gender identity. But the side of Stoddard that needed sexual expression kept him from ever keeling over into the clerical brotherhood. (He never aspired, even in fantasy, to priestly status.) Believing his desire for men was natural, and thus within the divine scheme, Stoddard also believed that the church, in its sacrament of penance, made allowances that the Protestants did not for human frailty. There is little indication, however, that Stoddard felt guilty about what he called his temperament. As he explained his religious conversion to James Whitcomb Riley: "I couldn't help it, you see; it was born in me and was the only thing that appealed to my temperament. I believe a man's religion is nessessarily [*sic*] a matter of temperament—I couldn't be anything else than a Catholic—except—*except* a downright *savage*, and I wish to God I were that!"[34] Catholicism, then, was as deeply "congenital" for Stoddard as his same-sexuality.

Stoddard's coming out as a Catholic in his conversion narrative, *A Troubled Heart* (1885), was symbolically equivalent, as Austen sees, to his revealing his sexual "temperament."[35] This equivalence remained inchoate for Stoddard because the idea of "coming out" would not crystallize in sexual, rather than religious, discourse until the category of "homosexual" had been fully established and enforced. However adrift in his sexual life, Stoddard remained firmly anchored to his religious faith, even when church officials (as at Notre Dame and Catholic universities) seemed to conspire against him.

An interesting contrast in this regard is Fr. Rolfe, the self-styled Baron Corvo, for whom "homosexuality" and Catholicism came more violently into collision than they ever did for Stoddard. Whereas Stoddard would have preferred being a "savage" to being the Pope of Rome, Rolfe transformed the latter fantasy into *Hadrian the Seventh* (1904), the embittered novel in which (as imaginary Pope) he avenged himself upon the church that had denied him ordination. ("Fr." stood, in fact, for "Frederick," not "Father.") In Rolfe's Manichean mind—he too was a convert to Catholicism from evangelical Protestantism—the flesh raged against the spirit. A seeker of spiritual friendships with fellow

Englishmen, he was also late in life a pander of Italian boys in Venice.[36] There was, as A. O. J. Cockshut says, "an absolute gulf" between Rolfe's conduct in Italy and his ideal of friendship:

> When Rolfe writes of homosexuality, he invariably does so in the coarsest, most brutal way. He can only write of it when all his higher aspirations, whether toward God or the imaginary friend, are laid asleep. His higher and lower nature can never be on stage together. There is absolutely nothing corresponding to the wistful talk about the love that dare not speak its name. And the imagined, long-desired, impossible perfect friendship is utterly chaste.[37]

Love, in Rolfe's view, had nothing to do with the flesh. As he wrote to Temple Scott about "heterosexuality":

> Carnal pleasure I thoroughly appreciate, but I like a change sometimes. Even partridges get tiresome after many days. Only besotted ignorance or hypocrisy demurs to carnal lust, but I meet people who call that holy which is purely natural, and I am stupefied. I suppose we all deceive ourselves. To blow one's nose (I never learned to do it) is a natural relief. So is coition. Yet the last is called holy, and the first passes without epithets. Why should one attach more importance to one than to the other? I don't think that I want to know.
>
> Some talk of wickedness, and vulgarly confound the general with the particular. Of course you're wicked, every instant that you spend uncontemplative of, uncorresponding to, the Grace and Glory of your Maker. That may be forgiven, for that Real Love forgives.[38]

Such logic, in Cockshut's opinion, plunged Rolfe into a self-destructive state of mind during his final years of penury and paranoia. He yielded to "an amalgam of two separate and partly opposite impulses: theological despair, and a desire, by piling sin on sin, to punish God for not taking him at his own valuation and making him a priest."[39]

In Stoddard's far sunnier Catholicism, which Rolfe would have considered self-deceiving, the spiritual and the carnal were happily wedded, without any sense that he was heaping sin upon sin. Publicly, of course, Stoddard seemed to conform to "the ideology of nonsexual Christian brotherhood," which "legitimized (nonphysical) intimacy between men by precluding the possibility that such intimacy could be defined as sexual."[40] As George Chauncey, Jr., has shown in regard to the Newport scandal of 1919 and 1920, in which Episcopal and other Protestant leaders leapt to the defense of a fellow clergyman accused by the United States Navy of "lewdness" in his ministry to sailors, the churchmen's stigmatizing of same-sexual *acts*, rather than individual dispositions, as "perverse" served to protect from suspicion those engaged in Christian devotion to youth. The navy's "inquiry had questioned the ideology of nonsexual Christian brotherhood that had heretofore explained their devotion to other men." The confrontation between the navy and the churches "represented fundamentally a dispute over the norms for masculine gender behavior and over the boundaries between homosociality and homosexuality in the relations of men."[41]

For Stoddard's generation, the battle lines in this dispute had yet to be drawn so sharply, if at all. No clear boundary existed between "homosociality" and "homosexuality" except within the ideology of Christian brotherhood, which Stoddard radically revised to suit his temperament. When he agreed to take a position at Notre Dame, in fact, he cited his devotion to young men as one of his strongest credentials. To his mind, there was nothing hypocritical in extending the lay ministry of his pedagogical office to include physical love itself. Indeed, Stoddard imputed no wrong to himself but only to those, such as the clergy at Notre Dame, who objected to his same-sex relationships. "How foul these brothers are," he wrote in his diary, "how prone to think evil and poison the minds of the lads."[42] The "palpable embodiment" of love, after all, was his "meat and drink" (D 19 Jan. 1885)—no less sacred to him than the spiritual sustenance of Holy Communion. With native boys and college lads alike, Stoddard felt that human love brought him only closer to the love of God. As the clerical defendant was to be described by his character witnesses during his 1920 Newport trial, so Stoddard could sincerely have characterized himself as " 'an earnest Christian man [who] was much interested in young men.' "[43]

Although some of Stoddard's sexual relationships *were* with young men, such as Frank Millet and Reginald Birch during the 1870s, his deepest and most sustained love affairs were pedophilic. As he once wrote in his notebook, "I thank God that I have no children of my own to worry me . . . but—O! how I long for those of others" (D 6 Oct. 1905).[44] In 1878, for example, Stoddard was employed as a male companion to young William Woodworth, fatherless scion of a wealthy San Francisco family, whom he took sailing off Monterey and botanizing in the Redwoods. (Woodworth was to become a distinguished naturalist and a professor at Harvard.) Stoddard later recalled his idyllic days with Willie, only the first of many youths to be dubbed his "Kid": "The Kid was the very thing—a youngster with happiness in heart, luster in his eye, and nothing more serious than peach-down on his lip; yet there was

gravity enough in his composition to carry him beneath the mere surface of men and things." In his way, Willie recalled the frontispiece
etching of Whitman in the 1855 edition of *Leaves of Grass*. Stoddard
wrote of a day when "The Kid" had returned from hunting rabbits with
a glow of moonlight in his eyes, a sunset flush on his cheek, and "the
riotous blood's best scarlet in his lips." The boy stood there, laughing
triumphantly, "a blue shirt open at the throat, hair very much tumbled,
and no thoughts of self to detract from the absolute grace of his pose."[45]

Both mentorial and erotic, Stoddard's relationship to Woodworth
bears some resemblance to "Greek love," as it was (re)understood by
John Addington Symonds in his privately printed *A Problem in Greek
Ethics* (1883). Sedgwick points out, in regard to Symonds's friendship
with the Italian gondolier Angelo Fusato, that the appropriation of
Whitman by upper-middle-class homosexuals in England could lead to
a "distinctive sexual-political narrative" in which the "potential political effects of 'Calamus' love" were described in "terms drawn from
chivalry, but appealing at the same time to the virilizing authority of the
Greeks." This narrative tended in Symonds to mystify his sexual exploi-
tation of proletarian men. His idea of Whitmanian "democracy," based
"on noblesse oblige and individual pastoralism and condescension,"
served to keep class barriers in place.[46]

As an American, however, Stoddard's class position was less fixed
than Symonds's, and he never invoked the idea of "Greek love" to describe his desire for youths whose backgrounds ranged from the upper
class (in the case of Woodworth), to the middle class (in the case of Tom
Cleary, Stoddard's "Kid" during his brief tenure at Notre Dame), to the
immigrant working class (in the case of Kenneth O'Connor, the boy he
"adopted" during his Washington years). In no sense did Stoddard think
of himself as an exploiter of Cleary, whose family sheltered him for two
years after he resigned his professorship. With Kenneth O'Connor, who
at the age of fifteen moved into Stoddard's Washington "Bungalow" in
1895, the narrative of their relationship derived less from the Greeks
than from American domesticity.

Like Woodworth, O'Connor was a fatherless boy for whom Stoddard
saw himself to be filling a paternal need. A dropout from school and
something of a street-corner tough (Stoddard preferred the term
"waif"), Kenneth drank and smoked and had his own desire for "Kids."
In the spirit of Horatio Alger, Stoddard wanted to "save" the youth from
a supposedly hellish family life and give him uplifting opportunities.[47]

Stoddard arranged for Kenneth to attend Georgetown Prep, and he lavished upon him the material bounty of bourgeois respectability. When Stoddard and O'Connor (along with Jules, the French cook and factotum, and Mexique, Stoddard's dog) took possession of their new home, Kenneth's mother helped to choose the kitchen equipment, Henry Adams sent over three Persian pillows, and even Bishop Keane, who had hired Stoddard for Catholic University, seemed to approve. Given to gushing about his "Kid" to whoever would listen, Stoddard described their life to Father Daniel Hudson, his enduring friend from Notre Dame, as "almost ideal," a domestic romance come true: "This is a rare house—a house of love."[48]

Although Stoddard had no biological son, his friends had no difficulty in recognizing him as Kenneth's "Dad" (which the boy was encouraged to call him).[49] Such a paternal role, as Lynch suggests, was to be proscribed for men like Stoddard under the paradigm of "homosexuality": "Pre-homosexuality 'homosexuals' entered the family structure by having children, but in the newly emerging role, the 'homosexual' would not be defined as a parent. Indeed, 'homosexual father' and 'lesbian mother' would come to be seen as self-contradictions." Here again Stoddard may be seen to mark a transition between Victorian and modern discourses on same-sexuality. Like Whitman, in his notorious claim to Symonds that he had fathered six children, Stoddard could avail himself of the idea of paternity. But whereas Whitman, as Lynch says, "assumed genetic fathering to be incommensurable with the new same-sex role he had done so much to articulate,"[50] Stoddard was closer to Symonds in finding no necessary contradiction between paternity and "homosexuality."

In one newspaper article, in the popular vein of the Author at Home, Stoddard's relationship to Kenneth was placed beside his fondness for native boys and found to be equally unexceptionable:

> "The kid" is the object of Mr. Stoddard's warmest affection; he is a fine-looking boy 17 years old—his other name is Kenneth—and he was adopted by Mr. Stoddard when quite a little fellow. The author of "South Sea Idylis," [sic] has all his life had a way of adopting boys, and he has watched over them with more than a father's love and care until they passed from him either by death or marriage. Some he has immoralized [sic!]: Kehele [sic], the young hero of Hawaii; Kana-Ana of Tahita [sic]; Hua-Manu of Pomotoe Islands, and others he has come across have deeply appealed to him.
>
> Mr. Stoddard's nature is an unique one; he has many souls in one and

through them all are strains of tenderness and melancholy. Boys of ardent enthusiasm and fervor of feeling are completely won over by him. Indeed, he wears his heart upon his sleeve at the disposal of whoever will take it.[51]

The untruths here—that Stoddard adopted Kenneth at a young age, that he habitually watched over his "Kids" until either marriage or death did them part—serve to trim the facts more closely to the narrative pattern of a male domestic idyll. The reporter is strikingly (to the modern reader) sanguine about what is called "more than a father's love": a term that seems less obscure if it is heard to resonate with "passing the love of women," the biblical phrase often applied to male romantic friendships in the nineteenth century.[52] Stoddard's "tenderness and melancholy," the traits common to his "many souls," qualify him, in fact, as an ideal guide for boys of like disposition, who require a "feminine" father.[53]

With such a father, what boy would need a mother? This is the unspoken question behind the reporter's jocular treatment of the misogynic spirit that pervaded "The Bungalow." " 'No woman can stand our whims—mine and the kid's,' " Stoddard told the interviewer, who adds that Jules, too, "has not much liking for 'these girls d'Amerique' who stop on their bicycles by the front gate to talk to 'the kid.' The fair lassies never dream of Jules' contempt for them nor of Mr. Stoddard's hearty laughter as he peeps out through the closed shutters."[54] Inaudible here is any nervous overtone to Stoddard's "hearty" laughter as he peeps voyeuristically at the "lassies" playing up to the "Kid." Of course, the joke is entirely on them, foolish enough not to recognize their superfluity to this decidedly male ménage: a house to which no angel need apply.

Enclosed by the shutters at "The Bungalow" were the rooms stuffed with souvenirs that Stoddard had accumulated through decades of travel. Part library, part shrine, part grass hut, the house was decorated to be emblematic of the major triad of its owner's life. Literature: photographs of celebrated authors; a collection of over three-thousand volumes, including deluxe editions and many inscribed books. Catholicism: a glass case containing relics of Father Damien (the veil and maniple he wore when saying mass for the lepers); a portrait of a Capucin monk vowed to silence; a crown of thorns; the rosary of a Franciscan friar; a picture in every room of a statue of Saint Anthony ("The Bungalow" was also called "Saint Anthony's Rest"). The South Seas:

"cocoanuts from the Fijis, fans and feathers from Hawaii, savage weapons and dancing skirts from Tahiti, and other bright pagan relics."[55]

Because it expressed a domestic ideal, "The Bungalow" was different from the more insistently "manly" environments to which Stoddard had gravitated: the Bohemian Club in San Francisco, where alcoholic high jinks were meant to set obstreperous young writers above the sober business class; Charlotte Street in London, where illustrator Wallis Mackay played genial host to an endless stream of male visitors; "Stag-Racket Bungalow" in Hawaii, where three young men-about-town took in "Charley" Stoddard as a boarder and good fellow; "Tuckanuck," the exquisitely appointed house of William Sturgis Bigelow on an island off Nantucket, where men took their ease, often naked, in an untamed natural setting; Carmel, where the California literati tried to combine art with physical culture. What Stoddard desired was a homosocial site in which his "feminine" tastes could be more fully expressed, one that literally brought home the worlds of art, religion, and tropical languor. He was most himself in a parlor that could double as a stage from which he retailed his adventures, for attentive visitors, from the comfort of an easy chair, surrounded by the curios that were his props.

Stoddard also possessed an extraordinary social grace in the homes of others. Wherever he went, either in male homosocial spheres or the domains of women, Stoddard was always welcomed merely for the pleasure of his company. As Howells said, Stoddard's "utter lovableness" endeared him to everyone who knew, "which is to say, loved, him": "He was so greatly and constantly beloved of hospitality that, as he complained once, he was being perpetually passed round on a plate, and there were none of his hosts who did not wish to add some special garniture to the dish."[56] As the metaphor implies, Stoddard readily adapted himself to a variety of social situations, masking his "temperament" when necessary. What remained constant, however, was his aestheticism "of Chopin at twilight, Oriental bric-a-brac, incense, lounging robes, and fragrant cigarettes."[57]

During Oscar Wilde's sensational American tour in 1882, in the course of which he arrived in California "wearing a Spanish sombrero, velvet suit, puce cravat, yellow gloves, and buckled shoes" and proceeded to drink members of the Bohemian Club under the table,[58] Isobel Strong wrote to Stoddard about her meeting the resplendent visitor in San Francisco:

He was delightfully entertaining, and said that the only thing he regretted about California was that he had not seen the Yosemite Valley and Charley Stoddard. But you, Charley, are the real aesthete—he affects what to you is natural and he has not your languour, grace, or beautiful voice and so the general verdict is that we have a better aesthete at home than this fellow who came all these miles to "show off."[59]

What was "natural" to Stoddard was soon, largely through the agency of Oscar Wilde, to seem all too "unnatural." Long before the scandalous trials of 1895, Stoddard had recognized in Wilde what "decent" people were later shocked to discover.[60] As he wrote to a friend from Hawaii in 1882: "Oscar Wilde! Shall I ever find him in this vague world? If you see him before I do, and of course you will, please say the unutterable things that stick in my throat—because here there is no one to spoon with, or to gush over, or to care a fig for and I am out of practice."[61]

"Spooning" and "gushing" were specialized words in Stoddard's vocabulary, used only in reference to his love for men and, outside of his diary, only in letters to fellow lovers of men. All such "homosexuals," whatever the variations in their gender identities, were subsumed during the 1890s, Sedgwick argues, under the aristocratic Wildean stereotype: "For the first time in England, homosexual style—and homophobic style—instead of being stratified and specified and kept secret along lines of class, became . . . a household word—the word 'Oscar Wilde.'" One consequence was that Symonds and Edward Carpenter, disciples of Whitman and proselytizers for a "middle-class-oriented but ideologically 'democratic,' virilizing, classicizing, idealistic, self-styled political version of male homosexuality," lost their consensus.[62]

The impact of "Oscar Wilde" on American "homosexuals" was perhaps neither so immediate nor so profound as it was in England. For Stoddard, in any case, Whitman, not Wilde, was the enduring idol. But Stoddard had never been political, and he was indifferent to the democratic Whitman. In retrospect, then, Stoddard may be seen, as literary historians *have* seen him, less as Whitman's heir than as a prototype of the Wildean aesthete.

At the end of his life, Stoddard was heartened by those breaking silence about their same-sexuality, curious about the terms being circulated to describe "the unutterable things" that had stuck in his throat and had remained unarticulated in his work. He became bolder in the homoeroticism of his later tales, and he projected, but never wrote, an autobiographical piece to be called "The Confessions of an Unnatural-ist." But Stoddard, born to another time, was not a modern "homosex-ual," and he was not to feel the full brunt of modern "homophobia." What his life offers is an invaluable clue to the formation of these categories during the crisis of gender and culture at the American *fin de siècle*.

Foreword

ROGER AUSTEN

Afuter they have been in their graves for a decade or two, it is a grand old American custom for homosexual writers to undergo curious transformations. Literary historians and critics and biographers set to work heterosexualizing or at least neutering these writers for posterity. Conveniently forgotten are all those nicknames that hinted vaguely at some form of hermaphroditism (James was called a "Miss Nancy," Whitman a "counter jumper," i.e., an "effeminate" creature of "weak depravities"). Passionate attachments to other males become innocuous, as Martin Duberman noted several years ago in the *New York Times Book Review:*

> The standard works on even celebrated literary figures (Gay Wilson Allen's biography of Walt Whitman, for example, or Leon Edel's *Henry James*) demurely bypass the question of sexual preference, presuming no

Written early in 1979, when Roger Austen was still attempting to place his book with a trade publisher, this "Foreword" was intended for the general reader. Austen believed that it would require revision should *Genteel Pagan* be accepted instead by a university press: "The tone of flippancy, so screeching in the last paragraph, would obviously have to be toned down." Because these pages reflect both Austen's intentions and their historical moment, I have chosen to include them as written.–ED.

· xliii ·

more than an occasional elevated "infatuation." But the presumption of *sex?*—Never! No one in our history, it seems, has ever been to bed with anybody of the same gender.

In place of boyfriends, girlfriends are discovered, frustrated heterosexual love affairs are hinted at, and irrelevant theories are offered to explain why these writers never chose to marry. And thus, *voilà!* These authors' lives and works may be safely examined by the schoolchildren of America.

Some gay critics have charged that this process is nothing less than an intellectually dishonest conspiracy, and they are right to the extent that literary historians have wittingly misrepresented the facts. In other cases, especially in the studies that were done a generation or so ago, it is possible that heterosexual scholars were simply too imperceptive to recognize a homoerotic clue when they saw one. But whatever the cause, the effect of all this whitewashing is the same: we are supposed to believe, as Martin Duberman says, that none of our writers ever went to bed with someone of the same sex.

This, of course, is nonsense, and it is time the truth was told.

But why tell the truth, the reader may well ask, about Charles Warren Stoddard? Since he was merely a minor author, does he warrant a full-length critical biography? No, not on the basis of his writing. Many of his books are admittedly second-rate, and some hardly merit rereading, let alone extensive literary analysis. *South-Sea Idyls* and *For the Pleasure of His Company*, however, do seem to warrant some degree of reevaluation in light of what is now known about Stoddard's life. In the past, these two books have been used as evidence to show that Stoddard was a somewhat "precious" stylist who could write charmingly but who didn't have very much to say. In fact, he had a good deal to say about a subject very close to his heart: men loving other men. And in *South-Sea Idyls* and *For the Pleasure of His Company* he said it, although at the time everyone had to pretend that he hadn't. In general, however, most of Stoddard's books deserve to remain in the background as their chief value is usually more biographical than literary.

It was how he lived, rather than what he wrote, that makes Stoddard of some interest to us today. All through his life he wore "his heart on his sleeve," as he used to say, falling in love with one good-looking young man after another. Since he felt it was his God-given right to love and be loved in return, he was seldom secretive about these affairs. On the contrary, when he had found a new "Kid," as he called these young men, he couldn't wait to share this good news with anyone who was willing to listen. By the time Stoddard was in his sixties, a British lady with whom he had corresponded for thirty years wrote to exclaim: "What a long line of Kids you have! . . . They 'stretch out to the crack of doom'!" In speaking out so freely about the love that otherwise "Dared Not Speak Its Name," Stoddard may be regarded as a homosexual touchstone among the writers in nineteenth-century America. Whenever he thought he detected a certain telltale quality in the lives or works of his fellow authors, he didn't hesitate to tell them so in letters or in person. Of course, he wrote to Whitman—*Leaves of Grass* was, after all, so *obvious* for one in the know. And with the same sort of sniffing intuition, he felt he detected something behind the facades of Rudyard Kipling, Bliss Carman, Yone Noguchi, Frank Millet, Jack London, and, yes, even of the Hoosier Poet himself, James Whitcomb Riley! An examination of Stoddard's life will be illuminating, then, simply on the basis of how he reacted to all of the famous and near-famous men he got to know—heterosexuals as well as homosexuals—and how they, in turn, reacted to him.

Let the misconceptions of the past be brushed aside. Those who still want to believe that Stoddard was in love with Ina Coolbrith (or was it Ada Clare or Lotta Crabtree?) should read no further. Those who will be affronted at finding Stoddard in bed with someone of the same sex should return this book to the public library. However, those curious to know what it was like to be a homosexual in nineteenth-century America may—with both pleasure and profit, it is hoped—read on.

Genteel Pagan

1

WITH WHAT he must have later regarded as remarkable prescience, Charles Warren Stoddard struggled against coming into the world in Rochester, New York, during the early morning hours of 7 August 1843. "I was born," he wrote sixty years afterward, "much against my will."[1] The infant had no way of knowing, of course, that his proud old family was in decline. He was to be told about the seventeenth-century Stoddards who had gone through Harvard to become doctors and ministers. Even in 1843, his paternal grandfather was a wealthy physician practicing in nearby Pembroke, New York. But Charles's father, Samuel Burr Stoddard, was in comparison an uneducated ne'er-do-well. In 1837, he had married a Pembroke girl, Sarah Freeman; he had fathered children in 1838 and 1841; and at the time of Charles's birth he was struggling to succeed in the paper-manufacturing business he owned with his father-in-law. For a while the firm of Stoddard and Freeman seemed on the verge of prosperity. In the late 1840s, the partners boasted in an advertisement that they offered "the largest assortment of Paper to be found in any house west of New York or Boston."[2] But in 1851 the firm failed, and after filing for bankruptcy, Charles's father left Rochester in search of a new job for himself and a new home for his family.

I

During his first seven years of childhood, Charles seemed to have every reason to feel secure in the family home. Along with Grandpa and Grandma Freeman, the Stoddards were living in a commodious, broad-fronted white house at 24 Frank Street. In addition to the older children, Ned and Sarah, he was to have younger brothers to play with: Sam, born in 1846, and Fred, born in 1850. A childhood friend recalled that it was always grand fun at the Stoddards'. In the large side yard there was a tent with flags, a cannon, a whirling contraption called "flying horses," and, on the lawn in a shady corner to keep it cool, a bucket of lemonade.[3]

For Charles, as he recalled, childhood had been difficult. Never a rough-and-tumble boy, he was "very timid and sensitive": "I hated most games, I liked better to lounge about, dream-building."[4] While the more rambunctious children played, Charles preferred to "steal apart . . . and, throwing myself upon the lawn, look upon them in their sports as from a dim distance. Their joy was to me like a song, to which I listened with a kind of rapture, but in which I seldom or never joined." For reasons that he could not then begin to understand, he just did not fit in. In spite of a doting family, he was a "lonely child . . . often loneliest when least alone," and his chief consolation was "intense and absorbing love, and love alone."[5]

The prevailing religious tone in the household was set by his mother and her parents, much to the boy's dismay. While Grandpa Stoddard over in Pembroke had become a comparatively liberal Unitarian, the Freemans and their daughters were God-fearing Presbyterians. Everyone was forced to attend Sunday services in a dreary unadorned church that Charles recalled with loathing for having offered nothing "for the eye to fall on with a sense of rest; nothing to soothe or comfort the heart" (*TH* 20). As it turned out, there *was* something. One day, while enduring the two-hour service in "dumb misery," Charles chanced to notice at the rear of the church a picture of an angel "floating through the air with a lute poised lightly upon his breast." Finding solace in this bit of beauty, he turned his back on the minister and gazed until "the man in the pew behind me seized me abruptly by the shoulders and turned me face about" (*TH* 22–23).

By contrast, the aura of the mysterious Catholic cathedral across from his home filled the boy with wonder. The music that wafted out of the stained-glass windows was strangely beautiful; and while standing across the street on Sunday nights, Charles sometimes caught "glimpses of clustering tapers, twinkling like dim stars through clouds of vapor" (*TH* 15). He longed to go inside, but he knew better than to ask his parents, who had no use for unsanctified religious practices. Without his parents' knowledge, Charles prevailed upon the maid to take him into the cathedral, where he was much impressed with the tapering columns, painted arches, rose windows, pictures, statues, and frescoes. "I saw an altar that inspired me with curious awe; a throng of worshipers, who knelt humbly and prayed incessantly, so that the quiet of the chapel was broken by the soft murmur of lisping lips" (*TH* 15–16). True, he was somewhat frightened by the dark-robed priests, who reminded him of the illustrations in a book at home picturing the most harrowing excesses of the Spanish Inquisition. But this surreptitious visit planted a seed that was to take root twenty years later. When it came to aesthetic beauty, Charles was convinced that the Presbyterians could not—and, of course, would not—hold a candle to the Catholics.

After 1850, the comforts of gracious living gradually gave way to the frightening reality that this branch of the Stoddard family was headed for the poorhouse. From his eighth to eleventh years, Charles moved with his family into increasingly narrow quarters: in 1850 to Fitzhugh Street in Rochester; then to a former wayside inn outside of town; then to Pennsylvania and back to Spencerport, New York; then, in 1854, back to Rochester to live near the railroad tracks. In and out of country schools at irregular intervals, Charles became a shy, self-conscious pupil, easily intimidated by his teachers. In the Presbyterian church every Sunday, Charles found his heart growing more and more troubled by a God indefatigably bent on visiting His wrath upon the sinful.

There were occasional moments of joy. Once in a while at school Charles would become attached to another boy, who would become his "chum"; and his family attended the marvelous traveling shows along the barge canal at Spencerport. But the steady decline of the Stoddards's fortunes and the incessant moving about had the effect of making Charles ever more sensitive, introspective, and insecure. In later life he jotted down some notes for his "Autobiography, Book First" that give a clue to his boyhood personality:

> A victim of emotional worries. The instant defender of the abused. A horror of the Insane—and of those who are under the influence of stimulants of any kind. Passionate attachments. Flights of Fancy. Dreams—by

day and night—more especially day-dreams. Shyness. Worldly detach-ment—life viewed as if from a distance, and not really entered into. School horrors—tyranny; anxiety over tasks; embarrassment in class. Supersti-tious. Testament under my pillow—perpetual prayer—If I get to the top of the stairs before anyone speaks *it* will happen![6]

II

Finally, late in 1854, Samuel Stoddard found a job in San Francisco with an importing and shipping firm, and the family prepared to join him on the West Coast. As the Stoddards awaited their boat in New York City, Grandpa Freeman, relaxing his usual rigor, took his daughter and the children to the "Lecture Room" at Barnum's Museum. As it turned out, the current attraction was not a lecture but a dramatic perfor-mance, the first one Charles was to see. Significantly enough, the play was *Damon and Pythias*, starring the great J. R. Scott, and little Charles was so enchanted that for some years to come he would act out scenes from this play with his brothers in their new San Francisco home.

In mid-December 1854, the Stoddard family boarded the *Star of the West*, the "ill-smelling, overcrowded, side-wheeled tub" that was to take them as far as Nicaragua.[7] Charles had brought along Defoe's *Robinson Crusoe*, a volume he would always treasure because it was a gift from a chum. The drama of Crusoe was brought to life one day when Charles saw, somewhere between the Florida Keys and the Caribbean, a lush green tropical island. Its peak was "sky-kissed," its valleys were "over-shadowed by festoons of vapor," and along its beach the "creaming breakers wreathed themselves, flashed like snow-drifts, vanished and flashed again" (*IFP* 8). Charles was as entranced as he had been at the performance of *Damon and Pythias*. He recalled that he had been filled with "a great longing" as he looked at the island and had wanted "to sing with the Beloved Bard: 'Oh, had we some bright little isle of our own, / In the blue summer ocean, far off and alone!' " (*IFP* 10).

Traveling across Nicaragua gave Charles his first taste of the exotic. As the flat-bottomed river boat headed west, the eleven-year-old boy was dazzled by "splashes of splendid color" against the vivid greens of the jungle. Macaws, with "scarlet plumage flickering like flame," flew nearby (*IFP* 16). The river banks were decked with "gigantic blossoms that might shame a rainbow" (*IFP* 22). There were oranges ("great globes of delicious dew"), mangoes, guavas, bananas, sugarcane, and other good things to eat that Charles had never seen before (*IFP* 19).

Equally fascinating was the "picturesque nudeness" of the people along the shore. The natives were not completely naked; they wore necklaces of shells and wreaths of blossoms, thus making themselves all the more beguiling to the rapt child (*IFP* 21). By the time the Stoddards reached the Pacific shore, Charles's latent voluptuousness had asserted itself; on the outside he might still be a Presbyterian, but he sensed that he was a pagan at heart.

Several weeks later the Stoddard family sailed through the Golden Gate, and Charles began living a life that was, especially compared with his memories of Rochester, exciting and romantic. Gold-seekers, adventurers, and desperate characters were everywhere; frame houses, tents, and a few brick buildings were springing up at every turn; and Market Street was sprawling westward toward the dunes of drifting sand. Most of the fifty thousand residents were fairly young men who had chosen to come west unencumbered by family, and merely his being a child made Charles something of an anomaly. Growing up in this rowdy frontier town must have been a particularly unusual experience for a soft, dreamy child like Charles Warren Stoddard. On the one hand there were the civilizing influences of church and school, but on the other—indeed, almost next door—there was the barely fathomable but irresistible allure of the Barbary Coast.

The Stoddards were, of course, a perfectly respectable family, and the children were expected to grow up as well-behaved Christians even in an outpost of civilization full of sin and shamelessness. At their first home near the eastern end of Union Street near Kearny, Charles's parents continued the traditions of family prayers and grace at table. Every Sunday found them in the First Presbyterian Church on Stockton near Broadway, where Mr. Stoddard taught a Sunday-school class.

The schools were modeled on the example of New England, and at the Union Street Public School Charles used readers and spellers that came highly recommended from the East. A major civilizing force in Charles's life at this time was his composition teacher, Mrs. Amelia Clappe, who was a graduate of Amherst Academy, a "relative of Julia Ward Howe, a friend of Emily Dickinson, and an admirer of Margaret Fuller."[8] Stoddard recalled that his "very first literary effort" had been an essay about a butterfly written for Mrs. Clappe.[9] Consistent with prevailing cultural standards, the fireside poets of New England and the sentimental English poets were upheld for San Francisco's school-children to emulate, and in a few years Charles began to do just that.

At the same time, beyond the protective limits of the family home and the school across the street, Charles was gaining quite another kind of education. Just a few blocks south of Union Street, at the bottom of Telegraph Hill and overflowing as far south as Portsmouth Square, lay a notorious area called "Sydney-Town," later to be known as the Barbary Coast. For decades it inspired fulminations from preachers, reformers, and editors alike. The following tirade is representative:

> The petty thief, the house burglar, the tramp, the whore-monger, lewd women, cut-throats, murderers, all are found here. Dance-halls and concert-saloons, where blear-eyed men and faded women drink vile liquor, smoke offensive tobacco, engage in vulgar conduct, sing obscene songs and say and do everything to heap upon themselves more degradation, are numerous. Low gambling houses, thronged with riot-loving rowdies, in all stages of intoxication, are there. Opium dens, where heathen Chinese and God-forsaken men and women are sprawled in miscellaneous confusion, disgustingly drowsy or completely overcome, are there. Licentiousness, debauchery, pollution, loathsome disease, insanity from dissipation, misery, poverty, wealth, profanity, blasphemy, and death, are there.[10]

And there also was young Charles Stoddard, drawn to the hurdy-gurdy attractions of the "El Dorado," the "Arcade," and the "Polka." The doors of such dives were, after all, open to the public, and there *did* seem to be "a vast deal of jollity within." So Charles, either by himself or with a neighborhood chum, ventured inside to get his eyes' fill. At the faro tables the dealers were "beautiful women in bewildering attire," plying their trade with devil-may-care "greasers" and thrill-seeking sailors, their eyes glazed with lust and liquor. On the walls were hung lewd pictures that "young and innocent eyes ought never to have been laid on" (*IFP* 64).[11] But young Charles took in everything and everyone and, in doing so, became less and less innocent, although he was unable then to grasp the significance of it all.

Charles had his share of conventional and wholesome boyhood experiences as well. There were family outings to "The Willows," a popular oasis offering animals in cages and an open-air theater, and to "Russ's Gardens," another resort out in the Mission District, which featured a German beer garden and acrobatic acts on Sundays. (Charles was especially struck by a muscular, near-naked tightrope walker named Blondin, who was later to become a partner of his friend Adah Isaacs Menken.) There were also jaunts with his neighborhood friends to the "Cobweb Palace" on Meigg's wharf, picnics at Fort Point and the Cliff

House on the ocean, and visits to the comparatively respectable "foreign quarters"—Chinatown, which always fascinated Charles, and the Spanish Quarter, where everyone seemed dressed "as if they were about to appear in . . . 'The Barber of Seville' "(*IFP* 59).

One thing was certain: compared to Rochester, San Francisco was colorfully cosmopolitan, even if it lacked as yet the patina of urbane sophistication. At school Charles could find himself sitting next to pupils who had been born in Europe, Australia, Russia, "Chili," or the Sandwich Islands—to say nothing of nearly every state and territory in the Union. In retrospect, Stoddard observed that there had been something "singularly bracing" about the climate of San Francisco: "the middle-aged renewed their youth, and youth was wild with an exuberance of health and hope and happiness that seemed to give promise of immortality" (*IFP* 101). In this regard, however, he was not speaking for himself. In his boyhood, as in later life, he had always been more of an observer than a participant in exuberance, and in spite of the general holiday spirit in San Francisco, still he was not happy. Beginning in January 1857, and for the next two years, Charles was to be even less happy.

III

On 4 January 1857, Charles and his seventeen-year-old brother Ned boarded the *Flying Cloud,* a clipper ship that would take them around Cape Horn to New York City.[12] At family prayers that morning, their father had read aloud from the Bible: "Then they cry unto the Lord in their trouble, and He bringeth them out of their distresses. . . . Oh, that men would praise the Lord for His goodness and His wonderful works to the children of men."[13] Goodness? Wonderful works? Charles had some reason to doubt; for it was thought that Ned was dying of a chronic alimentary disease, and this sea voyage had been prescribed in the hope of prolonging his life.

On the voyage Charles read his Bible faithfully, as his mother had bidden him do, although every day this reading made him "more and more perplexed." During the ninety-two days at sea, he also read *Uncle Tom's Cabin,* kept a journal, spied some more "pretty" islands, and noticed that Ned was not getting very much better. Charles was especially taken with the worldly-wise cabin boy from Paris who, when they arrived in New York, was even more impressive as a "perfumed exquisite" seen dining across the room at the Hotel Astor.[14]

After a night in Manhattan, the Stoddard boys journeyed to Little Valley, a village in western New York, where their Grandpa Freeman had a farm. Ned and Charles shared a room in the farmhouse attic, and Charles soon found himself dreadfully bored after the excitements of San Francisco. "What was there," Stoddard asked years later, "beyond brook trout and maple sugar in their season for the refreshment of farmers' sons?" Alas, he added, even "the sons were scarce."[15]

Charles kept himself busy decorating the attic with bric-a-brac from San Francisco—a Chinese kite adorned with a bird of paradise, little figurines in satin and silk with ivory faces, and other Oriental mementos—all of which soon became a "scandal in a house that was famed for simplicity and prayer."[16] The clicking of chopsticks and the clangor of gongs created consternation downstairs, where the Freemans were muttering that these heathen trappings had turned their attic into a cross between a junk shop and a joss house.

When Ned returned alone to California, Charles was left with only the nearby frogs and cows for company. He soon read through the Freemans' few books, which were along the line of *Fern Leaves from Fanny's Portfolio*. He killed some time by writing letters to his family on stationery that was most extraordinary for a little boy to use: "lavender or rose or orange or pea-green; gilt-edged of course, and perfumed"— redolent of the wintergreen he always carried in a phial, "because I was a child of Nature."[17] When spring came, it was pleasant to sit outdoors beneath the lilacs. But in general Charles found the atmosphere "blighting," and he dreaded Sundays, when he often had to sit through a morning and an afternoon and an evening service. He soon "took to sighing—a habit that has become second nature—and I must have been something of a burden to the old folks,—a kind of mild reproach, as if they were somehow responsible for my want of interest in life."[18]

Then, suddenly, Charles was sublimely happy. He had found a chum named Fred, a "mezzo-tinted" and "picturesque Spanish type that appealed to me," full of "quasi-Andulsian" [sic] charm.[19] Fred was to be his classmate and roommate when the fall term started at Randolph Academy, ten miles from Little Valley, where Grandpa Freeman had enrolled him.

For a fictional account of young Charles in those days, we can turn to "Hearts of Oak," a semiautobiographical novella that Stoddard wrote for the *Overland Monthly* some fifteen years later. In this work Stoddard casts himself as Paul Rookh, in his twelfth year and just on the verge of entering boarding school: "Some children are impressive at this period. Paul was not. He was too thin and too long for beauty; he was decidedly uninteresting, and remained so for two years or more. . . . His prospects were certainly dubious enough; so many things happened to him, and he himself was so spiritless and indifferent . . . How he longed for someone to fly to in his loneliness and sorrow!"[20]

In "Hearts of Oak," this role is filled by a boy named Rivers, who was probably modeled on Fred (and also Richard Waite and Edgar Montgomery, who were to become his chums the following year). Rivers embodies all the virtues to which, lacking them himself, Stoddard would be attracted for the rest of his life:

> They were nearly of an age, but of very different temperaments. Paul's mind veered with the wind, and quartered with the moon: he was passive, joyous, and downcast in turn; usually longing for something out of reach, and wondering why he could not obtain it. Rivers was evenly cheerful; not easily persuaded nor dissuaded, but having a mind of his own that spoke for itself. He had, moreover, the great and almost godlike gift of self-control, and that is equal to the control of others. Paul felt the power of his will, and submitted to it as patiently as the lamb to the shepherd. In fact, he would rather obey Rivers than be his own master. (361)

Physically they were opposites as well, as may be seen in this description of Rivers, stripped for swimming with some other boys from the academy:

> But there was one youngster in the group, whose *poses* were a study and a satisfaction to the observers. Modesty, without shame, was the characteristic that seemed to clothe him like a mantle. His chest was full and well cushioned with muscle; thighs, plump and sinewy; hips, not too broad nor too narrow; knees, small, and of that fine mechanism so different from the clumsy joints of many imperfect creatures born into the world denuded of the grace and strength which should be their birthright . . . It was he who was the living light in Paul's world of school, and all that Paul could find to love and respect in the motley crowd surrounding him. Of course it was young Rivers; and Paul was absorbed in watching him, as he stood there like a youthful Hercules. (361)

As a result of these differences, the boys to whom Stoddard was drawn were rarely attracted to him. Indeed, as Stoddard imagined, they were actually repelled. Rivers thinks of Paul: "It was a pity that boy was so stupid, when he seemed to be pleasant enough in other ways . . . He wished he wasn't so sickly-looking, and that he was a little bit wickeder than he was: good boys were so milk-and-watery, he really couldn't endure them" (360).

Thus hurdles had to be surmounted before an adored idol could become Charles's chum; but from time to time, miraculously enough, he seemed somehow able to leap these hurdles. Although he was crushed when Fred decided to leave the academy, Charles soon attached himself to another boy. "We showed one another a kind of devotion worthy of young knighthood," Stoddard recalled, and they could hardly wait for the Christmas vacation to begin. "I had been formally invited to spend the holidays with my bosom-friend . . . at their elegant home in the city. All the delights of the gay season in the metropolis had been promised us, and the vision of Christmastide was ever before our half-dazzled eyes. It seemed to us that the joyful day of our departure would never, never come" (*TH* 31, 33). It never did; Grandpa Freeman had other ideas for Charles.

In Rochester the year before, the famous evangelist Charles G. Finney had preached a revival that, in addition to bringing the city to its knees, had produced a number of edifying side effects. Throughout Monroe County renewed zeal was shown for Bible societies, the temperance movement, and religious education; indeed, Rochester began preening itself as a "banner city for Sunday schools."[21] Recalling the crusade in his autobiography, Finney noted that the "blessed work of grace extended and increased until it seemed as if the whole city would be converted."[22]

By late 1857, the waves from this revival had washed across western New York, engulfing Little Valley. Inspired by "conviction," Grandpa Freeman was concerned not only for his own salvation but also his grandson's: a strange lad, Charles, who always smelled suspiciously of wintergreen and who had shown a heathenish devotion to those graven images from China. The boy's mother had evidently allowed him to fall prey to godless influences in San Francisco; it was high time for him to be "saved."

Without at first knowing why, Charles was abruptly recalled from school. Heavy-hearted at the loss of his chum, he was further depressed by what was in store. Every night Grandpa Freeman drove him to the Little Valley church, where the revival was ablaze with the holy fire of an illiterate disciple of Finney. Long after he had become a Catholic, Stoddard recalled the scene:

There was a bench under the pulpit which was known as the "anxious seat"! All those who were willing to acknowledge themselves sinners—I remember that the large majority considered themselves not such;—all those who desired the prayers of the prayerful for their salvation; all those who were seeking, or desiring, or even willing to accept that "change of heart," which was pronounced the one thing needful, were requested to step forward in the face of the multitude and boldly station themselves on this "anxious seat"—or kneel by it if they preferred to do so,—and there undergo the ordeal of prayer. The spectacle was humiliating beyond expression. Nervous excitement and the loss of all self-control drove the timid and shamefaced forward upon this rack of torture. Some of them, embarrassed and bewildered, wrung their hands and cried aloud. Once there, they were not permitted to retreat, but, surrounded by half-frantic men and women, whose flushed faces and flashing eyes were fearful to behold, they were held forcibly upon the bench, where they suffered the torments of the damned, until the close of the session. (*TH* 37–38)

Rather than advancing to the anxious seat, as his grandfather had hoped, Charles retreated to a rear pew, "stupefied with fear" (*TH* 38). He was prodded toward the pulpit nonetheless and coerced into confessing his sinfulness, but "salvation" never materialized in any form that Charles could recognize. At first he was troubled. After the services, as he lay abed in the farmhouse attic looking at the frosty stars, he began to wonder when this mysterious "corporeal phenomenon" (*TH* 42)— the change of heart—would begin to manifest itself. It was some years later before Stoddard was able to convince himself that the heart he had been born with was perfectly all right.

During this dreary holiday Charles was delivered from his Slough of Despond by an invitation to visit Dr. Stoddard, his worldly grandfather in Pembroke. On the northbound train he felt much relieved: "Oh, the clouds that passed from before my half-blinded eyes; the millstones that fell from my neck; the shadow that was lifted from off my soul!" (*TH* 44). Unlike the hapless Grandpa Freeman, Dr. Stoddard had been a successful physician since 1810. Moreover, the doctor was rich—although he had lost a considerable sum in his son's Rochester firm. Most important, at least in his grandson's eyes, Dr. Stoddard was a gentleman, something that Charles yearned to be when he grew up; in fact, it was what he was trying to be even as a child.

In Pembroke no one was forced to go to church on Sunday, but Charles rather enjoyed the "light, bustling air" of the Unitarian services, which reminded him of declamation hour at school (*TH* 47). If he preferred, Charles could stay home on Sunday and play marbles or read anything he wished. Instead of grace at table, there was wine, with which Charles was occasionally toasted by Dr. Stoddard's dinner guests. Best of all, his grandfather took him to his first circus, where Charles, dazzled by the grace of the near-naked acrobats, concluded that they were "but little lower than the angels" (*TH* 46). Circus performers, male acrobats particularly, were to remain a lifelong fascination for Stoddard, who thirty years later in Honolulu frequented the tent where the young men changed their costumes.

According to the Unitarians, "man's chief end was to be sociable and satisfied" (*TH* 48), but during the last year of his "exile" in New York, Charles's efforts to be sociable and satisfied met with only occasional success. In the fall of 1858, after Grandpa Freeman had moved to another farm near Attica, Charles attended the Genesee and Wyoming Seminary in neighboring Alexander, a town that Stoddard remembered for its pleasant gardens. Here his chums were Edgar Montgomery, who, like Fred, reminded Charles of the olive-tinted Mexicans he had known in California, and Richard Waite, in whose father's barn the boys would often play. Charles also established a close friendship with a girl named Lizzie, with whose family he boarded. He and Lizzie read the *Waverly Magazine* with keen interest, especially after they had submitted their prospective contributions. Charles's romantically juvenile poem, "Helena," was accepted but never published—which is perhaps just as well.

Oddly enough for a bookish boy who was addicted to serialized novels—those of Mrs. E. D. E. N. Southworth being his favorites at this time—Charles did not care much for school. Recitation frightened him; spelling bees mortified him; and, small for his age, he stood target for the school bullies, one of whom pelted him with pebbles when he was not heralding his approach with sneering epithets. Charles took some satisfaction in editing the school paper, for which he worked up "personal items" in an "impertinent" style. He also looked forward to performing in the class play. Once again, however, Grandpa Freeman intervened: Charles was summoned home the week before final exercises, with "scarcely time to say farewell even to my bosom-friends" (*TH* 53). Joyfully, the boy learned that he was bound to rejoin his family in San Francisco.

First, however, there was something in Attica that Grandpa Freeman wanted his grandson to see: the corpse of a boy about Charles's age.

Apparently doubting the sincerity of Charles's religious "conversion," Grandpa Freeman believed that attending this boy's funeral would be a salutary experience. Thirty years later, Stoddard shivered to recall the "gloss of the rosewood coffin," the "sickly pallor of the memorial wreaths," the "mingled odor of fresh varnish and tuber roses," and the church choir's singing, "I would not live always, I ask not to stay / Where storm after storm rises dark o'er the way." But the funeral failed in its desired effect. Rather than being impressed with the "solemn fact that death is always with us, and that it is our first duty to be prepared for it," Charles felt only fiercer resentment toward his grandfather and the inexplicable and capricious God to whom he was always praying (*TH* 54).

The first stirring of Charles's rebellion came a few days later in New York, where he was to meet the boat for San Francisco. Despite his having been warned against the wiles of the city, Charles was determined to indulge his whims just as soon as Grandpa Freeman returned home. For two days the boy—smelling of wintergreen, no doubt—became a Broadway boulevardier, devouring the sounds and smells and sights with the voracity of a younger Walt Whitman. He dared to go to as many plays as he could afford, thrilled by the performances of both Laura Keene and James Wallack. "For the first time in my life," Stoddard remembered, "I felt a sense of absolute freedom and relished it heartily."[23]

On the way to San Francisco, via Panama, the fifteen-year-old boy had time to ponder his young life, and he came to at least two conclusions. First, he wanted nothing more to do with the religion of the Freemans; religious frenzy, he decided, simply weakened his faith in the frenzied. Second, he was finished with school. What would he do, then? He hardly knew, except to imagine staying home and becoming the Boy Poet of San Francisco!

2

S AN FRANCISCO had flourished during the two years Charles had
been away. Tents had been replaced by brick buildings that rose as high
as three or four stories. The Stoddard residence, now on Powell near
Clay, was in the center of the city, which was growing westward toward
the Presidio and southward toward the Mission Dolores. San Francisco
claimed to have a population of about sixty thousand, mostly men
between the ages of twenty and forty, who were reputed to be "easy
going, witty, hospitable, lovable, inclined to be unmoral rather than
immoral in . . . personal habits, and easy to meet and to know."[1] The
city had eight hundred liquor dealers, ninety-five hairdressers, eighty-
four restaurants, seventeen banks, and twelve daily newspapers.

The following items might well have attracted Charles's notice: Bayard Taylor was due to lecture on "The Arabs"; Norton I, the self-
appointed Emperor of the United States and Protector of Mexico, was
issuing outrageous and unheeded royal proclamations; a dramatic version of *Uncle Tom's Cabin* was opening, and the original Siamese Twins
were scheduled for exhibit; among the new books at the Mercantile
Library was Walt Whitman's *Leaves of Grass*, which "while full of rich,
nutty thoughts . . . are about as fit for general reading as Rabelais"; and

in Sacramento the legislature had approved the Bachelor's Homestead Bill, to the dismay of one editorialist who agreed that while homesteading "may be tolerated when confined to married persons, it becomes an intolerable public grievance when extended to those coreless knots on the trunk of society—confirmed and deliberate bachelors."[2]

I

The literary life of the city, which was formative of Stoddard's career in the decade ahead, may be described, in a somewhat oversimplified way, as an unstable mixture of Eastern elevation and frontier earthiness. The two traditions clashed, of course: first in northern California and later throughout the country. Philip Rahv's classic essay, "Paleface and Redskin," offers some usefully succinct generalizations about these two "schools" in American literature:

> The paleface is a "high-brow," though his mentality—as in the case of Hawthorne and James—is often of the kind that excludes and repels general ideas; he is at the same time both something more and something less than an intellectual in the European sense. And the redskin deserves the epithet "low-brow," not because he is badly educated—which he might or might not be—but because his reactions are primarily emotional, spontaneous, and lacking in personal culture. The paleface continually hankers after religious norms, tending toward a refined estrangement from reality. The redskin, on the other hand, accepts his environment, at times to the degree of fusion with it, even when rebelling against one or another of its manifestations. At his highest level the paleface moves in an exquisite moral atmosphere; at his lowest he is genteel, snobbish, and pedantic. In giving expression to the vitality and to the aspirations of the people, the redskin is at his best; but at his worst he is a vulgar anti-intellectual, combining aggression with conformity and reverting to the crudest forms of frontier psychology.[3]

Literary men who succeeded in San Francisco in the 1860s were generally those with more than a little of the "redskin" in their makeup. But as Charles Warren Stoddard grew to manhood in this decade, it was painfully clear to everyone that, at least in literary terms, he was a congenital "paleface."

When he got home, Stoddard was not so immediately concerned with the literary atmosphere of San Francisco as with his own future. He made it clear that he did not wish to attend the San Francisco High School, and he fancied that he might like a literary sort of job. This turned out to be not writing books, but selling them as a clerk in Chileon Beach's shop on Montgomery Street, a position he was to hold for two-and-a-half years. As the West Coast headquarters for the American Bible Society and the American Tract Society, the store ran heavily to religious stock, but miscellaneous literature was also at hand—although it was almost hidden on a back shelf. Charles favored poetry, and he began to keep a scrapbook of lines that impressed him and, ultimately, to submit his own poems to a new monthly magazine called the *Golden Era*. In the "Poet's Corner," where "the favorite Western themes of homesickness, praise of mountain and sea scapes, and tributes to nature's flowers—botanical or human—were treated over and over again by aspiring lyricists," verses by "Pip Pepperpod" (Stoddard's pseudonym) began to appear.[4] Charles, of course, was immensely pleased, sure that he had found his calling at last.

It was through his connection with the *Golden Era* that Charles began to meet people who would significantly affect him. Stoddard became a lifelong friend of Charles Henry Webb, a former regular at Pfaff's (the Bohemian beer cellar in New York), who had written for the *New York Times* and who was gaining popularity for his witty column called "Things." One of the most flamboyant members of the *Golden Era* circle was the sensitive and high-strung Fitz Hugh Ludlow, author of *The Hasheesh Eater*, who loved to talk about Charles Darwin, astrology, necromancy, and almost everything else. Another writer whom Stoddard grew to like was Ralph Keeler, a dashing young man who had run away from home, performed in a minstrel troupe, attended a German university, tramped barefoot throughout Europe, and who was currently teaching languages at a private school on Rincon Hill. Prentice Mulford, known throughout the state as the "Diogenes of the Tuolumne," had also taught school in addition to working in the mines, going to sea, and running for the state assembly.

Stoddard also met two unusual women who occasionally wrote for the *Golden Era*. The oft-married Adah Menken, a friend of Walt Whitman and a champion of free verse and free love, was soon to become notorious for her performance in *Mazeppa*, in which she impersonated a naked man strapped to the back of a horse. Accompanied by her illegitimate son, Ada Clare had come to San Francisco to appear in *Camille*, and Stoddard became one of her most devoted fans. There were other colorful characters passing through the *Golden Era* offices as well, but the three most important to Stoddard's life were Ina Coolbrith, Bret Harte, and Mark Twain.

Charles was about the same age as Ina, and they soon became like brother and sister. He loved the chats in which "Miss" Coolbrith confided a few mysteries about her past. No one was to know, she said as they sat in her cozy parlor, that she was the niece of Mormon prophet Joseph Smith and that she had come to San Francisco to escape a disastrous marriage in Los Angeles. Nevertheless, believing at this time and for many years to come that her friend was "normal," Ina told Charles that he would find true happiness only if he got "married and settled in life."[5] They probably talked a good deal about their poetry—hers was almost as delicate and wistful as his—which was appearing not only in the *Golden Era* but in the *Californian* and in *Outcroppings* as well. No doubt, they also compared notes on Bret Harte, who, when the *Overland Monthly* got under way, was to join them as a member of the "Golden Gate trinity."[6]

Stoddard's relationship with Harte was equally congenial, if never quite so intimate, as that with Ina. After all, Harte, who was six years older, would soon settle down as a married man and father, and he kept a certain reserve that held everyone at a distance. What the two men had in common on the surface was that they were both gentlemen; in fact, by California standards, Harte was regarded as something of a dandy. Beneath the surface Harte seemed to possess a compassion for the underdog that made him sympathize with Stoddard. One of his biographers has noted that Harte, being partly Jewish, was unusually sensitive to the plight of his fictional "breeds" and indeed to the plight of all the "weak creatures of the earth—animals, children, and oppressed races."[7] Having been driven out of the mining town of Arcata for his editorial stand against the slaughter of Indians, Harte had some personal basis for siding with outcasts, in and out of his stories. It would have been easy for him to make fun of dreamy Charles Stoddard; instead he took pains to encourage and to guide the younger man.

Although Stoddard and Mark Twain were eventually to become friends, it is unlikely that either made a favorable first impression on the other. Mark Twain might well have reminded Stoddard of the school bullies who once had tormented him. Around town the story was circulating that Mark Twain had a mean sense of humor: he and his roommate (who could "whip anybody that walked on two legs" in the

Nevada Territory) threw empty beer bottles upon the roofs of houses where Chinese lived, just to see the families swarm out and shake their fists.[8] As for literary talent, Charles was not likely impressed by Mark Twain's theater reviews for the *Morning Call;* and a tale about jumping frogs in Calaveras County was hardly Charles's idea of worthwhile literature. From Mark Twain's point of view, the youth who called himself "Pip Pepperpod" must have seemed too "milk-and-watery" to be a regular fellow. Years later he was to write publicly that Stoddard was "the purest male I have known," meaning, as he wrote privately, that Stoddard was "such a nice girl."[9] In short, Stoddard was a "sissy."

II

At the book shop San Francisco's rising young poet "did not take much interest in dusting," and when he had to wash the windows from the inside, he felt like a "freak on exhibition" (CRP). But what else was he to do? Toward the end of 1862, Thomas Starr King, a Unitarian minister and eloquent Unionist, suggested an answer: go back to school. King, who came into the book shop one day singing praises for the Pepperpod poems, urged that the discipline of the classroom would foster even greater mastery. "In my youth I was a hero worshipper," Stoddard recalled, "and Thomas Starr King seemed to me the most heroic of them all" (CRP). When his heroes spoke, Charles always tried to obey, and he enrolled in City College for the spring semester of 1863. Stoddard took the Reverend Mr. George Burrows's course in literature, which was a "gentle inspiration for us all." He also contributed poems to the *City College Journal,* still using the "secret" pseudonym of "Pip Pepperpod." But a single semester was enough to convince Stoddard that "city life in combination with City College was not calculated to especially benefit one of my temperament" (CRP).

That is, there were too many enticing diversions in San Francisco. At the theater, for instance, this was the era of Menken in *Mazeppa,* Edwin Booth in *Hamlet,* and Joseph Jefferson in *Rip Van Winkle;* of Miss Lotta Crabtree, "The People's Pet," singing such crowd-pleasers as "Willie, We Have Missed You" and "Dear Mother, I'll Come Home Again." Impresario Tom Maguire was bringing stars like Edwin Forrest, Charles Kean, and Madame Ristori to town, and in his newly opened Academy of Music he was presenting everything from grand opera to prizefights. Charles was also meeting more and more writers, artists, and "Bohe-

mians," all of whom were more exciting than his assignments for the
Reverend Mr. Burrows. There was "Orpheus C. Kerr," the satirist whom
Menken married after she had been deserted by John "Benicia Boy"
Heenan, the famous prize-fighter. Even more interesting was W. A.
"Comet Quirls" Kendall, who wrote scandalous poems in praise of
passion. Through Fitz Hugh Ludlow, Stoddard met Albert Bierstadt,
who was to become well known for his sketches of the Yosemite country.

Over in drowsy Oakland, no doubt, there would be fewer distractions.
After a family conference it was suggested that if Charles really desired
to prepare for college, he might cross the Bay to attend Brayton Academy. "There were classic groves and the town—it was little more than a
village then—was almost as quiet as a cloister," Stoddard recalled. "I
could return to the bosom of my family and revel in the pageant of the
streets that were so picturesque and peculiar in those days" (CRP). It
was decided he would enroll for the fall term of 1863, and, for once,
Charles actually seemed eager to go. Not only would the academy be an
escape from the workaday world, but also the idea of being "cloistered"
with other young men appealed to him mightily. Having "sighed" over
the pages of *Tom Brown's Schooldays*, Thomas Hughes's novel about
"the sweet influence of Arthur over the stalwart and impetuous Tom,"
Charles wondered if he might discover *his* Tom at Brayton Academy.

As it turned out, it appears, he did. But another discovery he made
during the 1863–64 school year was that he was never going to succeed
as a student. Virgil and the *Anabasis* were both his "delight" and his
"despair," and he was simply unable to "gather knowledge in the
conventional way." Once more Charles felt the embarrassment he had
known as a schoolboy in New York. "I conned my text-book by the hour
and honestly endeavored to make its contents all my own forever, yet in
the end I seemed to have accomplished little and that little left me when
the class was called" (CRP).

Outside the classroom, his emotional attachments continued to follow the pattern that had been established in early adolescence. As
usual, Charles was an outsider. Rather than living with the other boys in
the school dormitory on 12th Street, he lived apart in a vine-covered
cottage down by the water. But, of course, he wanted very much to
belong. At night he would stroll past the dormitory and "look up at the
long rows of lighted windows and wish myself a happy habitant—they
always seemed happy—for I began to feel that I was more like a parlor
boarder than a member of the fraternity." As an outsider, it was all the

easier for Charles to fantasize about the glamorous, self-assured young men who, as insiders, were the school's leaders and heroes. Stoddard recalled that boarding school had always seemed like an "enchanted realm," where "the manlier boys were natural rulers and all the others their willing votaries. I know that it is the nursery—not to say the hot-bed—of the emotions" (CRP).

In this particular "hot-bed," Charles apparently found the image of "Tom" in a classmate so spellbinding that Stoddard was to remember him for years and to confide about him in a long letter to W. D. Howells in 1892. Howells, with whom Stoddard had developed a warm friendship, had written playfully: "Whenever we feel gay or sad, we say, we wish Stoddard were here. Does everybody like you, and does it make you feel badly? Are you sure that you are worthy of our affection? If you have some secret sins or demerits, don't you think you ought to let us know them, so that we could love you less?"[10] In reply, Stoddard offered a sketch titled "The Spell-binder" as "one of the reasons why I should be despised and rejected." Although written in a tone of condescension and exaggeration meant to suggest that he was now greatly amused at his schoolboy silliness, the vignette has at its core an anguish that must at one time have been all too real. For what it reveals of Stoddard's inner life, it deserves to be quoted at length:

> Once there was a fellow at school who caught my eye and held it. He seemed to me little less than Godlike. I had never before seen such eyes, such curly hair, such a haughty mien in a youth of eighteen or nineteen. He had scorn of everybody and everything—save only himself.
>
> Me he ignored utterly even while I worshiped silently in his presence and secretly wished that I might die for his sake; for his briefest pleasure I felt that I would joyfully return to dust. Such is the heart of youth when it has been touched by the spirit of romance!
>
> At the close of his first term at school he, one day, wanted a match: we were all in the campus in Holiday attire; all in high spirits and most of the fellows were at his feet. I worship silently and apart—as was my wont.
>
> O, Blessed Day! It chanced that there wasn't a match in the crowd. But I was not in the crowd; I was never in the crowd; I had a match. Having become desperate in his fruitless search for a match he, at the last moment, discovered me. I thought I heard a voice from heaven crying for a match. Kismet! My hour had come! He asked me in the doubtfullest way if I had a match and I produced one. It was the proudest moment of my life. The dews of joy were damp upon my brow; my heart turned over with delight. I wished I were a match that he might strike my head against something and consume me at the tip of his cigarette.

He condescended to take my trembling match and turned away without uttering one syllable of thanks. Had I been a paper matchbox he could not have treated me with less [sic] indifference.

My admiration of his haughtiness was boundless. I felt that I had not lived in vain. The one word, the one moment had attoned [sic] for the draining of a cup of bitterness that was forever brimming over.

Although it seems quite likely that in reality the episode had ended here, in embellishing the tale for Howells, Stoddard added an improbable plot reversal and an obscure moral:

A second term was drawing to a close. I was still unnoticed; yet all this time I would have dragged myself at the wheels of his chariot—had he only given me the chance. In the last pathetic moments of commencement-day—when every heart was in its unaccustomed throat—suddenly the Match-King turned upon me—upon *me*, his abject slave—and protested love of me; and would have me pass my vacation at his Palace; and sit upon his right hand, that he might make mine enemies my footstool; other unspeakable attractions were offered too numerous to mention.

What did thy servant? With one momentary, far away glance that did not admit him or the likes of him within its range, I dismissed his overtures with a wave of my hand as something impossibly presumptuous, and soared away.

The spell was broken. My hour of deliverance had come. At that moment moment [sic] he crumbled before me—a creature of the commonest clay—and on the hights [sic] of Olympus there was loud laughter among the Gods.

Moral: We are ever human even if we seem divine.[11]

"The Spell-binder" describes the sort of relationship that Stoddard often sought and usually suffered through. Moreover, its self-deprecating subtitle—"one of the reasons why I should be despised and rejected"—abounds in implications for homosexual identity in the nineteenth century.

Until the day he died, Stoddard was almost constantly in love; and if there were no agreeable homosexual males nearby, which was often the case, Stoddard would, with a sigh, tumble for an attractive heterosexual male. With this point in mind, the streak of "masochism" that runs through "The Spell-binder" can be better understood. Time after time, falling in love had so conditioned Stoddard to expect rejection and suffering that he eventually accepted the proposition that, at least in his own case, a correlation existed between the two. The extent of his suffering seemed a measure and indeed a proof of his love. At least subconsciously, Stoddard felt he did not deserve to be loved by the godlike idols he worshiped; had they stepped down from their pedestals and loved him in return, his reaction would have been more consternation than joy. Renunciation became almost a way of life. He could, like Emily Dickinson, "wade Grief—Whole Pools of it," but "the least push of Joy" had a tendency to startle and unnerve him as he watched his accustomed universe turn upside down.[12]

III

How did Stoddard and others of his time define this kind of love that often brought with it such exquisite pain and so little pleasure? We have a clue in Stoddard's use of "should" in the phrase, "one of the reasons why I should be despised and rejected." As we have seen and will continue to see, many people of prominence and of various religious beliefs accepted rather than rejected Stoddard in spite of what must have been a general awareness that he was sexually "eccentric." To some extent, this acceptance is explained by the fact that Stoddard was a "Bohemian" at a time when people indulged the "sins" and eccentricities of Bohemians with the understanding that they were more affectations than signs of depravity.

More to the point, however, Americans in the nineteenth century simply lacked the terms with which to define people like Stoddard. True, various slang terms implying sissiness (e.g., "Miss Nancy," "Charlotte-Ann," "Aunt Fancy") were in use, but none was necessarily synonymous with "pederast" or "sodomite," words that were unsayable and almost unthinkable in the polite society in which Stoddard generally moved. If heterosexuals had a hard time defining the homosexual (a term coined in 1869 by a Hungarian doctor), it can be imagined how baffling it must have been for homosexuals to try to define themselves. In the mid-nineteenth century there was almost no published literature on this subject for the layman to read, especially in America. As a result, young homosexuals often felt they were the only ones in the universe so afflicted, and, quite understandably, a great number of their self-definitions were idiosyncratic.

In Stoddard's case, we find some relevant jottings in the "Thought-Book" he kept from 1865 to 1867. In one entry, he thinks of sketching a "romance of how my soul got into [Ada] Clare's body and was at rest," with the idea that the "physique" would thus be "made whole."[13] Coincidentally, this concept of a woman's soul trapped inside a man's body was the basis of Carl Ulrichs's theories in Germany at this time. By the end of the century in England, Ulrichs's *Urning* had been translated into Edward Carpenter's "Uranian," a member of an "intermediate" sex that, high on the evolutionary ladder, combined in one body the most noble aspects of the female and the male.[14] Thinking of himself as some kind of biological sport, Stoddard, at least at this time, seemed to experience very little shame or guilt about falling in love with other young men. In a few years he was to have Paul Rookh argue in "Hearts of Oak" that God-given instincts of whatever kind must be right; and in a "Thought-Book" entry for 27 May 1866, he expressed his belief in a God who is perpetually compassionate and forgiving. Later we will find that, in moments of depression, Stoddard tended to despise and reject himself. But in his young manhood he seemed to view the arrival of love as a tender and enchanting experience. Even when the love object was someone as indifferent as the "Spell-binder," Stoddard always tried to relish and enjoy the experience the best he knew how.

3

B Y THE end of the 1863–64 school year at Brayton Academy, Stoddard was a nervous wreck. What led to this condition we do not know
for sure; but, aside from Stoddard's aversion to his studies, his case of
nerves might have had to do with an especially devastating emotional
entanglement. Whatever the cause, the family doctor prescribed that
nineteenth-century panacea for any sort of mental or physical indispo-
sition: a lengthy sea voyage. So in August 1864, in order to recover his
equilibrium, Stoddard left San Francisco for a six-months' stay in
Hawaii.

Just twenty-one, Stoddard was still malleable, unformed, and uncertain from nearly every point of view. As a writer, he was a published
poet, but he had not yet discovered the type of writing that would bring
him more than local celebrity. As a searcher after religious truth, he was
wavering somewhere between the Unitarians and the Episcopalians,
occasionally visiting Catholic churches in order to hear the beautiful
music. As one drawn to his own sex, he was still no doubt very much of a
virgin, puzzled and saddened that most of those he loved so rapturously
seemed not to care too much for him in return. In several ways, this trip

to Hawaii was a turning point, destined, as Stoddard put it, "to influ-ence the whole current of my life" (CRP).

I

Charles was enchanted with the tropical kingdom of Hawaii. In the balminess of its climate, the sweep of its seashore, and the beauty of its flowers and people, it was to San Francisco as, some years before, San Francisco had been to New York State. A visitor to Honolulu about this time described the city as almost overwhelming in its lush and exotic foliage: "over-arching trees, through whose dense leafage the noon sunshine only trickled in dancing, broken lights; umbrella trees, caou-tchouc, bamboo, mango, orange, breadfruit, candlenut, monkey pod, date and coco palms, alligator pears, 'prides' of Barbary, India, and Peru, and huge-leaved, wide-spreading trees, exotics from the South Seas, many of them rich in parasitic ferns, and others blazing with bright, fantastic blossoms." The people of Honolulu were just as color-ful and picturesque:

> Such rich brown men and women they were, with wavy, shining black hair, large, brown, lustrous eyes, and rows of perfect teeth like ivory. Everyone was smiling. . . . Without an exception, the men and women wore wreaths and garlands of flowers, carmine, orange, or pure white, twined round their hats, and thrown carelessly round their necks. . . . Chinamen . . . "foreigners," half-whites, a few negroes, and a very few dark-skinned Polynesians from the far-off South Seas, made up the rest of the rainbow-tinted crowd.[1]

At first Charles was content to soak up such atmosphere in hopes of regaining the serenity he had lost at Brayton Academy. He spent days lounging in a hammock at the home of family friends who lived two miles from Honolulu in the Nuuannu Valley. Ada Clare's coming to town provided a pleasant distraction, but Charles was lonely enough to recall his life at Brayton Hall "with a touch of tenderness that verged dangerously upon the romantic." There had been an "emotional part-ing with certain of my school fellows," and during the next months he wrote them "a bag full of sentimental letters" (CRP). One, apparently written to a spellbinding friend, if not *the* "Spell-binder," asked plain-tively: "Have you entirely forgotten a fellow? Are there no reminis-cences of bygones wherein I figure?" For Charles there were memories:

of "the little chat" in the dusk of his friend's quiet parlor, of the "ramble through the beautiful garden" and his gift of flowers. "Perhaps you don't know that I kept those flowers in a little white vase, till the leaves fell apart and then I knew it was time to walk again toward you and your garden" (IH 17, Sept. 1864).

Charles snapped out of his nostalgia one day when, in Whitney's bookstore, he was introduced to a "slender but well proportioned gentleman, clad in white duck." This "godsend" turned out to be Charles Derby, the thirty-eight-year-old manager of the Royal Hawaiian Theater. The two became "fast friends at once, and it was my custom to lounge under the window in the green-room hour after hour, while he talked of the vicissitudes in his extraordinary career." Derby had been "delicate and effeminate" as a youth, but, "possessed of much physical grace," he became a circus acrobat and later a versatile actor. He excelled in light comedy and eccentric character parts, and he loved to perform in drag ("the prima donna in burlesque opera was a favorite assumption"). On the side he raised botanical specimens and instructed young men in music, dancing, fencing, boxing, and gymnastics. Known for being charitably disposed toward the young, Derby invited many homeless youths to take temporary shelter under his roof. Over glasses of lemonade, he enthralled Stoddard with tidbits of backstage gossip. Years later in "The Drama in Dreamland" Stoddard was to capture Derby in a description that was in some ways a self portrait: "a man of the most eccentric description; greatly loved by a few, intensely disliked by many, and perhaps fully understood by no one. He had learned to hate the world, and at times to irritate himself very much over it; doubtless he had cause" (*CSS* 53, 56, 62–64).

An even greater godsend was the chance to accompany Enoch Wood Perry, an American painter in his early thirties, on a tour of the island of Hawaii, the highlight of which was a week spent in Hilo, which was even more luxuriantly green than Honolulu. Stoddard and Perry stayed at the Protestant Mission House (since there was no hotel in Hilo), and every afternoon Stoddard went to a nearby pool to watch the young natives swim. The setting was breathtaking: "The stream that flows down from the mountain over a bed of lava as smooth as glass, there leaps from the brink of a cliff and buries itself in foam at the top of a deep pool half a hundred feet below. It was like pouring cream from the lip of a mug the way that stream slid off into the air, and 'twas whipped cream for sure when it struck the rim of the pool" ("Kane-Aloha," *CSS*

69). The swimmers of Hilo, who have been likened in physique and comeliness to "the bronzes of the Naples Museum,"[2] were breathtaking, too. "And the greatest of these," Stoddard decided, perched on a rock above the pool and eyeing each young man in turn, "was Kane-Aloha" (*CSS* 71).

In a sketch written about Kane-Aloha ("well named the Loving Man" [*CSS* 81]), Stoddard says that before long he and the young native were "inseparable," explaining that "friendship ripens quickly in the tropical sunshine" (*CSS* 71). But the Protestant missionary's wife was suspicious, making it her business to interrogate young Stoddard about his doings. In the sketch, however, it is not the woman but, rather surprisingly, Enoch Perry who tries to come between the two young men. Perry suggests leaving Hilo; Stoddard counters with the idea that Kane-Aloha be hired as their guide for a horseback trip to the other side of the island. Finally acquiescing, Perry assumes the role of watchful chaperon and insists that everyone stay together during their journey. Stoddard outwits Perry by straggling behind with Kane-Aloha, conveniently getting "lost," and the two are separated from Perry for several delightful days and nights.

The noonday heat induced Kane-Aloha to shed his garments one by one, and it was "evident that presently there would not be a solitary stitch left for propriety's sake. Nobody seemed to care in the least." Especially Stoddard, who, after all, was the only one around *to* care: "Is there anything more soothing, more cleansing, more ennobling and refining than the caress of the pure, cool air when it comes in immediate contact with the human body as God created it? O, Ye Tailors! Ye Men-Milliners! Ye Out-fitters of the Unfit! Ye Padders, and Upholsterers, and Repairers and Remodelers of the human form divine, out upon Ye!" (*CSS* 76).

If the days spent riding with Kane-Aloha through the jungle greenery were enchanting, the nights were literally indescribable. Stoddard became an "easy convert to the untrammelled delights of barbarianism." He and his "loving man" not only engaged in "riotous living," they reveled in it (*CSS* 76). Although they "transgressed the unwritten law," they were "not in the least sorry for it" (*CSS* 78). At twilight they slept together in little thatch huts along the roadside; and as the "indolent zephyr breathed upon us freighted with the narcotic aroma of cocoanut-oil," they "yielded to the seductions of the hour" (*CSS* 76). Stoddard may well have lain awake for a long time, glancing at the beautifully naked youth sleeping beside him and marveling at his great good luck after all these years. What fun it would be to write about these experiences! But could such a tale ever be published?

II

Stoddard did write about Kane-Aloha several years later, and the sketch was published. But in 1865, he was bracing himself for one more try at Brayton Academy, where he enrolled again soon after his return from Hawaii. By glancing at college freshman Paul Rookh in "Hearts of Oak," we can understand why Stoddard's student days soon came to an end. They were simply a pose. Paul develops a "taste for the niceties in dress, and an inclination to swaggering and indifference." He chooses his cravats with care; he smokes and drinks and wants to impress everyone on campus as being blasé and altogether comfortable with his dandified worldliness. "Instincts are given us," says Paul. "Why are they given us, unless we are to follow their guidance? God does not instill into us desires which are awakened only to be smothered. That would be a mistake of God and Nature, and neither God nor Nature can err."[3] A revealing rationalization for Stoddard to make as an unorthodox libertine, but a disastrous one for him to follow as a would-be student. By the end of 1865, he had left Brayton Academy for good and devoted himself to love and poetry.

The last chapters of "Hearts of Oak," along with the early chapters of the autobiographical novel *For the Pleasure of His Company*, provide a glimpse into Stoddard's Bohemian affairs at this time. Of special interest in the latter is the story of Paul Clitheroe's romantic fling with a mysterious young man named Foxlair, whose real-life model was Wylde Hardinge.

Data is scarce on this slippery adventurer's activities on the West Coast. In Civil War histories, however, Hardinge gets footnote mention as the first husband of "Rebel Spy" Belle Boyd. In the spring of 1864, Miss Boyd fell in love with one of her captors, Samuel Wylde Hardinge, a lieutenant in the Union navy. According to Miss Boyd, this dark-haired New Yorker was irresistibly magnetic: "The fascination of his manner was such, his every movement was so much that of a refined gentleman, that my 'Southern proclivities,' strong as they were, yielded for a moment to the impulses of my heart."[4] In June 1864, Hardinge was dishonorably discharged, and two months later he and Belle were married in London. Returning to America alone, he was arrested, imprisoned, and then released in 1865. According to Louis Sigaud's *Belle Boyd, Confederate Spy*, Hardinge was eager to rejoin his wife in England, but he never did. Sigaud insists that he must have died in the attempt, thus paving the way for his widow to marry again, which she did several times. In fact, Hardinge was in San Francisco about this time.

The impression he made on Stoddard's persona, Paul Clitheroe, matches the account of Miss Boyd. This dashing stranger is "swarthily handsome, with the physique of a trained athlete." He is "possessed of strong personal magnetism; there was no manner of doubt about that." Foxlair's air of mystery is enhanced by "all kinds of romantic rumors . . . that he had been a Rebel Spy, or the husband of a Rebel Spy, and a privateersman in the Spanish Main, etc., etc. Of all these he could speak most entertainingly."[5] In the novel Paul yields to the impulses of his heart and falls in love with this charmer, with whom he drinks, dines, carouses, and sleeps. In real life, Hardinge apparently left the Bay Area as mysteriously as he had arrived. After an exposé was printed in one of the dailies, the "Prince of Frauds" vanished, taking with him a piece of Stoddard's heart—and some of his clothes as well!

While the details of the Wylde Hardinge affair remain obscure, Stoddard's career as "Boy Poet" can be charted clearly. He made his poetic debut in book form with the publication of *Outcroppings*, the first anthology of California verse. A small quarto in gilt and purple, the book was edited by Bret Harte and published in December 1865, in time for the Christmas trade. Of the forty-two poems in the volume, four were Stoddard's, and these received mixed reviews in the local press. The Sacramento *Union* praised Stoddard's "Keats-like" quality, while, contrarily, the Virginia City *Territorial Enterprise* found that his verses were "frequently constructed without skill." A spirited controversy soon erupted over the book as a whole, along the lines that divided the "redskins" from the "palefaces," who dominated the anthology. The book smacked of a "mutual admiration society," complained the *Parajo Times*.[6] The Gold Hill *Daily News*, according to George Stewart's *Bret Harte*, "called the whole collection effeminate, unworthy of the virile West, and epitomized it as 'purp-stuff,' an epithet which thirty years later still stuck in Harte's memory."[7] Franklin Walker has noted that the "he-men among Pacific Coast poets were outraged." Where, they asked, was John Swett's "In the Mines"? And they sniggered at the inclusion of Stoddard, "who was so much like a girl that he blushed when the fellows told dirty stories in his company." Other "redskin" reviewers charged that the book was a "feeble collection of drivel" and "hogwash ladled from the slop-bucket."[8]

Apparently undaunted by the epithets hurled his way (at least indirectly) by the he-man critics, Stoddard persisted in writing "purp-stuff," doing all he could to advance the only career he had. He hardly cared what the ignorant miners in Nevada thought; he was bent on getting the attention of respectable writers back East and in England. To this end (and also to collect their autographs) he sent out proof sheets of seven of his poems, along with a cover letter, to all the famous people he could imagine might be sympathetic. "I was eager to know what the opinion of those whose reputations were established beyond question might be concerning my feeble efforts," Stoddard later explained, "and it was not long before I was pretty thoroughly informed" (CRP).

Among these poems were: "My Friend," a set of couplets in praise of the "deathless soul"; "The Secret Well," which turns out to be the poet's "fount of memory"; "At Anchor," a sentimental effusion about a sailor's homecoming; "Madrigal," an insipid pastoral scene, complete with brook and blushing maid; and "At the Spring," the climax of which is the discovery that a water snake has been spoiling a fountain. "A Rhyme of Life" epitomizes the verse Stoddard was writing at this time:

> *If life be as a flame that death doth kill;*
> *Burn little candle lit for me,*
> *With a pure spark, that I may rightly see*
> *To word my song and utterly*
> *God's plan fulfill.*

> *If life be as a flower that blooms and dies;*
> *Forbid the cunning frost that slays*
> *With Judas-kiss, and trusting love betrays:*
> *Forever may my song of praise*
> *Untainted rise.*

> *If life be as a voyage, or foul, or fair;*
> *Oh! bid me not my banners furl*
> *For adverse gale, or wave in angry whirl,*
> *Till I have found the gates of pearl*
> *And anchored there.*

In "Cherries and Grapes," however, Stoddard struck the sensual, exotic note of his later South-Sea prose:

> *Not the cherries' nerveless flesh,*
> *However fair, however fresh,*
> *May ever hope my love to win*
> *For Ethiop blood and satin skin.*
>
> *Their lustre rich, and deep their dye,*
> *Yet under all their splendors lie—*
> *To what I cannot tribute grant—*
> *Their hateful hearts of adamant.*
>
> *I love the amber globes that hold*
> *That dead-delicious wine of gold;*
> *A thousand torrid suns distill*
> *Such liquors as those flagons fill.*
>
> *Yet tropic gales with souls of musk*
> *Should steep my grapes in steams of dusk:*
> *An orient Eden nothing lacks*
> *To spice their purple silken sacks.* [9]

Stoddard was especially interested in hearing from Herman Melville, whose *Omoo* had so excited his imagination. Melville responded that he was "quite struck with the little effusion entitled 'Cherries & Grapes,'" adding, apparently in response to Stoddard's mention of his recent voyage to the South Seas, that he did "not wonder that you found no trace of me at the Hawaiian Islands." [10] Many of the replies were at least as faintly praising as Melville's. [11] Tennyson "liked" the verses; Longfellow found "a deal of beauty and freshness"; Emerson judged them "good and interesting"; while Fr. John Henry Newman thought them "elegant and touching." Other responses were tactfully critical. William Cullen Bryant detected a "certain unpruned luxuriance"; Henry Ward Beecher looked forward to "other maturer works"; John Stuart Mill cautioned against publishing any poetry "but what is of the very highest quality." Bayard Taylor hesitated to prophesy whether Stoddard would "become a part of our literature," and Thomas Wentworth Higginson said it was too early to tell if "verse is to be your appointed means of expression"—a view seconded by Thomas Hughes, who wrote that he did not think "poetry will prove to be your vocation after a few years."

Like most young writers, Stoddard thirsted for hearty encouragement, not disheartening caution, such as Oliver Wendell Holmes's
frank advice to "think well" before relinquishing "any useful occupation . . . for the life of an artist in verse." But Stoddard had no useful
occupation, and being a poet seemed the only vocation open to one of
his temperament. Encouraged by the more favorable comments and by
Bret Harte's willingness to help him, Stoddard decided in 1866 to have
a book of his poems published in San Francisco.

This slim volume of forty-five poems, underwritten by subscriptions,
illustrated by his friend William Keith, and published by Anton Roman,
appeared in the fall of 1867. The poems were grouped under six head-
ings: "Of Nature," "Idyllic and Legendary," "Of the Heart," "Of Fancy
and Imagination," "Of Meditation," and "Of Aspiration and Desire." In
the last group, two are of some interest. In "Unrest," Stoddard alludes to
"My heavy woe I may not name," but in "The Awakening," set in
Hawaii, Stoddard pretends that his experiences during that trip were
significant for spiritual as opposed to sexual reasons.

When *Poems* was about to appear, Anton Roman had the foresight to
send the jittery young Stoddard into the mountains "on the pretext of
wishing me to set Yosemite to song." He was relieved to have some place
to flee to, especially when he thought about the critical brickbats that
had been thrown at *Outcroppings*. Stoddard planned to stay at Yosemite
until "the agony was over," hoping that he could return to San Francisco "with peace in my heart and my brow bound with victorious
wreaths" (CRP).

The wreaths had thorns. While a few local reviewers praised him,
many others made sport of Stoddard and his book, often in the Wild-
West spirit that was conventional among San Francisco critics. One
reviewer had it both ways. In the *Californian*, James Bowman praised
the *Poems* in grandiose style and then savaged this review and Stoddard
in an anonymous piece in the *Dramatic Chronicle*. The reviews from the
East, on which Stoddard so counted, were no more encouraging. *The
Nation*'s critic felt only "imitation spasms" of someone in plight to the
Spasmodic School, and Edward Rowland Sill averred in the *New York
Round Table* that Stoddard had merely done "well what Tennyson has
done so infinitely better." In later years Stoddard came to agree with the
critics who "saw little or nothing in my verses save extravagance, rather
than those who professed to see in them evidence of great promise."
Poems, he conceded, had been a "mere wind-fall of unripe fruit."[12]

In 1867, the American poet whose approval Stoddard most desired, for reasons that did not have everything to do with poetry, was Walt Whitman. Stoddard's first reaction to Whitman's rude yawps had been a gentleman's cool disdain. In 1866, however, Stoddard wrote: "I have been reading *Walt Whitman* and him I thought a fool—and him I am growing to glorify." In the "Calamus" poems, Stoddard felt a temperamental kinship to Whitman that was far more important than their poetic differences. "Who shall say we are not all babes and fools; and that this one and the other one who are declared gross and rude— because their eyes see all things clearly and their lips speak out—who shall say they are not prince and king among us—and shall by and by shine brightly and be understood" (IH 21, 22 May 1866). Although Stoddard had hardly spoken out in his poems, he was hopeful that they might still ring a responsive chord in the heart of this man who had the courage to champion love between comrades.

Apparently, Stoddard's book of poems did not impress Whitman, who chose not to reply. Disappointed and frustrated, Stoddard tried a flank approach, sending an ingratiating note to John Burroughs, whose *Notes on Walt Whitman as Poet and Person* had just been published. How grateful he was, Stoddard wrote, for Burroughs's book on "the glorious Walt Whitman," from whom he was so eager to hear. Might Burroughs be willing to serve as a go-between?[13] But Whitman was not to break his silence until 1870, when, after reading "A South-Sea Idyl," he recognized Stoddard as a fellow worshiper at the altar of "manly love."

III

As the hostile reviews of *Poems* continued to come in, Stoddard felt hurt and depressed. He had done his best, and that had fallen short of his ambitions. He hardly knew where to turn. More than ever before, Stoddard needed a source of comfort, a refuge that would protect him in a way that his family and friends could not. He found that refuge in the Roman Catholic church, into which he was baptized at Saint Mary's Cathedral in San Francisco on 2 November 1867.

Several literary historians have written perceptively about what may have led Stoddard to become a Catholic. Kevin Starr attributes the conversion to Stoddard's aesthetic as well as emotional need for "an altar before which he could prostrate himself in adoration." The symbols of Catholicism "met the needs of his imagination and the hungers of his heart. Romanism was part of a total *mise en scène*. The Latin liturgy, the Italian Jesuits of Saint Ignatius Church where he went for instructions, his developing interest in the civilizations of Southern Europe, the very Mediterranean metaphor of California itself, all massed themselves on the borders of his imagination, moving him to an assent that was an act of religion, the election of a culture—and a vision of beauty."[14] Starr is right not to overlook the role of those Italian Jesuits at Saint Ignatius. Some were young and dark and beautiful; others were old and white-haired and venerable; all were soft-spoken and comforting and kindly. With equal insight, Franklin Walker views Stoddard's conversion in light of both his postpublication depression and his need to find a creed elastic enough to allow for his "pagan love of life." Catholicism "answered for him, as nothing before had done, the question which was with him constantly: 'What shall I do to be saved?' When he was baptized, he felt that all his problems were solved."[15] Stoddard himself gave an explanation twenty-four years later in a letter to James Whitcomb Riley: "I couldn't help it, you see; it was born in me and was the only thing that appealed to my temperament. I believe a man's religion is nessessarily [*sic*] a matter of temperament. I couldn't be anything else than a Catholic—except—*except* a downright *savage*, and I wish to God I were that!"[16]

When Stoddard spoke of his "temperament," he was alluding to the love of beauty that Walker and Starr recognize. But he was also suggesting to Riley the psychosexual implications of the word. In this regard, the consolation of Catholic confession was especially important to Stoddard, who knew very well from childhood what the Calvinists had to say about Sodom and Gomorrah. What the Presbyterians had seemed to damn in self-righteous fury the Catholics seemed to have the grace to forgive; and Stoddard sensed that one of his "temperament" would need a good deal of forgiveness for the rest of his life. Equally important to Stoddard was the "haven" aspect of the church, the sense that all over the world Catholics were warm and loving and hospitable. Years later Stoddard could recall the special balm of a young priest's touching him lightly on the shoulder, and it was mainly his sense of the church's loving embrace that made him happy to be drawn to its "majestic bosom."

In his comments on the conversion, Franklin Walker is not exaggerating when he says that Stoddard felt "if he could not find a place in lay society, he would become a monk."[17] For the rest of his life, Stoddard relied on the comforting idea that Catholics take care of their own; and in 1867, he asked assistance from Father Accalti, the Jesuit who had been in charge of his religious instruction. He explained to this good man that although he was not quite ready for the monastery, he needed some secular employment that would be comparably contemplative.

In *For the Pleasure of His Company,* there is a scene in which Paul Clitheroe turns to the Clergy House for an answer. Father A. Venerable (modeled on Father Accalti) gives this advice:

> It seems that many young men are seeking positions where they may make a respectable livelihood; they are willing to accept anything that is offered to them; there are in many cases young men of some experience; hardy, accustomed to manual labor, and stronger in body than you are, my child. . . . You cannot shovel coal; you cannot trundle freight upon the docks; you cannot drive a carriage for the coach companies in the city. . . . You are fitted to do another class of work; you are fitted to adorn literature.

It is a shame, the priest continues, that the public does not provide for struggling geniuses as it does for orphans and other unfortunates, especially since literary talent and reputation are widely considered to be insurmountable obstacles to worldly advancement: "Business men will not for a moment have a poet in their counting room, and they are no doubt right." But Father Venerable does know of one suitable opening: "There is a gentleman here who owns vast tracts of land in the southern part of the State; his flocks and herds wander broadcast over it; one might say that the 'Cattle upon a thousand hills are his.' He can offer you the lot of a shepherd" (*FPHC* 46–47).

A *shepherd?* Stoddard made other plans, turning at last to Harry Edwards, the actor-manager at the Metropolitan Theater, who had noticed his flair for the theatrical and had floated the idea of his going on the stage some day. Edwards's wife, an equally good friend, had commented favorably on Stoddard's voice and way of posing; she sensed he was a born actor. Less than thrilled by the prospect of appearing before the same local critics who had ridiculed his *Poems,* Stoddard asked to join Edwards's company in Sacramento, where he could break in with minor roles.

On 13 March 1868, Stoddard made his debut as the priggish Arthur Apsley in Dion Boucicault's *The Willow Copse.* The Sacramento *Daily Union* found his appearance "encouraging," his articulation "clear and full," and his manner "natural and self-possessed."[18] Something of a hit, Stoddard, like his character Paul Clitheroe, noticed that on the streets he was an "object of interest" to some of the young men of that city. In a rare reversal of roles, Stoddard became the idol of a star-struck young clerk, who was "never so happy" as when the actor "would consent to accept a late supper at his hands, and permit him to share the midnight oyster and musty ale which usually followed the labors of the evening." Soon, however, Stoddard/Clitheroe began to struggle in memorizing all of his different parts, and he wondered if he were truly cut out for a life on the stage. The star of the company told him that "an actor who hopes to reach the top of his profession must not only have talent, voice, figure, health, energy and application—he should have a steam engine at the base of his brain." Stoddard's reaction to this was despair. He soon found that he could not concentrate at all. During the afternoons he slipped off to the riverbank to sun himself and to "pore with listless eyes over the hateful text he was endeavoring to memorize"—a task all the more difficult for his having chosen the very spot where the young men of Sacramento came to swim (*FPHC* 59, 65–66).

Stoddard's listlessness increased, and when he heard there was an opening on the *Californian* in San Francisco, he hastily took it. The job turned out to be a menial one. The *Californian* was about to fold; and instead of writing, Stoddard was charged with keeping the books and mailing out subscribers' copies. But at least he now had rent money. At this time he was living in Oakland at the Hotel de France in grand Bohemian style. In the evenings he and other residents, including Prentice Mulford and James Bowman, would dine and drink alfresco while overlooking the Oakland waterfront. The *Californian* job also led to introductions to many of the new literary celebrities in the city, one of the most interesting of whom was Ambrose Bierce.

In 1868, Bierce was a twenty-six-year-old bachelor, "one of the handsomest men in town, with almost angelic good looks. He was a six-footer, with an erect carriage, a mop of curly golden hair, a sweeping gunfighter's moustache, fierce blue eyes, and baby-pink cheeks."[19] These attributes alone were sufficient to commend the former Union army lieutenant to Stoddard, but there was more. They could swap stories about their harrowing religious experiences as boys—although Bierce had been more resistant to revival hysteria than had Stoddard, having once broken up a camp meeting by galloping through the congregation on a horse. Bierce also impressed Stoddard with his sardonic sense of humor. Although Stoddard prided himself on tossing an occasional *bon mot*, there was no one sharper than Bierce in stinging repartee. His epigrams were quoted everywhere, and his "Town Crier" column in the *News Letter* was enormously popular. By the late 1860s, Stoddard was cultivating a lifelong fondness for drinking, something that appealed to Bierce as well.

In *Ambrose Bierce,* a slightly perplexed Richard O'Connor tries manfully to fit Stoddard into Bierce's circle of drinking cronies. "Among his favorite companions were Jimmy Bowman, a hard-drinking and determinedly Bohemian writer, and Charles Warren Stoddard . . . a wispy youth with a delicate manner; 'such a nice girl,' as Mark Twain called him. Yet he must have been made of sterner stuff than Twain believed in order to be accepted as a fellow tankard-man by the likes of Bierce and Bowman."[20] Like the biographers of Stoddard's other friends, O'Connor seems at a loss to explain the wispy youth's acceptance by "normal" people who, it is implied, should have known better. But, as we shall see, Stoddard was accepted as a "fellow tankard-man" by a wide variety of people, ranging from the ultrafeminine to the ultramasculine of both sexes; and his acceptance was based on criteria other than who happened to be made of "sterner stuff" than someone else. Stoddard was an appreciative listener; he enjoyed a good joke; but most of all—and this predilection had nothing to do with gender—he simply liked to get drunk.

At about this time, Stoddard was also getting acquainted with another man who was to leave a distinctive mark on West Coast literature: Joaquin Miller. Through a series of friendly letters, written from Grant County, Oregon, this country lawyer cemented a bond with Stoddard that was to become one of the most peculiar in the history of American literature. Like Bierce, Miller had been born in the Midwest, but unlike Bierce, Miller's talent was less for writing than for melodramatizing himself. Miller wrote at first to entreat Stoddard to boom his rough-hewn poems in the *Overland Monthly;* and upon receipt of a "gushing" reply, he confided to Stoddard that "I have not wrote much yet that I like." One day soon he and his wife would like to keep "open house for all free Bohemians. Wouldn't it be nice for you and Ina [Coolbrith] to come up and spend a Summer with Minnie Myrtle and I?"[21]

Instead of going to Oregon to visit this strange man, however, Stoddard decided to go back to the Islands. He had been invited to visit his sister, who had just married Parker Makee, son of a wealthy Maui plantation owner. From Sarah's description of their fifteen-thousand-acre estate, Stoddard concluded that being a coddled houseguest amid so much wealth and beauty would be a most welcome change. Then, too, he had been commissioned by the San Francisco *Evening Bulletin* to write a series of letters, to be published under the heading of "Hawaiian Island Notes." (He had already quit his job at the *Californian*, a position that was, after all, quite beneath his dignity.) Finally, there was the chance of meeting another Kane-Aloha and once more of loving and perhaps being loved in return. At this time in San Francisco, there was neither freedom nor opportunity to act as his "nature" prompted him. Doing so, as he would tell Walt Whitman, "would not answer in America, as a general principle,—not even in California, where men are tolerably bold."[22] He set sail for Honolulu toward the end of October 1868.

4

For the next eight months Stoddard roamed the Hawaiian Islands looking for news copy and also for obliging young men. Part of this time he was a guest at Rose Ranch, the Makee estate, which stretched from Makena Bay to halfway up Mount Haleakala. There, with his sister, brother-in-law, and other relations, he enjoyed a life of leisure and luxury to which he adjusted without difficulty. There were peacocks on the lawn, pianos in both the parlor and the schoolroom, and, should a playful mood strike him, a billiard room, a bowling alley, and a tennis court. And there were sailors to play with.

Stoddard's visit coincided with that of an American naval vessel, and he was seated often next to officers at the "long table in the long, long dining hall" (*ITD* 168). As Stoddard remembered, there was "nearly always a glimmer of brass buttons in the tableaux of social life. Ah, me! Many a youthful mariner, beautiful in broadcloth, gorgeous in gold lace, and surcharged with those graceful accomplishments that are forever associated with the aspiring off-shoots of Annapolis, found his way as if by instinct into the rose-garden of Ulupalakua" (*ITD* 176). Stoddard loved Rose Ranch for its commanding views of earth, sea, and sky, and he soon succumbed to the soft atmosphere, "the melting humidity, the permeating fragrance, the sensuous warmth, and the surprising beauty bursting at intervals upon the enraptured vision, that nourishes the voluptuous element in our nature" (*ITD* 181–82).

I

Stoddard could fully indulge *his* voluptuous element only when he was beyond the watchful eyes of his relatives on the estate. No doubt he found his way into the rose garden for chats with the better-looking officers, but if he wanted to sleep with the savages, he would have to go where they were. So he traveled up the coast of Maui to Lahaina and then on to the islands of Oahu and Molokai. Usually on horseback, sometimes with a guide, and other times alone, Stoddard had the wondrous experiences he described to Walt Whitman on 2 March 1869. Still chagrined that Whitman had never bothered to acknowledge his *Poems*, Stoddard began with a disarming plea:

> May I quote you a couplet from your Leaves of Grass? "Stranger! if you, passing, meet me, and desire to speak to me, why should you not speak to me? And why should I not speak to you?"
> I am the stranger who, passing, desires to speak to you. Once before I have done so offering you a few feeble verses. I don't wonder you did not reply to them. Now my voice is stronger. I ask—why will you not speak to me?

To prove his kinship with Whitman, Stoddard then described his *modus operandi* for finding superb young men:

> So fortunate as to be traveling in these very interesting Islands I have done wonders in my intercourse with these natives. For the first time I act as my nature prompts me. It would not answer in America, as a general principle,—not even in California, where men are tolerably bold. This is my mode of life.
> At dusk I reach some village—a few grass huts by the sea or in some valley. The native villagers gather about me, for strangers are not common in these parts. I observe them closely. Superb looking, many of them. Fine heads, glorious eyes that question, observe and then trust or distrust with an infallible instinct. Proud, defiant lips, a matchless physique, grace and freedom in every motion.
> I mark one, a lad of eighteen or twenty years, who is regarding me. I call him to me, ask his name, giving mine in return. He speaks it over and over, manipulating my body unconsciously, as it were, with bountiful and unconstrained love. I go to his grass house, eat with him his simple food, sleep with him upon his mats, and at night sometimes waken to find him

watching me with earnest, patient looks, his arm over my breast and around me. In the morning he hates to have me go. I hate as much to leave him. Over and over I think of him as I travel: he doubtless recalls me sometimes, perhaps wishes me back with him. We were known to one another perhaps twelve hours. Yet I cannot forget him. Everything that pertains to him now interests me.

You will easily imagine, my dear sir, how delightful I find this life. I read your Poems with a new spirit, to understand them as few may be able to. And I wish more than ever that I might possess a few lines from your pen. I want your personal magnetism to quicken mine.[1]

Stoddard closed this letter with a request for a photograph, and in June, Whitman complied, adding a short note: "I cordially accept your appreciation, & reciprocate your friendship. . . . Those tender & primitive personal relations away off there in the Pacific Islands, as described by you, touched me deeply."[2]

One of the unforgettable young men was Kána-aná, whom Stoddard met while riding through the Halawa valley near the eastern coast of Molokai. With "ripe lips," eyes that were "perfectly glorious," and "not a bad nose," Kána-aná was perhaps a "young scion of a race of chiefs" ("Chumming with a Savage," *CSS* 33). According to the tale that was to appear in the *Overland Monthly* in September 1869,[3] Stoddard stayed with Kána-aná for a couple of weeks, during which they gave themselves up to nearly every sensual delight. When they were not splashing in the ocean, they were lying naked on the beach, laughing, talking, and watching wild poppies nod in the breeze. They slept together in a huge bed, its posts charmingly festooned with wreaths of sweet-smelling herbs, quite as if it were their honeymoon. Stoddard could not help admiring the sleek, supple physique of his companion, who wished to hug him all night long. "I didn't sleep much," Stoddard confessed. "I think I must have been excited" (*CSS* 36). Again and again, Kána-aná "would come with a delicious banana to the bed where I was lying, and insist upon my gorging myself, when I had but barely recovered from a late orgie of fruit, flesh, or fowl. He would mesmerize me into a most refreshing sleep with a prolonged and pleasing manipulation" (*CSS* 41). Stoddard was so "beguiled" that he grew to like Kána-aná "altogether too well" (*CSS* 39).

It is likely that on this same trip Stoddard met "Joe of Lahaina," whom he also sketched for the *Overland Monthly*.[4] "I saw a figure so fresh and joyous that I began to realize how the old Greeks could worship mere physical beauty and forget its higher forms" (*CSS* 47). Joe possessed not only a well-formed physique but also a handsome face, something, to his considerable disappointment, that Stoddard did not always find in the native youths. Best of all, Joe seemed "inclined" to enjoy homosexual lovemaking.[5] Stoddard "borrowed" Joe from his uncle, and for a time they kept house in a hut near Lahaina. On a typical evening—so Stoddard's story goes—he and Joe would sit on their lanai, watching the waving banana leaves, listening to the sea and smelling the intoxicating odor of grape. Charles would look over and say, "Joe, housekeeping *is* good fun, isn't it?" Joe would agree. Then they would finish their cocoa-milk and bananas and go to bed because, as Stoddard put it, "we had nothing else to do" (*CSS* 47).

By July 1869, Stoddard had seen enough of the Islands for a while. Tanned, fit, and feeling well loved, he was ready now to write, and possibly to lecture, about these picturesque people. When, after returning to San Francisco, he submitted the story of Kána-aná to the *Overland Monthly*, he was delighted to hear Bret Harte say, "Now you have struck it. Keep on in this vein and presently you will have enough to fill a volume and you can call it *South Sea Bubbles!*"[6] Harte was correct in this assessment. Now that Stoddard was taking sides with the savages, he could almost be called an honorary "redskin." True, his South-Sea fiction did not fit the Wild-West formula, but it showed an anticivilized wildness in Stoddard; and Hawaii was even farther west and more barbarous than the mining camps in Calaveras County. He was appealing to the irreverent spirit of the frontier in a way that "Pip Pepperpod" never could.

In addition to contributing sketches to the *Overland Monthly*, Stoddard began writing a weekly column for the *Golden Era* in September 1869. In composing his "San Francisco Feuilleton," Stoddard adopted the persona of a debonair man-about-town, affecting a world-weariness quite remarkable in one so young.[7] Addressing "my dear *Era*" as if he were the Eustace Tilly of the West Coast, Stoddard wrote languidly of trips to the country, Saturday afternoons at the Cliff House, and clambakes at Sausalito. In the Christmas issue he hinted that gifts might be left for him at the *Golden Era* office, his preference being for "elegant dressing gowns." His pet topic was show business—he evidently attended every opening night in town—and occasionally he chided his readers for breaches of etiquette in the theater. He praised Adah Menken as one "who dared to live up to her nature," compared the cancan with the hula, and sentimentally marked the passing of a trouper. Circuses and carnivals continued to have a special fascination, and he closed one column with this confession: "I wish I were a circus-boy in shapely tights, to throw my double-summersault under the dome of the theatre in a blaze of flashing spangles!"

In another column, titled "The Pet of the Circus," he revealed that in Rochester, when he was about six years old, an older child (an "Ethiop!") had forced him to play "circus" for several hours, with the youth assuming the role of whip-wielding master and Stoddard being submissive as the "horsey." Stoddard seemed to have loved it, although he pretended otherwise in this column. The youth's whip had been "well applied," and soon the "irresistible web of his magnetism was spun about me and I was wholly in his power." Stoddard claimed that he would never forget his persecutor: "I feel that he will yet plunge upon me from some obscure corner and claim me as his own."[8]

Whereas Stoddard was rapidly advancing as a writer, his plans for lecturing on the Sandwich Islands led him nowhere. In late July, he tried to exploit his extensive literary acquaintance by asking correspondents throughout the country to advise him about lecturing in their areas—in the company of "a couple of little *Native boys* who should at the close of the evening, sing, dance and entertain the people with some of their picturesque and grotesque mannerisms."[9]

The replies were not encouraging. Although George Henry Boker, for one, thought that Stoddard and his "Sandwich Island niggers" would be "heartily received," Thomas Wentworth Higginson noted the extra expense of traveling with "native boys." Joaquin Miller cautioned that only circuses could draw a crowd in Oregon. Ralph Keeler, who had lectured in the East about his show-business days, warned against the venture: "You never had, and I will never again have, the 'brass' and impudence to go through what I did to challenge public attention. Stay where you are if you can Charley, and grow up with the country."[10]

Stoddard concluded that if he could not make a lecture tour, at least he could write about one. In "My South-Sea Show," published in *The Overland Monthly*, the show is a fiasco—Zebra, the Wonder Boy, dies after swilling too much cologne—much as it may have been if Stoddard had actually gone on the road.[11]

II

By spring 1870, he was making other plans: to escape to the South Seas again, this time to Tahiti. As he wrote to Walt Whitman, "in the name of

Calamus": "I know there is but one hope for me. I must get in amongst people who are not afraid of instincts and who scorn hypocrisy. I am numbed with the frigid manners of the Christians; barbarism has given me the fullest joy of my life and I long to return to it and be satisfied." Sending Whitman his Kána-aná story on 2 April, Stoddard begged for a reply "within the month": "I could then go into the South Seas feeling sure of your friendship and I should try to live the real life there for your sake as well as for my own."[12]

Whitman did respond within a month, but not in a way that left Stoddard altogether sure of his friendship, even though he ended with a declaration of love and the hope to meet his young admirer some day. After praising the "sweet story," Whitman added: "As to you, I do not of course object to your emotional & adhesive nature, & the outlet thereof, but warmly approve them—but do you know (perhaps you do,) how the hard, pungent, gritty, worldly experiences & qualities in American practical life, also serve? how they prevent extravagant sentimentalism? & how they are not without their own great value & even joy?"[13]

In broad literary terms, Whitman was suggesting that Stoddard stop flitting about like a butterfly to exotic locales and come down to earth. Earthiness, as Whitman had experienced it, meant loafing on the grass, walking along Broadway, resting on the beach, drinking in a tavern, and loving men like Peter Doyle. But if he had to deflect suspicion from his poetry, by interposing male "comrades" with female ones, Whitman would do so. In more specifically sexual terms, the fifty-one-year-old poet was writing from the vantage point of his wider experience. He had not needed to go to Hawaii to find the "real life" that could be enjoyed any night of the week, wherever he was. Whitman could recall evening strolls up Fifth Avenue that would end with his sleeping with farmers, policemen, deck hands, soldiers, and black-smiths.[14] What stranger miracles, he might have asked, *are* there? For the twenty-seven-year-old Stoddard, however, the "hard, pungent, gritty" experiences of everyday American life had brought little satisfaction of any kind. They were more to be lamented and escaped than celebrated. At this stage in his life, at least, Stoddard lacked Whitman's sexual *savoir faire*. In order to love other males freely, he felt he had to go to "barbaric" countries.

Whatever Stoddard's reaction to Whitman's letter may have been, it did not divert him from going to Tahiti and writing up his adventures in the style that suited him. While he was waiting for the *Chevert*, a French training vessel, to sail, he shared the society of a few friends who were, no doubt covertly, trying to pursue the "real life" in San Francisco. Two such men he was getting to know at this time were Eben Plympton and Theodore Dwight.

Plympton was a professional actor who had been hired to play juvenile roles at the California Theater. He and Stoddard may have been introduced by Mrs. Jenny Spring MacKaye Johns, an extraordinary woman attracted to all things theatrical, including self-dramatization. In *For the Pleasure of His Company*, "Little Mama," who was modeled on Jenny, plays cupid for the Stoddard and Plympton characters: "I arranged this meeting; I chose to bring you two together; my boys must always meet; and they must always let me plot for them" (*FPHC* 134). In real life, the two men had an intense relationship—"too intense to last"[15]—after which they kept in touch for the rest of their lives. In later years the actor lived on a country estate in Massachusetts to which interesting men of various types, including Stoddard, would be invited.

Dwight was gradually becoming a member of the Harte-Coolbrith-Stoddard circle as a result of his contributions to the *Overland Monthly*. Although the native of Auburn, New York was merely a bank clerk at the time, he had literary ambitions and, more important, good connections with some of the "better" families on the East Coast. During the early years of their friendship, Dwight and Stoddard had two passions in common: autograph collecting and theatergoing. After Dwight had moved back East and begun to dabble in photography, they came to share a more illicit hobby—collecting pictures of naked young men.

Another person who may have been tempted to pursue the "real life" while visiting San Francisco was Bayard Taylor, with whom Stoddard had some good times that June. The forty-five-year-old Taylor was a poet and travel writer, and he had also tried his hand at fiction. Some of his books were colored by a homoeroticism that Stoddard must surely have noticed, especially in the novel that came out that year, *Joseph and His Friend*.[16] In this book, dedicated to those "who believe in the truth and tenderness of man's love for man, as of man's love for woman," Taylor's young heroes share a twilight kiss and the dream of living together in California amid the orange and olive groves. Although Taylor had enjoyed tender relationships with young men while visiting Europe in the 1840s, he gave Stoddard the impression that he was no longer allowing himself to love as freely as he was tempted to. Years later Stoddard wrote of Taylor: "I fear his life, not withstanding the honors that fell to his lot, was a disappointment to him and left his heart unsatisfied" (CRP).

Just before Stoddard sailed for Tahiti, Joaquin Miller finally came to town, hoping to take Stoddard and San Francisco by storm. The self-styled "Byron of the Rockies" deposited himself on Stoddard's doorstep one morning, dressed in sombrero, linen duster, blue denims, and beaded moccasins. He was full of liquor, ingratiating compliments, and, most of all, myths about himself. Claiming to be Stoddard's age (he was actually older), he insisted that he had established a utopian Indian republic on Mount Shasta and had served with General William Walker in Nicaragua. He pressed upon Stoddard the poem, titled "To the Bards of San Francisco Bay," that he had written expressly for the occasion. After lunch, Miller wanted to "go and talk with the poets," all of whom, he assumed, were eager to meet him. As it turned out, they were not. Ina Coolbrith found him striking, but Bret Harte detected a talentless poseur. Others thought his resemblance to Byron was limited merely to his impulsiveness and recklessness. Stoddard nevertheless stood by this colorful masquerader, as he would for the rest of his life. Here was someone, he may have thought, who was even more outlandish than himself. For posterity Stoddard wrote: "Never had a breezier bit of human nature dawned upon me this side of the South Seas than the Poet of the Sierra [sic] when he came to San Francisco in 1870."[17]

III

Stoddard finally boarded the *Chevert* on 7 July 1870. His official reason for making this trip to Tahiti was the notion that he might once more play the role of traveling correspondent; but, in fact, no one had commissioned him to write articles. Unofficially, he had two reasons for going. First, he needed material for a few more tales that could, after appearing in the *Overland Monthly*, fill out "South Sea Bubbles," the book he and Harte had discussed. Second, his mind was, as he admitted, "saturated with romance" (*ITD* 13). Having read about the incomparably beautiful and amorous young men in Melville's *Omoo*, Stoddard was determined to have his share of barbarian satisfaction.

The atmosphere aboard the *Chevert* was so thickly homoerotic that Stoddard must have wondered if Tahiti was going to be anticlimactic. According to his account of this voyage, punningly titled "In a Transport," his fellow passengers consisted of forty "bold" young French sailors on a training mission, a soft-eyed first officer and his clinging black aide-de-camp, and *Monsieur le Capitaine,* whose "hard, proud" face "unmanned" everyone when he paced the quarter deck with "the shadow of a smile" (*CSS* 146–47). It is little wonder that the captain smiled. When the members of his crew were not busy hugging each other, they skipped about like a "ballet scene in *L'Africaine*" (*CSS* 144). His shameless first officer was the "happy possessor" of Nero, a handsome "tight little African," whom he kissed in front of everyone with a defiance "calculated to put all conventionalities to the blush" (*CSS* 151–52). (With marvelous delicacy, Robert Gale has described this "manifestly homosexual pair" as being guilty of "miscegenating.")[18]

There was also that dreamy-eyed American passenger who spent so much of his time pressed to the bosom of Thanaron, a French sailor whose "handsome little body" everyone on board loved to squeeze (*CSS* 149). Stoddard hints that his intimacies with Thanaron went so far that "by the time we sighted the green summits of Tahiti, my range of experience was so great that nothing could touch me further" (*CSS* 147). When they docked at Papeete on August 9, the "fruity flavor in the air" was so narcotic that the disembarkment was nearly orgiastic: Thanaron was hugging Stoddard; the first officer was hugging Thanaron; and Nero, the first officer's lover, was somewhere in the vicinity of "his master's knees" (*CSS* 156–57).

Stoddard's courtesy interview with the American consul in Papeete was not a success. Although he introduced himself with the "ingenuous air" that "had won me troops of friends and invited not a few adventurers to capture and lay me waste," the consul, cool and correct in his white flannels, was not impressed (*ITD* 15–16). Stoddard "showered" him with letters of introduction (*ITD* 16). Still suspicious, the consul warned Stoddard that as long as he was in Tahiti, he would be expected to keep his distance from the natives.

Not surprisingly, Stoddard did just the opposite. He knew quite well what he was risking, of course. It was one thing for white men to sleep with the native women; it was quite another for a white man to sleep with young Tahitian men. Hiding behind the euphemistic phrase, "of the climate," Stoddard asks: "What if the gentleman in white flannel should discover me yielding for a moment to the seductions of the climate?" Answering this question, he imagines himself overhearing the reactions of civilized Christians: "Disgusting! Who ever heard the like? Positively beastly!" (*ITD* 18–19). But in the soft, limpid air there seemed to be the indulgent atmosphere of "aita peopea," which has been translated as "a kind of happy 'Who cares?' " Stoddard was quick to sense this attitude, and he decided that the risks were well worth taking. After all, he had come four thousand miles for the chance.

Allowing for a certain amount of wish-fulfilling fantasy, which makes his stay in Tahiti seem altogether *too* sexually successful, we can still infer from Stoddard's Tahitian pieces that he must have enjoyed more than purely imaginary intercourse with the natives. His partners were found mainly in the villages outside of Papeete, away from the watchful eyes of the American consul. Setting out on a walking tour that would take him along the eastern and southern coasts of the island, Stoddard seemed to meet gallant natives at every turn. As he describes it, there was a sort of "Bali Hai" magic and mystery to these providential encounters. If there was a stream he could not ford, he had only to wait, and he "was invariably picked up by some bare-backed Hercules, who volunteered to take me over the water on his brawny brown shoulders" ("A Prodigal in Tahiti," *SSI* 338).[19] His luck at finding companions for the night seemed almost a matter of preordination: "As I walked I knew something would cause me to turn at the right time and find a new friend ready to receive me, for it always does. So I walked slowly and without hesitation or impatience until I turned and met him coming out of his cage, crossing the rill by his log and holding out his hand to me in welcome. Back we went together, and I ate and slept there as though it had been arranged a thousand years ago; perhaps it was!" (*SSI* 341).

What special appeal did the young men of Tahiti have for Stoddard? First, they possessed an almost Mediterranean beauty: they were "not black . . . not even brown" but "olive-tinted and this tint was of the tenderest olive; of the olive that has a shade of gold in it" (*ITD* 27). Second, like the Italians in John Horne Burns's *Gallery*, the Tahitians "had the gift and the voice and the eyes of love" (*ITD* 31).[20] They were *simpatico:* "I was a stranger in their midst; even the blind might have seen that; they pitied me for the sorrows I had known, the effects of which I could not laugh away; they pitied me again for the sufferings I had endured among the enlightened of the earth and for the indelible scars I bore in form and feature, these unmistakable evidences of civilization" (*ITD* 26). Third, at least in some cases, they were sexually dashing and daring, as we can gather from this series of rhetorical questions: "Was I not seized bodily one night, one glorious night and borne out of a mountain fastness whither I had fled to escape the sight of my own race? Was I not borne down the ravine by a young giant, sleek and supple as a bronzed Greek god, who held me captive in his Indian lodge till I surfeited on bread-fruits and plaintain and cocoanut milk? And then did we not part with a pang—one of those pangs that always leave a memory and a scar?" Furthermore, as he goes on to claim, "this happened not once, but often" (*ITD* 20)—which, if true, suggests that as he wandered from village to village, his reputation may well have preceded him.

How long did Stoddard luxuriate in these "mysteries undreamed of?" His answer is: "Well: Really, I cannot tell you. No one kept tally . . . and, as for pinning me down to so fine a point, I'd as soon think of someone who had been in Paradise for a while suddenly sitting up and asking: 'What time is it?' " (*ITD* 33). In fact, Stoddard stayed in Tahiti less than three months, and his stay, moreover, was not one long honeymoon.

There are other aspects to this story that range, in Stoddard's fictional rendering, from the darkly humorous to the pathetic. Stoddard's only friend during the first week in Papeete was an imbecilic, misshapen cripple he called "Taboo." With this fellow outcast he took in the sights of the *Fête Napoléon* on August 15; but after a while Taboo, who could only grunt, became a rather depressing sort of companion ("Taboo—A Fete-Day in Tahiti," *SSI*). When his money began to run out, Stoddard appealed to the local Catholic church, to which he was always to turn in times of extremity. The bishop, however, gave only "a blessing, an autograph, and a 'God speed' " (*SSI* 348). In desperation Stoddard took a menial job with a French merchant, in whose chicken coop he was allowed to sleep. Not feeling up to the task of hauling sacks of potatoes, he soon quit. Eventually his clothes were in rags, and he was so downcast that he was tempted to throw himself into the ocean—except that he was afraid of the water ("A Prodigal in Tahiti," *SSI*).[21]

One day the American consul stopped Stoddard on the street and suggested that he think about going home. The *Chevert* was about to sail, and if Stoddard could promise that his fare would be paid when he reached San Francisco, he could sail with it. Stoddard made this promise, much to the pleasure of the consul, who said he was going to be making the trip as well. Once on board, Stoddard sensed that the tables had been turned: now it was the consul who was trying to be charming. It all began when Stoddard was airing the contents of his trunk on the deck: there were his dainty souvenirs, his beloved copy of *Leaves of*

Grass, a number of signed photographs of young men. Noticing Stoddard's possessions, the consul "grew more friendly" by the hour. They
discovered they "had hosts of friends in common," and together they
"unmasked the mystery" of Stoddard's "nature," which must not have
been much of a mystery to either of them. As Stoddard blossomed like
the "night-blooming cereus," the consul began lavishing gifts upon
him. "Accept, dear boy," said he, "these pearls, a trifling souvenir of
our friendship." Toilet soaps and "prettily plaited" native cloths were
pressed on him, as well as a standing invitation to return to Papeete and
stay at the consul's plantation (*ITD* 34–35). As in his "Spell-binder"
narrative, Stoddard decided to punish the master-turned-supplicant for
his earlier indifference. The consul had "struck fire" too late, when his
hour was past. Nevertheless Stoddard tucked the pearls safely into his
trunk. If the captain was looking down on this scene from the quarter
deck, he was likely smiling, as usual.

5

EARLY IN November 1870, Stoddard returned to San Francisco and to the several Bohemian circles in which he moved. One of these, composed chiefly of contributors to the *Overland Monthly*, was on the verge of breaking up. With the completion of the transcontinental railroad in 1869, San Francisco was no longer an outpost, and its "Golden Era" of frontier literature was on the wane. By the end of the year, many of Stoddard's literary friends either had moved to the East or to England or were planning trips there. Bret Harte was headed for Boston, where the *Atlantic Monthly* had lured him with a ten-thousand-dollar contract. Joaquin Miller was in London bearding the Pre-Raphaelites, who were less taken by his poetry than by his Wild-West antics. Mark Twain had married and settled in Buffalo, where he was editing a newspaper and making a name for himself as a humorist and lecturer. Ralph Keeler was still in the East, where Prentice Mulford and Ambrose Bierce were shortly to go, en route to England. Even Ina Coolbrith was thinking of jumping an eastbound train. But Stoddard was still gazing westward toward Hawaii, Tahiti, and Samoa as he continued to plan his "South Sea Bubbles."

I

In addition to his Tahitian sketches, Stoddard was writing his auto-biographical novella, "Hearts of Oak," which ran serially in the *Overland Monthly* from April to July 1871. Stoddard also resumed his career as a newspaper columnist, thanks to the kindly intervention of Bierce, in the *Alta California*. Titled "Swallow Flights" and bylined the "Swallow," the column was similar to Stoddard's earlier one in the *Golden Era*. The persona he adopted of a lavender dandy was so congenial that for the rest of his life, regardless of circumstances, Stoddard was to think of himself and to impress others in these terms.

Even literary historians have tended to color Stoddard in pastel tones. Albert Parry, for instance, casts him as a Bohemian aesthete: "He was then as yet pale and slender. People imagined thrilling things about his sojourn in the Hawaiian Islands in company with the Queen of Bohemia [Ada Clare]. When he played the piano, they took him for a young god. The more cynical remarked that his music was quite suitable to tea and twilight."[1] More recently, Kevin Starr has divided the California Bohemians into two types: one, personified by Jules Tavernier, was "assertive," living a wine-filled "risqué life" in the traditional garret or studio; the other, represented by Stoddard, practiced a "genteel" Bohemianism of "Chopin at twilight, Oriental bric-a-brac, incense, lounging robes, and fragrant cigarettes."[2]

Stoddard himself was as responsible as anyone else for the idea of his being ever so *spirituel* and sinless in San Francisco. Given the naïveté and complacent heterosexuality of most of his otherwise "Bohemian" friends, he was obliged to revert to this role when he came home, to hide behind a mask as much as possible. For instance, in a "Swallow Flights" column about a bay cruise, he feigned disinterest when several of the all-male crew, resembling Greek gods, strip to go swimming. In another essay, he minimized the homoeroticism in the Turkish baths, and he felt obliged to give "Hearts of Oak" a vaguely heterosexual ending. All this camouflage was effective. Ina Coolbrith continued to believe in his heterosexuality, as did most of his friends in the Bay Area. In a testimonial poem written some years later, Richard Savage epitomized this view of Stoddard in calling him a man "of gentle ways" that had "never led to wrong."[3]

Stoddard behaved one way in the South Seas and in quite another way in California. Yet since Stoddard's writings made no secret of his falling in love and sleeping with the natives, one has to wonder how his friends could persist in misapprehending him. True, Bierce once crudely asked if Stoddard had fallen "in love with another nigger boy" in the Islands, but this was an idea that could only be expressed—in a jeering allusion at that—in private communication.[4] For nearly everyone else, the only imaginable reason for Stoddard's inordinate interest in savages was that he cared for their beautiful, childlike spirits. Thus George Wharton James's explanation of why a "man of such culture" would "so demean himself" as to sleep with Hawaiians: "He became one of them. . . . He saw the inner and beautiful things of the soul,—the purest affection, the devotion, the simplicity, the tenderness, the gentleness, the innate poetry and instinctive religious feeling of the child of Nature."[5]

But what of all the fondling that Stoddard had described? Most nineteenth-century Americans regarded members of the brown races as more or less noble savages who, if they engaged in sexual demonstrativeness, did so simply because they did not know any better. It was assumed that Stoddard, being not only a civilized man but a rather prominent Roman Catholic, *did* know better. His San Francisco friends were happy to believe that he had behaved as chastely in the Islands as he seemed to live at home, and that when he wrote of spending the night with a young native, he was merely indulging a harmless fancy.

Behind his protective coloration, Stoddard longed to return to the South Pacific. By the winter of 1871–72, he was eager to dispense once more with clothes and pretenses. "Friends become common," he complained in his farewell "Swallow Flights" column, "and a common thing is not the cure for a malady so deep seated as mine." "I'm pining for new faces and new people," he continued, "voices that have an unfamiliar ring to them; footsteps that are not recognized the very moment they strike the front door steps. . . . I mean to embrace every fresh opportunity that presents itself."[6]

Stoddard boarded the *Witch Queen*, bound for Samoa, on February 10. Capricious and sometimes beastly midwinter weather, ranging from eerie calms to stupendous squalls, made this voyage one of the worst experiences of Stoddard's life. The passengers were not reassured when a "crusty old sea-dog" began spinning yarns of "wrecks and marine disasters of every conceivable nature" ("In the Cradle of the Deep," *SSI* 10). To distract himself, Stoddard wrote a play, which Harry Edwards was later to pronounce not stageworthy. By the time the schooner reached Honolulu harbor—after thirty-one days—Stoddard was in no mood to sail on to Samoa; and for the last few stories to finish his book, he would rely once more on Hawaiian inspiration.

After a few days at Waikiki, where he was a guest of Hawaiian royalty, Stoddard crossed over to Lahaina to visit his younger brother, Sam. Within a year Sam would die of tuberculosis; within a few months Stoddard's older brother, Ned, would finally die of the ailment that had plagued him since boyhood. Intimations of his brothers' mortality contributed, perhaps, to the uncharacteristically subdued tone of "The House of the Sun," "The Chapel of the Palms," and "Kahéle," the three sketches derived from this trip. For whatever reason, Stoddard was unusually pensive during his stay on Maui.

One of his most poignant experiences was meeting two French Catholic priests who served the villages on the eastern coast of the island. After inspecting Haleakala, the huge crater in the center of Maui, Stoddard and his guide Kahéle encountered Père Fidelis, a self-sacrificing "martyr" whose devotion to his "dusky worshippers" was deeply touching. This priest in turn introduced them to Père Amabilis, who, despite his own spartan habits, provided Stoddard with the best of everything. After a delicious luau, strong French coffee, and a smoke under the stars, the priests insisted that Stoddard sleep in the only bed while they slept on the bare floor. Such kindnesses touched him to the quick: "I wonder why the twin fathers were so very careful of me that morning? They could not do enough to satisfy themselves, and that made me miserable; they stabbed me with tender words, and tried to be cheerful with such evident effort that I couldn't eat half my breakfast, though, as it was, I ate more than they did—God forgive me!—and altogether it was a solemn and memorable meal" ("The Chapel of the Palms," *SSI* 256).

In Stoddard's eyes there were two kinds of missionaries in Hawaii and throughout the world: the self-important and prudish Protestants, who were harassing the natives to adopt clothes and abjure the hula; and the Catholics, such as these priests on Maui and, later, Father Damien, who were well-educated, tolerant, and selfless, and who impressed Stoddard as being uncanonized saints. Their example made him wonder if serving the church might not be the answer for him after all. If only he could put off his worldly cares, resign ambition, forget the past, and dwell joyfully under the palms with the good priests for the rest of his life!

Stoddard soon overcame such sentimental revery as he and Kahéle traveled on to the Meha valley, where the natives greeted them with a warmth that was amusing as well as a little embarrassing. In his companion's changeable ways, Stoddard recognized not a little of himself: "Kahéle, the chameleon, whose character and disposition partook of the color of his surroundings; who was pious to the tune of the church-bell, yet agile as any dancer of the lascivious *hula* at the thump of the tom-tom. . . . He was, moreover, worthy of much praise for his skill in playing each part so perfectly that to this hour I am not sure which of his dispositions he excelled in, nor in which he was most at home" ("Kahéle," *SSI* 281–82).

II

When Stoddard returned from Hawaii during the summer of 1872, he was feeling some urgency about defining his own place in the literary world. True success seemed to depend on his collection of South-Sea tales, and he began searching for a publisher. Through Harte and also Howells, Stoddard attempted to interest James R. Osgood in Boston. Meanwhile, Bierce promised to use his influence with Tom Hood in England. What Stoddard desired was not only a reputable publisher but one who would promote the book and, more important, pay him an advance.

In San Francisco, Stoddard joined a convivial group of writers, artists, and actors that had been formed while he was in Hawaii. Adopting the motto, "Weaving Spiders Come Not Here," the Bohemian Club glee-fully blackballed the president of the Bank of California. Years later, Stoddard recalled that "we scorned the mighty dollar and it was easier for a camel to go through the eye of a needle than for a rich man to enter the Kingdom of Bohemia."[7]

To support himself during this period, Stoddard resumed writing "Swallow Flights," this time for the *Golden Era*. Topics included "High-Jinks" at the Bohemian Club, boating on the bay, a balloon trip over Woodward's Gardens and, as always, the local theater. But the Swallow was growing flight-weary, and it showed in the columns. Stoddard's restlessness increased when Bierce and Joaquin Miller began to urge him to come over to England. "If you will only wake up, use some *snap* and *nerve*," Miller exhorted him. "Sell your autographs if you can get anything from them and come over here. No magazine article will bring less than $25. And there are 20 a man can write for. You can get here cheap—"8

Stoddard was drawn to England not entirely for literary opportunity. Writing articles would be, just as they had been in Hawaii, merely the means to the end. As Carl Stroven has observed, Stoddard "desired companionship above all else, even a literary career."9 By 1873, Stoddard was eager to experience the companionship, sexual and otherwise, that Europe might offer. There he could love and be loved in comfort, as opposed to "roughing it" in Hawaii. He had always loathed roughing it, in truth. Two events clinched the trip to Europe. First, Stoddard's old Powell Street School friend and owner of the *San Francisco Chronicle*, Charles De Young, agreed to hire him for a year as the paper's roving reporter in England and on the continent. Then James R. Osgood and Company agreed to publish his book, which would appear in the fall of 1873, under the title that Osgood proposed: *South-Sea Idyls*.

By 1873, American readers had come to expect ripe romanticism in books about travel to foreign lands and perhaps even overripeness when these books described life in the tropics. Some readers still relished the charming sensuousness of *Typee* and *Omoo*, which were, according to popular opinion, better than anything Melville had written since. When it came to sketching the natives, authors often reflected the ambivalence Americans felt toward the darker races. On the one hand, white men mildly condescended to the "quaint" life of the barbarians. Everyone knew that the natives talked funnily and acted funnily, and readers wanted to smile at their outlandishness. On the other hand, Americans embraced the sentimental notion that the savages, communing daily with nature, were somehow more "noble" than people who had been shaped by civilization. Readers liked to entertain the idea that somewhere on earth there still existed a prelapsarian Eden.

On the surface at least, *South-Sea Idyls* seemed to adhere to these social and literary conventions—except that Stoddard's narrator is less consistently "civilized" than usual in this genre. Whereas at one moment he seems to be as aloof and bemused as Irving's Geoffrey Crayon, Gent., at another he more closely resembles Walt Whitman, taking off his clothes and lounging about slothfully, as if his sense of propriety were no more cultivated than that of the native youths with whom he always seems to be chumming. Indeed, unlike other literary tourists to the South Seas, Stoddard's narrator does not merely flirt with the joys of barbarism and then retreat into civilized decency. In Stoddard's tales, there is a deep undercurrent of feeling that life in the Islands is, in fact, infinitely preferable to life in the United States. Stoddard's narrator is genuinely fond of eating and sleeping with the natives; he is sincere in his devotion to paganism; and he fiercely resents having to put his clothes on and return to the restrictions of Christian civilization.

Of course, these restrictions included a taboo on the very homoerotic experience that, as we have seen, lay behind many of Stoddard's tales. Granted, Stoddard's homoeroticism does not dominate every one of the sixteen sketches included in the book. In "The Chapel of the Palms," for example, he devotes himself to another of his themes: the beautiful, self-sacrificing lives of the Roman Catholic priests who have found an enviable serenity in their service to the church. Nor is there anything very sexual in "The Last of the Great Navigator," which recalls the final days of Captain Cook in Hawaii. But in most of the pieces, either in the background or the foreground, there is at least one handsome young pagan who captures Stoddard's eyes or heart or both. For instance, in "Taboo," the narrator is not interested so much in his misshapen companion as in the perfectly shaped, "naked and superbly built fellows" who shinny up a greased pole, and in the sight of the hundred young men in their war canoes, all "stripped to the skin and bareheaded; their brawny bodies glistening in the sun as though they had been oiled" (*SSI* 97, 99). In "Joe of Lahaina" the young man's significance can hardly be overlooked. But of all the tales in this book, perhaps the greatest degree of homoeroticism may be found in "Chumming with a Savage" (based on Stoddard's 1869 visit to Molokai), "Pearl-Hunting in the Pomotous," and "In a Transport" (both based on his 1870 trip to Tahiti).

While the significance of Stoddard's unabashed delight in seeing and touching and being touched by handsome, naked males seems rather obvious now, it is understandable why *South-Sea Idyls* caused few eyebrows to be raised over a hundred years ago. The combined innocence and ignorance of nineteenth-century readers was a key factor, of course, but another was Stoddard's half-shrewd, half-bumbling technique of constructing sentences and paragraphs so as to cover his tracks with confusion. The governing pattern in the following examples of this technique can be compared with a squirrel's venturing out, farther and farther, to the leafy end of a branch. When swaying signals danger to the squirrel's brain, it stops short and leaps back to safety as nimbly as it can. Likewise, instead of crossing out and revising passages of telltale homoeroticism, Stoddard merely retreated, hoping he could scurry back to safety under the cover of misleading explanations.

The first example is taken from the paragraph in "Chumming with a Savage" that describes Stoddard getting into bed with Kána-aná for the first time: "Over the sand we went, and through the river to his hut, where I was taken in, fed, and petted in every possible way, and finally put to bed, where Kána-aná monopolized me, growling in true savage fashion if any one came near me. I didn't sleep much, after all. I think I must have been excited." Rather than deleting that last sentence, Stoddard gropes for some suitable reason for the excitement. The paragraph continues: "I thought how strangely I was situated: alone in the wilderness, among barbarians; my bosom friend, who was hugging me like a young bear, not able to speak one syllable of English, and I very shaky on a few bad phrases of his tongue" (*SSI* 31–32). The idea that he is distressed at the thought of sleeping among barbarians is belied, elsewhere in the text, by his depiction of the hospitable Hawaiians, who pose no threat to him at all. Nor under normal circumstances would a sudden awareness of impending language difficulties likely induce much emotion. Most revealing of all, however, is Stoddard's dropping his mask in midflight. The concealment of an explanation that is no explanation is itself undone by the suggestive, but comically turned, detail about hugging, which points again to a sexual cause for the excitement.

In another example from this tale, Stoddard is still in bed, now peering at the sleeping body of Kána-aná: "He lay close by me. His sleek figure, supple and graceful in repose, was the embodiment of free, untrammelled youth. You who are brought up under cover know nothing of its luxuriousness. How I longed to take him . . ." What Stoddard goes on to say is surely the last thing he must have had in mind at the time. After having described, in euphemistic terms, the joys of being naked, he contradictorily suggests that they go to America and put on some clothes: ". . . over the sea with me, and show him something of life as we find it. Thinking upon it, I dropped off into one of those delicious morning naps" (*SSI* 33).

In midparagraph in "Pearl-Hunting in the Pomotous," Stoddard again realizes he has tipped his hand. During the "balcony scene," Hua Manu begins "making vows of eternal friendship," vows that are "by no means disagreeable" to the narrator, now playing Juliet. But why are these vows not disagreeable, or, rather, why are they so agreeable? Is it the beauty of the native's Herculean physique that compels the narrator to reciprocate? No, Stoddard wants us to believe, it is Hua Manu's intimidating size: "He was big enough to whip any two of his fellows, and one likes to be on the best side of the stronger party in a strange land. . . . I leaned over the stern-rail . . . assuring that egg-boy that my heart was his if he was willing to take it at second-hand" (*SSI* 153).

A final example may be cited from "In a Transport," which is surely one of the most lavender pieces of prose published in the nineteenth century. In the following paragraph, Stoddard wants to show both the cause and the effect of the ship's crew and passengers being "un-manned" as they catch sight of Tahiti: "There was something in the delicious atmosphere, growing warmer every day, and something in the delicious sea, that was beginning to rock her floating gardens of bloom-ing weed under our bows, and something in the aspect of *Monsieur le Capitaine* . . . that unmanned us; so we rushed to our own little cabin and hugged one another . . . ." Stoddard seems to realize that the con-junction "so" is not strong enough to stand alone in explaining why he and Thanaron are hugging each other. How to finish this sentence in order to satisfy, or at least to confound, the reader? ". . . lest we should forget how when we were restored to our sisters and our sweethearts, and everything was forgiven and forgotten in one intense moment of French remorse" (*SSI* 309). This conclusion is, of course, nonsense. Nonetheless, the spray of words following "lest" may have convinced most nineteenth-century readers that the narrator and Thanaron are embracing for reasons that, if not perfectly clear or convincing, are at least quaintly amusing.

Reviewers were generally pleased with *South-Sea Idyls*, often com-paring Stoddard with Melville as to subject matter, and with other Western writers as to style. In the *Overland Monthly*, an anonymous reviewer (who likely knew the author) evaluated the book in light of Stoddard's personality, with which readers were presumed to be well acquainted:

> Being young and poetical, ardent in his love of the beautiful, and really bored with civilization—by spells—Stoddard was "enthused" over the lovely islands of the Pacific—over their coral shores, their palm-groves, their water-falls, their deliciously tinted peaks, their remoteness, and their amiable, sensuous people, who treated him like a brother, because he fraternized with them in the mood of a poet and a humanitarian. Hence his

ecstasy was not an affected one. He wrote from the inspiration of a dreamy nature, keenly sensitive to every charm of form, and color, and perfume, yet melancholy, and not so much of the Puritan that he could not play the prodigal.

About Stoddard's style, this reviewer concluded with an optimistic (but, unfortunately, inaccurate) prediction: "If it is thought sometimes too exuberantly descriptive, or too florid and sensuous, these are qualities that will be corrected or tempered by experience."[10]

In the *Atlantic Monthly*, W. D. Howells found some of Stoddard's sketches to be written in such a "dreamy" and "vague" manner that he could not tell whether they were supposed to be fiction or nonfiction. However, Stoddard was given the benefit of the doubt: "You must rest satisfied with your inference that at several times Mr. Stoddard visited Tahiti and the islands of the Hawaiian group; for there is no historical *resumé* of the facts of his goings or comings." Howells wished for "a little more structure in the book, something more of bone as well as marrow, of muscle as well as nerve"; but he conceded that "the tone for writing about the equatorial, lotus-eating lands has been set, and we are not sure but Mr. Stoddard gains a charm by holding to the traditional vagueness."[11]

The reviewer in *The Nation* was also troubled by Stoddard's style. There was, he found, "something disagreeably jarring" in the uncertain tone of this writer. At the same time he was able to tolerate Stoddard's unfathomable peculiarity by placing it within the tradition of the "California humorist," whose business is "to make us laugh by humorous distortions of the common tongue of Shakespeare and Milton." The review concluded by warning readers that the tone of the book was not entirely wholesome: "We ought to say, however, that life in the Southern Seas is such a peculiarly non-moral life, that we cannot recommend 'South-Sea Idyls' as a book of invigorating and purifying tone. The Southern Seas—as it used to be said of Paris—are not a good place for deacons."[12]

If the urbane tone of the last sentence is any clue, *The Nation*'s reviewer was not truly shocked by anything in *South-Sea Idyls*. Neither was Howells, who took the pose of "unrepentant" prodigality merely as a convention of Western humorists who wrote chiefly to amuse each other: "It all strikes us as the drollery of a small number of good fellows who know each other familiarly, and feel that nothing they say will be lost or misunderstood in their circle." Howells, then, thought that Stoddard was only teasing in the homoerotic scenes. Indeed, "In a Transport" was singled out for special commendation. The paragraph depicting the first officer's kissing Nero was quoted to illustrate Stoddard's gift for characterization, and this whole piece about the "amiable" French sailors was thought to be full of "airy humor." Howells concluded by welcoming the book "as a real addition to the stock of refined pleasures, and a contribution to our literature without which it would be sensibly poorer."

That Stoddard could *not* be serious when he touched on same-sex love and demonstrativeness was entrenched in nineteenth-century reviewers' and readers' minds; and, as earlier pointed out, Stoddard's stylistic sleight of hand contributed to this impression. More recent commentators on *South-Sea Idyls*—perhaps because they could not or preferred not to recognize the homoerotic undercurrents—have chosen to dwell on the safer and milder (that is, the genteel) qualities of the tales. When Van Wyck Brooks, for example, painted a landscape of all the things Stoddard had loved best in the tropics, the young men who dominate *South-Sea Idyls* were scrupulously excluded:

> He loved the dreamy days of calm in the flowering equatorial waters, the booming of the surf on the beaches, the clashing of the palm-fronds, the twilight glow on the yellow shores and the cane-fields and banana-thickets, the slopes of the distant headlands and the sickle of the sea. He never tired of the winding roads, the groves with their seventeen shades of green, with the huts of the natives half-hidden like voluminous nests, or the foam-girdled reefs of the great lagoons where exquisite sea-gardens blossomed in splendor under the tranquil waves.[13]

These young men are also missing from a Catholic critic's account of the book. "The 'Idyls' are filled with boundless sympathy, a tender, reverential awe," said Father Francis O'Neill, in a 1917 review in the *Catholic World*. O'Neill went on to claim that this volume "will remain the most popular of Stoddard's books, for in them is blended tranquil, yet enthusiastic joys, soul stirring pathos and a spiritual vision that counts the trappings of artificial living not worth striving for."[14]

In 1939, Franklin Walker summoned enough courage to point out the obvious. "The emphasis in this unusual picture of island life," he wrote, "is not on the customary brown maidens with firm breasts, lithe limbs, and generous impulses, but on the strong-backed youths, human porpoises who drive their canoes through the mists of the storm and share their joys and sorrows with the prodigal from California."[15]

Having mentioned the "strong-backed youths," Walker engaged in a Stoddard-like retreat, edging toward the idea that the appeal of these muscular young men was related to their capacity to guide canoes through misty storms.

Not surprising, it was a fellow homosexual who first said in print what these others could not bring themselves to utter. Stoddard's "predilections" were instantly recognized by "Xavier Mayne" (the pseudonym of Edward I. Prime-Stevenson), whose *Intersexes* was an overview of "similisexualism" and "philarrhenic literature" throughout the world. In this book, which was privately published in Naples in 1908, Stevenson quotes a long passage from "Chumming with a Savage" as exemplary of a "uranian complexion."[16] By Stevenson, then, *South-Sea Idyls* could be fully appreciated for what it was: a joyous celebration of what we now call "coming out," thanks to the obliging young men of Hawaii and Tahiti.

Charles Warren Stoddard during the 1870s

Frank Millet during the 1870s

6

WHEN STODDARD arrived in London on 13 October 1873, none of his California friends was in town to welcome him. Eventually he did find Mark Twain, who was lecturing that week about the Sandwich Islands. Twain was soon leaving for America, but he planned to return to England in December, and he invited Stoddard to become his companion-secretary at the Langham Hotel. Meanwhile Stoddard stayed with Prentice Mulford, who showed him the city. From Bierce, who was in Paris for a month, he received a letter imploring him to behave himself. "You will, by the way, be under a microscope here," Bierce cautioned, "your lightest word and most careless action noted down, and commented on by men who cannot understand how a person of individuality in thought and conduct can be other than a very bad man. . . . Walk, therefore, circumspectly . . . avoid any appearance of eccentricity."[1] London, in other words, was not Hawaii. In the worldly-wise company of publisher Tom Hood and newspaperman George Sala, Bierce had learned something new about homosexuality, namely that people went to prison for it in England. He did not want Stoddard to do anything to embarrass the American literary community in London.

The delightful thing about being in England, however, was that

Stoddard could play the "swell" without being ridiculed, as he had sometimes been in San Francisco. In the streets the peddlers and shop-keepers called him "sir," and he loved it. At the same time, he willingly deferred to his "betters" when he met them in London's drawing rooms. Attending George Eliot's reception or Lady Hardy's "Saturday Evenings" in St. John's Wood was instructive as well as fascinating. Stoddard quickly learned the nuances of class stratification and the degree of ingratiation proper to a Sir Thomas Hardy or to an Indian prince or to a poet like Phillip Marston. Nevertheless, the British, accustomed to such "Californians" as Joaquin Miller and Mark Twain, rather expected Stoddard to conform to the Wild-West stereotype, and they were no doubt disappointed when he so obviously did not. As he recalled:

> We chat as well as an American is expected to do under the circumstances; we talk dirk and gulch and wild, wide West, because this is the sort of thing that we are bullied into by bevies of London maids who have never heard anything better of California. We grieve that we have never "dropped our man," for this is expected of us. We run out of bear stories and get bored with questions; and, in despair, turn the current of conversation back to the centre of civilization.[2]

I

During Stoddard's six-week engagement as Mark Twain's secretary-companion, the conversation ran to gossip and drollery. Stoddard's job consisted of little more than opening the mail and keeping a scrapbook of newspaper clippings. Afternoons were spent walking through the parks, and before dinner Twain would often play and sing spirituals at the piano, "rolling his vowels in the Italian style." After dinner they strolled to the Queen's Concert Rooms in Hanover Square, where Twain gave his lecture, "Roughing It on the Silver Frontier." Stoddard usually watched from the seclusion of the royal box. Afterward, accompanied by George Dolby, Twain's manager, they would pull up their easy chairs to the sitting room fireplace and smoke and drink and swap tales until well after midnight. During these boozy, mellow evenings, Twain talked so candidly about himself—"his boyhood, his early struggles, his hopes, his aims"—that Stoddard felt that he "could have written his biography at the end of the season" (*EE* 65, 70).[3] As Twain recalled the same evenings, there had been no drinking to speak of, and Dolby's (but not his own) tales had been "indelicate" enough to "distress" Stoddard, "the pensive poet," who was "refined, sensitive, charming, gentle, generous, honest himself and unsuspicious of other people's honesty"—this in contrast to Dolby, the "gladsome gorilla," who was "large and ruddy, full of life and strength and spirits, a tireless and energetic talker, and always overflowing with good nature and bursting with jollity."[4]

Literary historians have not failed to note the obvious personality differences between Mark Twain and Stoddard; and when the two men are compared, it is never to Stoddard's advantage. Fred Lorch, for instance, asserts that "Twain was fond of the Californian despite the fact that he was somewhat effeminate, unworldly, and given to religious enthusiasms."[5] Paul Fatout agrees that Stoddard was "a gentle, un-worldy man, good-hearted, sensitive, somewhat effeminate, yet hearty enough to have been the 'Prince Charlie' of boisterous San Francisco adventures in the sixties."[6] What Lorch and Fatout ignore is that Mark Twain liked having Stoddard around not despite, but because of his difference from the California "redskins." If anyone was slightly out of place in London, it was Mark Twain, not Stoddard. It made good sense for him to hire a "paleface" secretary to deal with the British. Lorch and Fatout also do not perceive that it was precisely Stoddard's androgynous nature that made him not only charming company in general but also a welcome companion to a man whose own sense of masculinity could be enhanced by Stoddard's apparent lack of it.

In January 1874, after seeing off Mark Twain at Liverpool, Stoddard stopped in Chester on his way back to London. There he had a chance encounter with a young man, Robert William Jones, to whom he be-came attached. The feeling went deeper for Bob Jones, who was later to besiege his "dearest friend" with passionate letters. Stoddard, however, was by then preoccupied with the pleasures of Charlotte Street, where the *Punch* illustrator Wallis Mackay kept his rooms. Mackay lived with a drama critic and an actor; with the addition of Stoddard, the four made up a "community of confirmed stags." Their dedication to the joys of bachelorhood was so strict that "women were forbidden the prem-ises." Certain young men, on the other hand, were always welcome, and the revels sometimes ended—and here Stoddard is surely exaggerating again—with fellows sleeping "about six in a bed."

With these new friends, Stoddard proceeded to violate all of Bierce's canons for good behavior. Stoddard recalled that there had been a good deal of mutual, and often drunken, affection. It is likely that Stoddard slept with some of these young men. He also "took an occasional prowl in the dark parks, where we saw the shadow of much that was past finding out, and caught fragments of human history from the lips of woe that were wonderfully tragic and impressive" (*EE* 344–45). The "fragments of human history" were possibly similar to those being collected by Krafft-Ebing, tales that would serve both to sadden and to excite a visiting American. One of the most tragic and impressive stories then making the rounds concerned Simeon Solomon, the promising Bohemian artist, who had been convicted earlier that year for committing an "indecent act" in a public lavatory. Whatever else happened to Stoddard during his evening prowls, he avoided arrest.

During his stay with Wallis Mackay, Chatto and Windus brought out *South-Sea Idyls*, under the title *Summer Cruising in the South Seas*, in a handsome edition that seemed to please Stoddard at the time. "It will be very pretty," he had told his sister before Christmas 1873, "with twenty-five illustrations and fancy cover."[7] Many years later, however, W. D. Howells recalled that Stoddard had been "scandalized" by these illustrations, which so "grossly misrepresented the nature of the harmless story."[8] In his "Introductory Letter" to the 1892 edition of *South-Sea Idyls*, Howells wrote: "Your London publisher defamed your delicate and charming text with illustrations so vulgar and repulsive that I do not think anyone could have looked twice inside the abominable cover."[9]

Apparently, some readers did not look twice; for Stoddard, in an inscription in one copy of the book, referred to "an air of vulgarity that frightened the Critics" and that led them to call him "an immoral person."[10] But Stoddard seemed also to dissociate himself from such reactions in the very reporting of them; and it is unlikely that he had ever been "scandalized"—although he may have allowed Howells to think otherwise—since the illustrations in question had been drawn by none other than Wallis Mackay. As to their being a "vulgar and repulsive" misrepresentation, Howells probably meant not that Mackay had homosexualized the drawings—something that would have been unsurprising, given the atmosphere of his Charlotte Street chambers—but rather that Mackay had *heterosexualized* the sketches, showing many more naked maidens than actually appear in the "harmless" tales. In fact, the drawings do not seem to be very sexy from any viewpoint. They are, as Carl Stroven has noted, simply "bad,"[11] the products of an uninspired and untalented pen that make Stoddard's characters look weird and pathetic rather than charming.

I I

Soon after the publication of *Summer Cruising*, Stoddard decided to visit Joaquin Miller in Rome. "O God! Here is peace! Cross The Rubicon," Miller had urged; and Stoddard was ready to explore new territory for his *Chronicle* sketches, for which he had nearly exhausted his impressions of England. Stoddard's first days in Rome were not altogether merry, as he had managed to lose not only his luggage but also his jacket, which contained his money and Miller's address. He finally spotted Miller at the English bank near the Spanish Steps, "where one is pretty sure to meet most of the Americans in town." Their accounts of the meeting differ. According to Stoddard, Miller was unrecognizably

> wrapped in a long cloak, with a broad-brimmed, high crowned hat slouched over his eyes. He seemed to limp without limping, and heaved his shoulders like a stage-sailor in a heavy sea. . . . I wondered who he was, and had concluded to class him with those modern artists who do the picturesque professionally, when, to my amazement, he stalked toward me, unshrouded himself, stretched out a hand loaded with massive gold rings, and greeted me with a smile which was half a welcome and half a reproof.

With this "modified edition of the original Joaquin, adapted to continental circulation," Stoddard icily "froze together, as it were; and, with scarcely three words of greeting on either side."[12]

According to Miller, Stoddard seemed on the verge of a nervous breakdown: "a pale, slim ghost" who "crept out of the shadows . . . and laid its head on my shoulder, while tears ran down its face. I rated him soundly and roundly for depending on his saints all the time. But he excused his saints by saying he had forgotten his saints for a second to think of me and so got into trouble. I marvelled that he did not take the fatal Roman fever and die."[13] At any rate, Miller wined and dined the hapless Stoddard and offered him temporary lodgings in his own dingy room, which smelled like a stable and was decorated with cheap gimcracks. Stoddard soon moved elsewhere, but he continued to rely on Miller to show him around Rome, and they spent a lot of time drinking wine at the Cafe Greco.

As a Catholic, it was Stoddard's duty and, of course, his great pleasure to play the role of pilgrim in Rome. He especially enjoyed visiting the American College, where he soon made friends among his countrymen who were studying for the priesthood there. More than anywhere else in Rome, Stoddard felt completely at home among the "strapping big fellows from the Far West, the angular fellows from the East, the elegant fellows from the South."[14] For his chum Stoddard chose a "gentle, trustful, sympathetic" seminarian named Dan Paul, of Hazleton, Pennsylvania. The two spent the week after Easter on a walking tour of Genzano and Lake Neimi, using the *casino* of a marchesa as their headquarters. It was Dan Paul who told Stoddard about the *Ave Maria* and its editor, Father Daniel Hudson of Notre Dame. Sometimes Stoddard would dine with the other seminarians at the American College. "You would have thought I had taken orders myself," Stoddard recalled, "if you could have seen the brotherly way some of those novitiates and I nodded to each other over our glasses!"[15]

The idea of taking orders, always in the back of Stoddard's mind, often came to the fore during these Roman days. In May 1874, he wrote to a friend that he was greatly tempted to "bury myself out of this world in the seclusion of one of these monasteries. I never pass one here but I keel a little over to that side."[16] When he was presented to Pope Pius IX, His Holiness told Stoddard, "with a twinkle in his eye," that he "should try to be good."[17] But just as he felt drawn to the spiritual element in Rome, he also responded to the sensual side of the city, especially as spring turned into summer.

Not so voluptuous as Hawaii, perhaps, Rome was intoxicating just the same. The police were "gorgeous"; the Swiss Guards, who looked "like nothing else under heaven," were "gorgeous"; everywhere Stoddard saw gorgeous Italian men who made him sigh and melt.[18] He wanted someone who would be as sympathetic as Dan Paul but physically demonstrative as well. He was apparently able to find such men, at least for a few hours. In May he wrote that "friends follow me or meet me wherever I am, and friends blossom out in a night—new friends, like the night-blooming cereus, full of strength and fragrance and satisfying beauty." Alas, he added, these friendships "*don't last any too long.*"[19]

Somewhere between the spiritual and the sexual extremes of Rome was the sometimes brilliant social life in which Stoddard was eventually caught up. He made the rounds of artists' and sculptors' studios, enjoying a glass of wine and a smoke with such men as William Graham, Randolph Rogers, and Charles Carrol Coleman. In company with some of these American Bohemians, Stoddard often spent his evenings at the opera or the theater. Fete days and carnivals were always of special interest, especially when they required everyone to don elaborate costumes. At the "Fete of the Stags" in the Campagna, Stoddard hardly knew where to look first: men in fourteenth-century costumes were walking arm in arm; "Greek sailors" were sporting scarlet caps and brief trousers; and prancing on horseback was an elaborately gowned man pretending to be Queen Elizabeth.[20]

The American artist of greatest interest to Stoddard—"the man I like best in Rome"[21]—was Eugene Benson, who had already achieved some recognition in America for his essays in the *Atlantic Monthly*. In a studio adorned with Damascus tiles, Japanese screens, and draperies from the Levant, Benson painted souvenirs of his recent trip to the Mideast. He had recently married Henriette Malon Cooley Fletcher, a charming, cultivated, and wealthy woman of Swiss extraction, who was old enough to be his mother. But it was Mrs. Fletcher's eighteen-year-old daughter, Julia (nicknamed "Dudee"), who made the greater impression on Stoddard and who years later was to appear in *For the Pleasure of His Company* in the guise of Miss Juno. Attracted to "Dudee's" androgynous qualities, Stoddard engaged with her in animated and philosophical discussions about the mysteries of masculinity and femininity. Stoddard also helped her to launch a literary career that summer. Under the pen name of "George Fleming," she later wrote a number of novels and plays, including *Kismet* (1877).

Meanwhile, Stoddard was concerned with advancing his own literary career. "I was never so full of projects as at this moment," he wrote to his sister Sarah in July 1874; "I have material for a half dozen volumes."[22] He sought Bierce's advice on the possibility of collecting his nontropical, "and therefore moral," tales from the *Overland Monthly*. "Hearts of Oak," he thought, might be issued separately as a novel for children.[23] In addition, he wrote to John Carmany of the *Overland Monthly* that he had an idea for what he was to begin calling his "San Francisco novel." Carmany was already publishing some of Stoddard's British sketches in the *Overland Monthly*, and every Sunday the *San Francisco Chronicle* was featuring (in the upper left corner of the front page) his articles about Italy. They ranged from "Interviewing the Pope" to "The Theaters of Rome." Then, suddenly, they stopped; for Stoddard had been thrown by a horse!

The mishap occurred one June night while he was riding across the campagna with two Italian youths. Stoddard shattered his left forearm, and after surgery he remained in a hospital until July. For the rest of his life he could not fully bend that elbow. After he recovered, he began sending home sketches of Naples and then, in the fall, columns about the cities he passed through on his way to Venice: Ravenna, Bologna, and, perhaps most interesting of all, Loreto.

Stoddard's chief reason for stopping at Loreto was to visit the "Holy House," which Catholics believed to have been the home of the Virgin Mary at the time of the Annunciation. (The shrine was miraculous in that the house had supposedly been carried to Loreto by angels in the thirteenth century, when Mohammedans were overrunning the Holy Land.) At the local church his confessor turned out to be a progressive young Franciscan from Terre Haute, Indiana, who had been banished abroad for disciplinary reasons. With his "coalblack eyes that sparkled like jet," Father John was "quite unnecessarily good looking," and as a devotee of boxing and fencing, he had "more shape than he knew what to do with."[24] Delighted to see another American, the priest played host to Stoddard for the next few days. The muscular priest let Stoddard feel his "knotted biceps," and Stoddard let the priest drive him around to the many shrines in the area. Like the selfless French missionaries on Maui, Father John struck Stoddard as the personification of everything that was beautiful and admirable about the Catholic church. With reluctance Stoddard left this winsome priest and continued his train ride northward, more hopeful than ever that someday he too would become a monk—if only the church would have him.

III

Enervated by the heat, Stoddard had been unable to write well in Rome, where he would "lie in bed till two or three in the afternoon, smoking, reading and dreaming over the work I hope to do before long."[25] He promised himself that he would get to work in Venice, where the weather would be more bracing. Venice also held an answer to the vexing questions of whom to live with and whom to love. One night, during intermission at the opera, a young man quietly joined Stoddard in his box. "We looked at each other," he recalled, "and were acquainted in a minute. Some people understand one another at sight, and don't have to try, either."[26] This young man, whom Stoddard had met once before (in Rome), was twenty-eight-year-old Francis Davis Millet. Like everyone else, Stoddard called him "Frank"; his nicknames for Stoddard were "chummeke" and, later, "you butterfly."

Born in Mattapoisett, Massachusetts, in 1846, Millet had been a Civil

War drummer boy, serving beside his surgeon father. After the war he earned a master's degree in modern languages and literatures at Harvard, where he was elected to Phi Beta Kappa. Millet had come to Europe to study at the Royal Academy of Fine Arts in Antwerp, where he had also done well. Now in Venice, he was painting, writing travel sketches for the papers back home, and looking for someone to love. That night at the opera, when he invited Stoddard to come and live with him, there was never any doubt as to the answer. Looking back on this experience, Stoddard mused, "Isn't it a delightful 'Divinity that shapes our ends, rough-hew them how we will'?"[27]

During the winter of 1874–75, Stoddard lived with Millet in an eight-room house that featured a *loggia* and windows opening on the Grand Canal, the Guidecca, the Lagoon, and the Public Garden. The other occupants were Giovanni, the servant-cook-gondolier, and another American artist or two interested in keeping "bachelor's hall" for a while. Millet had taught Giovanni to fix baked beans and codfish balls, and during the frosty winter days, Stoddard loved dining on this New England fare in the cozy kitchen. An added attraction was the view from the kitchen windows of half-nude artisans at work in an adjoining shipyard. During the days Millet painted on the *loggia*, and Stoddard dozed and smoked and wrote his *Chronicle* columns. They dined early and usually took a sunset spin in their gondola, and at night they slept together in Millet's bed in the attic chamber with a commanding view of this enchanting city.

Local color was everywhere in Venice, of course, and Stoddard wrote column after column on every aspect of Venetian life: the afternoon band concerts on the Piazza San Marco; Florian's Cafe, where people gathered to gossip over chocolate and ices; the colorful peddlers who kept plying him with matches, flowers, and chestnuts. Most rapturously of all, he wrote about Venice after dark: "the divinely beautiful evening of that almost divinely beautiful city;—tranquil, moonlit, with a shimmer of waters, and a shadow-haunted labyrinth of canals walled in by white, silent palaces, half in deep shade and half pallid in the moonlight."[28] *Chronicle* readers were perhaps learning more than they wanted to know about the city. There were accounts of "Beautiful Venice," "Afloat in Venice," "Lingering in Venice," "Venetian Vignettes," "The Mother of Venice," "The Venetian Islands," "The Gayeties of Venice," "The Venetian Fetes," and "Farewell to Venice."[29]

In order to gather fresh material for his columns, Stoddard took a three-week tour of Northern Italy in February. Frank went along as guide and "companion-in-arms." In Padua they were struck by the sight of "lovely churches and the tombs of saints and hosts of college boys." On the way to Florence Stoddard sympathized with a display of passionate male friendship often seen in Italy. A gigantic young fellow had just parted with his friend at the station.

> As soon as they had kissed each other on both cheeks—a custom of the country,—the traveler was hoisted into our compartment, and the door locked behind him; but no sooner did the train move off, than he was overcome, and, giving way to his emotions, he lifted up his voice like a trumpeter, and the echoes of the Apennines multiplied his lamentations. For full half an hour he bellowed lustily, but no one seemed in the least disconcerted at this monstrous show of feeling; doubtless each in his turn had been similarly affected.[30]

In Florence, Millet explained the art to Stoddard, who was much taken by the "Venus de Medici" and "The Wrestlers." Outside the city they visited La Certosa, the monastery where chartreuse was made. They were so amused by the strange, indirect ritual by which the monks were served their meals that they later played at being monks, handing "invisible provisions in to each other through the little hole in the wall" of the monastery garden. In Siena the two men slept in a "great double bed . . . so white and plump it looked quite like a gigantic frosted cake— and we were happy."[31] When they got to Pisa, Millet wanted Stoddard to see the leaning tower from just the right angle, so that he would be duly impressed. He was. Highlights of Genoa included sampling the *capo magro* and the Turkish punch, and taking a sunset stroll on a terrace overlooking the harbor. Stoddard regarded Milan as the "Paris of Italy"; he reveled in the glass-roofed Galleria, and enjoyed going with Millet to the opera.

Back in Venice, the two men were often invited to dinner by American friends eager to hear of their recent adventures. In those days the social life of the American colony seemed to revolve around the consulate, where one had to suffer Dr. Harris, a "perambulating corpse," and "Mother" Harris, who was, fortunately for her husband, an ex-army nurse. This woman was kind enough to have "the boys" over for Thanksgiving dinner but squeamish enough to regard *Summer Cruising in the South Seas* as distasteful. When Frank offered her his copy of the book to read, she glanced slyly at the illustrations of "several naked figures dancing" and handed it back with a "maiden blush." "From what they say," she added, "I don't think I should care to read it."[32]

That spring Stoddard's heart was set aflutter by the appearance of A. A. Anderson, an exquisite American artist whose beauty and wealth were noteworthy, even in Venice. Anderson called on Millet one lazy Sunday in a long black cloak "of Byronic mold" (one corner of which was "carelessly thrown back over his arm, displaying a lining of cardinal satin"), a damask scarf of a gold-threaded fabric, and a slouch hat with tassels. But Anderson was most striking to Stoddard for his "comely face of the oriental-oval and almond-eyed type." He dubbed him "Monte Cristo." By contrast, Frank Millet now seemed less interesting.

Millet's "butterfly" had taken flight; Stoddard was fascinated by the dashing young Anderson. "Before we parted I had learned to pass half the day with him in his gondola, reading, chatting, writing, dreaming, or merely drifting with him while the tide swung lazily between the meandering canals and the Lido. The rest of the day we were ashore, but usually in each other's company." One night Anderson gave a dinner at the Danielli Hotel, where Stoddard felt he "must have had the suite of the royal princess, it was so ample and so richly furnished." The menu was "the realization of a sybarite's dream," with "wondrous wines" and "viands from the four quarters of the globe." Anderson gave Stoddard a fez as a souvenir of this dinner and a sketch of a Venetian canal as a memento of their warm friendship. Then he left Venice as abruptly as he had arrived.[33]

IV

With Anderson gone, Stoddard began to grow restless with Millet, and he decided to leave for Paris, telling Frank he would rejoin him in Brussels in July. "I feel there will come a time when I shall find it quite impossible to recall anything unpleasant in my whole Italian experience," Stoddard wrote en route.[34] He was looking forward now to a tour of the British Isles, in part to see Bob Jones. During his stopover in Paris, Stoddard encountered an old family friend from Oakland, Mrs. Preston Moore, who attached herself to him despite his protestations that he preferred to travel alone, for reasons that he would rather not explain. In London, Stoddard was "busy day and night showing her about," and he could not manage to leave her behind when, failing to keep his rendezvous with Millet, he went on to Chester—and to Bob Jones, who for over a year had been sending letters that were quite as impassioned as those Stoddard was now beginning to receive from Frank.

"Miss you? Bet your life," Millet had written after Stoddard's departure from Venice. "Put yourself in my place. It isn't the one who goes away who misses it is he who stays. Empty chair empty bed, empty house."[35] But Millet reluctantly resigned himself to Stoddard's ways. "You know that I only feel whole when you are with me. Is it magnetism? I'm sure it is the magnetism of the soul that can not be explained and had better not be analyzed," he later wrote. Then he added: "Go ahead! You know I'm not jealous, if I were I should be of 'Bob.' Anyone who can cut me out is welcome to. Proximity is something but you know I'm middling faithful."[36]

Since their parting, Bob had bought a puppy that he called "Charles Warren Stoddard"; the namesake was anxious to see them both. In Stoddard's account of his reunion with Bob, Mrs. Moore was kept out of sight and out of mind, as she may well have been; for Stoddard moved in with the young man for the rest of his stay in Chester. "Ah!" Stoddard was to recall fondly, "What days of lazy leisure, what moonlight on the Dee; what strolls down the Liverpool road after vespers; what high-jinks and what not!"[37] After the "high-jinks and what not," Stoddard and Mrs. Moore went over to Ireland for a few days and then to Scotland. There they were joined by an Oxonian who assumed they were married. When Mrs. Moore asked him why he thought Stoddard was her husband, the Oxonian replied, "Because he pays so little attention to you, madame!"[38]

In London again around the first of August—and finally rid of Mrs. Moore—Stoddard spent his days visiting Bierce and others while awaiting the arrival of his *Chronicle* check, which allowed him to spend the next five months touring Western Europe. (Egypt was in the back of his mind; for he had heard glorious things about it from Eugene Benson and, particularly, A. A. Anderson.) From the male-only nude beach at Ostend, aptly known as "Paradise," Stoddard wrote to Bierce that he was as "red as a herring and as jolly as a clam."[39] He especially enjoyed watching two Italians ("lovers possibly, and organ grinders probably"), who were such "guileless, olive-brown, sloe-eyed, raven-haired, handsome animals."[40] Stoddard continued by train to Brussels and Cologne, sailed down the Rhine to Frankfurt, then went up to Leipzig and Berlin, and finally down through Dresden and Vienna on his way to Munich.

With guidebook in hand, Stoddard inspected all of the tourist attractions at each stop, writing up his impressions for the *Chronicle* in a style that was sometimes world-weary and other times strangely disarming. A typical column described works of art in the museums, music in the squares, food in the restaurants, and accommodations in the hotels (usually unsuitable). Stoddard also dropped the names of any San Franciscans he happened to see.

When he got into scrapes or simply wanted the comfort of human companionship, Stoddard depended on attracting new friends by virtue of his "animal magnetism": "I believe I am peculiarly unaccountably fortunate; someone is sure to come to my relief at the right moment; I have only to hang out signals of distress and I awaken a response in a bosom whose horizon has, perchance, never before lapped over mine."[41] Here he seemed to be echoing his accounts of his providential experiences in Tahiti, where he had enjoyed such good luck with the native men; for when he spoke of a "response" in a stranger's bosom, he hinted at more than the ordinary kindness of strangers. With his sad blue eyes transmitting a gaze full of helplessness and longing, Stoddard's signals must have been instantly recognized by those who knew what they meant.

By the middle of October 1875, Stoddard was in Munich, where he spent several weeks living with two American students he apparently met through Toby Rosenthal, who had lived in Munich for about ten years and who seemed to know everyone in the art world there. The two young men, Joseph Strong and Reginald Birch, were to play important roles in Stoddard's later years. Stoddard took immediately to Joe Strong, who also had lived in the East, in San Francisco, and in Hawaii. They joked, in regard to their comparably shaky finances, that perhaps they would both end by having to "take the veil" and join a monastery. The cream of the jest was Stoddard's posing in clerical robes for a remarkable oil portrait by Strong.

While Joe had a personal charm that was quite irresistible to Stoddard, Reggie Birch was downright lovable. Born in London, young Birch had more recently lived in San Francisco, where he became well known as a designer of theatrical posters. Stoddard found himself falling in love again. Reggie became his "Kid," and their friendship was sustained for the next twenty years. Meanwhile Stoddard stopped writing to Frank Millet, who had returned to America and was now languishing in East Bridgewater, Massachusetts. "My dear old Chummeke," Frank protested, "Two weeks in Munich spooning! spooning! SPOONING! and couldn't find time to write me. Che diavalo! . . . I haven't spooned a bit since I got back, you know I haven't, but you [butterfly pressed on the page] you have had one solid spoon. . . . Now then you butterfly if you don't write more I'll cut your ——— off so you won't flutter about anymore."[42]

Undeterred by Millet's transatlantic threats, Stoddard left Munich for Paris, where he continued to spoon as often as he could. He moved into a Latin Quarter hotel that catered to American art students; it seemed like a "great boys' boarding-school" (*M* 19). To some degree accepted as one of the boys—one of the older boys, to be sure—Stoddard adjusted his daily routine to that of the Left Bank artists:

> Breakfast is quite like a noon dinner, with soups and dessert, if we prefer them. It begins shortly after twelve o'clock and lasts an hour or two. . . . The affairs of the day are duly canvassed; we plot a thousand pleasant things and live up to about half of them; we discuss art, literature, the *prime donne*, music, and the masque. We burn the fragrant weed over tall glasses of black coffee, and grow boisterous, perchance, in argument or repartee. (*M* 14–15)

Some nights, when he was feeling particularly bold, Stoddard went to the Boullier dance hall to watch the gyrations or to the "Valentino," where he was surrounded by people who were either depraved or at least pretending to be. Here the "wickedest" dances were performed; in the satanic glow of red, blue, and green lights, "Frou Frou" did the cancan in the center of the floor. The special appeal of the "Valentino" was that everyone came in costume and, even more intriguing, some of the dancers cross-dressed. In describing those in drag for the *Chronicle*, however, Stoddard affected moral detachment:

> We boys of the Quarter, who come only to look on and to renew our feeble but I trust virtuous indignation at such sights, turn at last from the girls in boys' clothes, and the boys in girls' clothes; from the jaunty sailor girl-boy who has just ridden around the room on the shoulders of her captain; from the queen of darkness who swept past us in diamonds and sables, and never so much as suffered her languishing eyes to rest for a moment on any one of us; from the misery of the jealous one in the corner who has been robbed of his prize, and the melancholy of the two who are advising one another to go home.[43]

Stoddard's indignation was "feeble" indeed, belied as it was by the perspicacity and sympathy of his description. It seems likely that many of these dancers were homosexuals and that Stoddard knew it.

When Stoddard wasn't socializing with the other "boys of the Quarter," he was sometimes in the company of Americans he had known in California. But the American he was most desirous of seeing was A. A. Anderson, who had just returned to Paris after a visit to New York. Beckoned by a pale pink invitation, "faintly perfumed as if it had been stored in a casket of sandalwood," Stoddard arrived at Anderson's opulent home on the other side of the Seine. He felt "transported to the realms of the Arabian Nights" when a corner of "a tapestry heavy with gold embroidery was lifted" and he found himself "at once in the embrace of Monte Cristo." After a lantern-lit "feast that might have been served in a kiosk of the Khedive," the two men sipped their coffee, smoked their water pipes, and talked about going together to the "fabulous East," where Anderson would illustrate the exotic sketches Stoddard would write. In the clear light of the next morning, no longer "intoxicated with the incense of smoking pastilles," Stoddard realized that such Arabian pipedreams were nothing more than that.[44] Anderson was not serious about accompanying him to Egypt, and Frank Millet could not afford to join him. But Stoddard set out nonetheless— off to Marseilles, where a ship was waiting to take him to Alexandria.

V

From January to July 1876, Stoddard made a semicircular tour of the countries bordering the eastern Mediterranean. If what he expected to find was a grand panorama that lived up to what he had read in travel books, he was often disappointed; for what he generally found were appalling poverty and decay: beggars with outstretched hands, and crumbling shrines at every turn. But Stoddard was a seasoned traveler by now, and he bore delays and mishaps with equanimity. He could usually find something amusing or beautiful enough to fill his *Chronicle* columns.

In Egypt, Stoddard tried to enter into the spirit of a culture he scarcely understood. One day in Alexandria he joined a funeral procession that was making its noisy way through the streets. "It is thought well of a man," he explained knowingly, "if he helps to swell a funeral pageant." But, as it turned out, the mourners did not think too well of Stoddard, for they made him march in the rear with "the children of the Prophet" and denied him admission to the cemetery (*M* 62). In an adventurous mood one night in Cairo, Stoddard began strolling alone through the dark streets and ended up lost in a remote quarter. He noticed with some satisfaction that "many an eye was turned on me in surprise." Then, suddenly, he was surrounded by a "mob" of rock-throwing youths, forcing him to make "as speedy a retreat as possible" (*M* 80). While in Cairo, he tried the baths, which abounded in sensual delights, although he felt obliged to write of them as if they were a bewildering ordeal.

After visiting the pyramids, Stoddard embarked on a leisurely cruise up the Nile on a flat-bottomed barge named the *Nitetus*. Sailing southward always seemed to produce the same effect on Stoddard; as on his trips to Hawaii and Tahiti, the closer he came to the equator, the more he was tempted to turn into a languorous voluptuary. "The delicious days," he noted, "drift by unreckoned. Hour by hour we cast off the customs of our time, one after another, and grow luxurious and sensuous, taking in the landscape as if it were something that was provided for our physical enjoyment" (*M* 151). It would not be difficult, he fancied, "to turn heathen in this heathenish land" (*M* 139).

One "heathenish" aspect of Egypt that left Stoddard unmoved, however, was the seductive dancing of the "ghawazee" in the "fleshpots." Before a performance in Luxor, the audience gradually lost consciousness of "the absurdity of our situation" and began "to look about us as if we had some business here." Stoddard and his fellow thrill-seekers sat "in solemn rows on each side of the hall . . . apparently waiting for some one to lead us in prayer" (*M* 189). When the women began to undulate, Stoddard observed with disdain that their light garments were "excessively ugly" and that their dancing was little more than an "awkward shuffle over the floor from one end of the hall to the other" (*M* 190–91). While the ghawazee "very much bored" Stoddard (*M* 191), his soul was "satisfied" in Egypt by the sight of "handsome men and lovely boys" (*M* 159).

Back in Cairo early in April, Stoddard almost dissolved in the heat. "Under its enervating influence I subsided into a hasheesh frame of mind, and passed my time between the bath and the nargileh, the victim of brief and fitful moods" (*M* 217). After a few days he was headed north to tour the Holy Land with a couple of American friends.

Stoddard, playing the penitent and reverent pilgrim, visited the most sacred shrines during Easter week. But he found in Jerusalem "a lack of color, a want of vitality, a drowsiness of spirit noticeable everywhere"— as if an "eternal Sabbath," the "awful hush of the deep-blue New England Sabbath," brooded over the city "like a curse."[45] Always critical of tourists and tourist attractions, Stoddard found much to bewail about the biblical landmarks. At the Church of the Holy Sepulchre, he was disappointed to find "no grotto, no semblance of a tomb—nothing, in fact, but gaudy sculpture and a blaze of golden lamps." While kneeling in the church, he was "rudely" jostled by two American tourists— "noticeably non-Catholic" (*CUC* 166). The crypt at the Church of Saint Mary in Bethlehem was "gaudily decorated in the worst possible taste" (*CUC* 85). But Stoddard, who sometimes wept when he thought of the cross he had to bear in life, felt quite at home in the Garden of Gethsemane.

Stoddard shook the dust of the Holy Land from his feet and sailed up to Syria, where he also shook off the role of pious pilgrim and reverted to his sybaritic self. In Damascus, orange water thickened with snow was served to him by the deposed Emir, who gave him a beautiful autograph in "arabesque" (*CUC* 199–201). Beirut had its pleasures as well, although the belly dancers there were no more appealing to Stoddard than they had been in Egypt. The last cities on his itinerary were Athens and Stamboul. In Athens, he lamented the ruins of the Acropolis: "It is not unlikely that in the flight of the gods mankind lost his reverence for the purely beautiful; they took with them that finer faculty—the sentiment is called feminine to-day, it may be considered infantile tomorrow—for the want of which the world is now suffering sorely" (*CUC* 254). Stamboul seemed a lively combination of East and West. The baths were especially pleasant, and for once Stoddard did not pretend otherwise: "They are one and all forbidding when viewed from the street, but within they offer the chief delights of the Levant—delicious waters that cleanse you and babble to you, pipes that tranquilize you and couches that invite you to repose" (*CUC* 286).

When Stoddard arrived back in Venice in July 1876, he was cheered by the sight of his old American friends (minus Millet), but all was not well. He had little money, and he worried about the future. Should he stay in Europe or go home? Could he find a publisher for a book of his recent travel essays? The news from America was not encouraging. Millet had written that money was so tight that people had no ready cash to pay for his paintings. Not only was there economic depression, but the prevailing philistine atmosphere was oppressive to the creative artist. Millet advised Stoddard to stay in Europe if at all possible: "You do quite wrong to come home. I have a good constitution, a mercurial temperament and a naturally hopeful disposition. Yet I can tell you that

I have never suffered so much, mentally, as in this place. Kick, kick against the pricks of popular ignorance, conceit and worst of all politics."[46]

The news was no better from Mark Twain, who had tried to interest his own subscription-book publisher in bringing out Stoddard's travel sketches. He had gone to Elisha Bliss, Jr., he reported, "to see if he could do anything, but he shook his head—says he has got more books than customers, & doesn't want any more of the former." In fact, Bliss was postponing the publication of *Tom Sawyer* in hopes of a "livelier market" after the fall presidential election. But Twain had another idea: "Hayes will be elected; Hayes has strong literary taste & appreciation; Howells has written Hayes's biography for campaign purposes; Mrs. Howells is Hayes's own cousin. Suppose you write to me or to Howells & say you want a consulship somewhere, & let us try & see if we can't manage it."[47]

Although Twain and Howells joked to each other in private about Stoddard's hapless career, the latter did try to obtain him a consulship— to no avail.[48] In any case, what Stoddard needed was immediate income; and he finally decided that if he were to pad his *Chronicle* columns with ancient history and guidebook data, he could make them last long enough to subsidize his stay in Italy. Meanwhile, perhaps, he could seek new material. In fact, the *Chronicle* continued to run his columns until July 1877. Meanwhile Stoddard lived as cheaply as he could.

Most of 1876 he spent in the vicinity of Naples, making several excursions to Sicily and Capri, sometimes in the company of that ubiquitous and indefatigable traveler, Mrs. Preston Moore. In the fall he toured Sicily with Mrs. Moore, who was called "M. M." in his *Chronicle* letters and later transformed into "Pythias" when he wrote of Sicily for the *Ave Maria*. He was delighted with the "heavenly" town of Taormina, where Baron von Gloeden was later to snap the nude photographs that would gladden Stoddard's heart in the 1890s.

Stoddard was keeping in touch with Joe Strong and Reggie Birch, who were continuing to study art in Munich. Strong had to disagree with Stoddard's assertion, in a letter, "that girls are well enough in their way, but not to go to bed with." At the risk of seeming "absurd," Joe retorted, "I think that is the place where they are *perfectly charming.*"[49] Frank Millet, who tended to agree with Charles, was back in Paris, urging Stoddard to join him, his cousin, and her three children: "The most I can find time to write you in the hurry of apartment hunting is that 'I want you.'. . . You can live very cheaply here in this quarter and I am sure you would work hard. You know I think you don't do half as much as you ought to."[50] Millet was not the only friend to twit Stoddard for his lackadaisical attitude toward serious writing. After visiting him in Rome, Charles Webb wrote, "It seems to me that you are undergoing a process of growth just now, of which you are not yourself aware. Full of a man's ambitions and aspirations, you've not as yet gathered your-self together for the jump. Lotus eating has still too strong a charm for you."[51]

In a peculiar and perverse mood throughout the spring of 1877, Stoddard was not sure when or where he would leap. He toyed with the idea of living in the monastery at Monte Casino, but he was told there would be no room for him until summer. A. A. Anderson was in Paris—but with his new wife in tow—and he was not sure he wanted to see Frank just yet. It was in this state of indecision that he wrote to a California friend in March:

> As for myself, I have torn up my roots so often that they do not strike into any soil with much vigor. The warmer and the softer it be, the better my chance—but I was ever an airplant. . . .
> You will find me changed, I fear, and most likely not for the better. My enthusiasm has boiled down; man delights me not, nor woman either . . . but there is more grit in me than of old and I feel my ribs bracing themselves against the day when I shall come breast to breast with the world.[52]

Later in the spring he decided that he was ready to come breast to breast at least with Frank Millet, and he went up to Paris. In the middle of this visit, however, Millet left for Romania to cover the Russo-Turkish war for the London *Daily News* and the London *Graphic.* Writing in June from the front, Frank told Stoddard that he was "spooning frightfully with a young Greek."[53] It was Millet's turn, finally, to be "inconstant."

By the time Stoddard read this letter, he had already decided to go home, if there was still such a thing as "home" waiting for him in San Francisco. For one thing, he was tired. He felt like a leaf that had been "whirled hither and thither" for the past four years, and he hoped to find some stability, repose, and security in the United States. For an-other, he was out of money. In July he began a farewell tour of Europe:

first to Venice and northern Italy, then to Naples and Marseilles, and finally to Paris, by way of Lourdes, where he hoped that the Blessed Virgin might heal his crippled left arm in a way the Italian surgeons could not. (She did not, but Stoddard left Lourdes with his belief unshaken.) Then it was off to London and Liverpool and the steamship home. Stoddard reached Philadelphia on 26 August 1877.

The Bungalow Boys and the Strongs, Hawaii, 1883. Joe Strong
(*far left*), Charles Deering (*front left*), Austin Whiting
(*center*), William Sproull (*standing*), Belle Strong, Charles
Warren Stoddard (*far right*).

On the beach at Monterey, November 1905. Left to right:
Joaquin Miller, George Sterling, Charles Warren Stoddard.

7

"EUROPE IS like a picture book—good to look at and think about,"
Stoddard had written to a friend from Italy, "but how lacking in the
genuine life we know at home, especially in the West."[1] Now that he
was back in the midst of "genuine life," however, Stoddard had no idea
how he would fit, even in San Francisco. He could always write more
"Swallow Flights," but that would be a retrogression in his literary
career: precisely what he did not want to do for the rest of his life.
Stoddard decided to stay in the East for a while; and for three months
during the fall of 1877, he was the houseguest of Mrs. Jenny Johns, who
had been so fond of him and Eben Plympton years before. Following
the suicide of her latest husband, Jenny had moved to her parents'
estate, "Eagleswood Park," near Perth Amboy, New Jersey. Jenny regarded Stoddard as a harmless "Babe in Christ," someone who was
almost silly-simple. Stoddard regarded her as good material for the San
Francisco novel that was still in the back of his mind.

While staying at "Eagleswood Park," Stoddard sent a brief note to
Father Daniel Hudson at Notre Dame, mentioning their mutual friend,
Dan Paul, and suggesting that if Father Hudson would send him the
Ave Maria, he would be happy to contribute to the paper. With Father

Hudson's encouraging reply began a steady correspondence and a friendship that would last for over thirty years.

Stoddard was also in contact with Joaquin Miller, whose *Danites in the Sierras*, a revenge drama about a Mormon massacre, was becoming a hit on Broadway. Stoddard wanted to see the play, and he decided to leave "Eagleswood Park" and spend the winter with Miller in Manhattan. In Miller's hotel room they led a "kind of camp life," cooking over "a bed of live coals in the parlour grate" (*EE* 230ff.). It is likely that Miller told Stoddard of his meeting Walt Whitman in Boston, where neither of them had hit it off with the local poets as well as they had with each other. With Miller as a literary connection, it would not have been surprising had Stoddard wished to make a pilgrimage to Camden. For some reason, however, it appears that Stoddard never made an effort to visit Whitman, although in the years to come he often found himself passing through the Philadelphia area.

During his stay in New York, Stoddard saw old friends, such as the Prentice Mulfords, and made some new ones among Manhattan's literati. William H. Rideing recalled the impression Stoddard had made on the set that did their drinking at Oscar's on Fourth Avenue, a group consisting of Maurice Barrymore, H. C. Bunner, Edgar Fawcett, Frank Watson, Richard Watson Gilder, George Parsons Lathrop, and others. Stoddard was "one of the gentlest and most plaintive of little men," with a "beseeching, wistful, propitiating manner, shot with gleams of humor that played as the sun plays through clouds. When he smiled at you, it was with a mute entreaty for sympathy." Rideing added that " 'Charley' would take from us anything he wanted and we could spare as he took the air, or as a child takes things, as a natural right, without constraint or the awkward protestations of gratitude of the ordinary received: a night's, a week's lodging, the freedom of one's table, one's pipes, one's gloves, one's money, but when his ships came home—they were always belated and unlucky—restitution never failed and what was his at once became ours."[2]

Stoddard made a similar impression on the poet Edmund Clarence Stedman, who was by this time no longer a Bohemian but an established member of both the literary establishment and the stock exchange. After Stoddard had dined with the Stedmans one March evening, his host made this notation in his diary: "Lonesome and hard up. Is a Catholic and talked of taking orders. Cheered him up, and must get him some money."[3] Joaquin Miller had also been trying to help Stoddard by asking railroad officials to give him a pass to the West Coast. But Stedman finally obtained an advance of two hundred dollars from Scribner's, and by the end of March 1878, Stoddard was on his way back to San Francisco.

I

He was welcomed home by a writer for the *Alta California*, who exclaimed that his visit to the editorial rooms was "like a streak of sunshine after a long season of cloudy weather." Five years of absence and travel had "changed the pale, slight boy, in appearance to an enlarged man, with a healthy and ruddy countenance."[4] At last Stoddard was beginning to resemble the self-possessed man of the world that he had tried so hard to be; but when he went "home" to 42 Hawthorne Street, much of his confidence deserted him. In this dreary house, located in a working-class neighborhood "South of the Slot," he found his parents and his brother Fred struggling against destitution. His father had a menial job in the custom house, and his brother—unmarried, unskilled, and often unsober—was thinking of becoming a photographer. "Trust that the day is coming," Stoddard had grandly written to his mother from Rome, "when the ancient glory of the house of Stoddard will shine again."[5] In 1878, that day seemed not very close at hand.

While a "restless wandering youth is appropriate and agreeable to witness," Stedman wrote to Stoddard from New York, "a Bohemian after thirty has a frame badly suited to his picture."[6] That year Stoddard would turn thirty-five, and some of his married Californian friends expected him to find a wife, get a regular job, buy a house, and start a family. If he was unhappy as a rootless bachelor—and he often conceded he was—then surely the solution was to settle down like everyone else.

For Stoddard, of course, the ordinary heterosexual rules did not apply. Women were all right in their place, as he had told Joe Strong, but he certainly would never want to marry one. As for children, he once wrote in his diary: "I thank God that I have no children of my own to worry me . . . but—O! how long for those of others."[7] The young man for whom Stoddard soon began to long was William Woodworth, whom he called the "Kid."

Born in San Francisco during the Civil War, Woodworth came from a wealthy family. His grandfather had written "The Old Oaken Bucket," and his late father had been an officer in the United States Navy. "Willie," who had been privately educated in Europe, exuded a great "personal fascination," according to a friend, who added, however, that Woodworth was also "perverse, exasperating, high tempered and overwhelmingly generous. . . . He offended his dearest friends whenever he pleased, safe in his infinite resource in winning them back, for there was no resisting his fascination when he chose to exert it."[8] Mrs. Woodworth must have sensed that her fatherless boy would benefit from older male companionship and guidance. As a budding naturalist who planned to study this field at Harvard, Woodworth was especially eager to take outings into the countryside.

During the summer of 1878, Stoddard was more than happy to oblige by accompanying Willie, then fourteen, on camping trips up into the Redwoods and down the coast to Monterey. Stoddard recalled one such trip to Sonoma County: "The Kid was the very thing—a youngster with happiness in heart, luster in his eye, and nothing more serious than peach-down on his lip; yet there was gravity enough in his composition to carry him beneath the mere surface of men and things." The days that followed were idyllic. While Stoddard wrote, Willie went swimming and hunting and chasing dragonflies. "One night, the Kid set out for the stubble-field and lay in wait for wild rabbits; when he came in with his hands full of ears, the glow of moonlight was in his eye, the flush of sunset on his cheek, the riotous blood's best scarlet in his lips, and his laugh was triumphant; with a discarded hat recalled for camp-duty, a blue shirt open at the throat, hair very much tumbled, and no thoughts of self to detract from the absolute grace of his pose" (*IFP*r 214–15, 217).

Back in San Francisco in the fall, Stoddard was in fairly good spirits even though he had no income beyond the sixty dollars a month from the *Chronicle* for his weekly column of European anecdotes, plus whatever he was paid for an occasional piece in the *Atlantic, Scribner's,* or the *Ave Maria.* It was enough for Stoddard to begin looking for an inexpensive room of his own, where he could write and entertain with the privacy he lacked with his family on Hawthorne Street. He found his atmospheric "Eyrie" at 3 Vernon Place, on the once fashionable Rincon Hill. His rooms in the slowly decaying Gothic house seemed "suspended in midair" because of the huge, deep cuts that had been made on nearby Second Street, and there was a touch of faded glory about the house and the neighborhood. But Stoddard found this ambience entirely appealing, and the rent was only ten dollars a month.

The place was to be lovingly recalled at the start of *For the Pleasure of His Company*. In the sitting room with a bay window were several easy chairs, a faded carpet, books everywhere, water colors and oil paintings above the bookcases, statuettes, busts, medallions, a Florentine lamp, an idol from Easter Island, signed photographs of famous people, spears, war clubs, pots of ferns and creepers, Japanese lanterns, oriental fans, and a skull with faded boutonnieres stuck in the eye sockets. In the bedroom (the former conservatory that was now "half doll's house and half bower"), the "ivy had crept over the top of the casement and covered his ceiling with a web of leaves." Above the bed's headboard was a "holy-water font—a large crimson heart of crystal with flames of burnished gold set upon a tablet of white marble." The whole effect, Stoddard felt, was one of "harmonious incongruity" (*FPHC* 19).

After he moved into the "Eyrie," Stoddard's daily routine no doubt resembled that of Paul Clitheroe in *For the Pleasure of His Company*. Mornings were usually serene, devoted as they were to reassuring rituals. After slipping into sandals and an angel sleeve robe (which made him resemble something between a "Monk and a Marchioness"), he opened the bay window shutters, watered the ferns, patted a few favorite books on their spines, and went out for the mail (*FPHC* 23). Then breakfast; then reading letters from all over the world; then working on his next *Chronicle* column or answering letters.

Afternoons and evenings were often less predictable. Like Clitheroe, Stoddard would wander down to the Bohemian Club on Pine Street "for a bit of refreshment which was sure to be forthcoming, for his friends there were ever ready to dine him, or more frequently to wine him, merely for the pleasure of his company" (*FPHC* 23). He was often someone's supper guest as well; and then, after musical entertainment in his host's home or a visit to a theater, Stoddard would sometimes have a beer at a picturesque rathskeller and arrive home by midnight. He was not, however, always alone. Once in a while an attractive art student named Rudolph Muller came for the night, as did, perhaps, the actor Will Stuart, when he was performing in San Francisco.

Stoddard's merrymaking was usually under the auspices of the Bohemian Club, which was always up to high jinks or low jinks or some kind of tomfoolery that amounted to lots of wine, speeches, pranks, laughter, and alcoholic fellowship. That June, Stoddard had gone to Camp Taylor on the B. C. ("Bully Crowd") train for the first Midsummer "High-Jinks," which included swimming in the "buff" and general silliness during the day, and music and drinking around the campfire at night. For a later Jinks, with "The Devil" as a theme, Stoddard wrote and recited an eight-stanza poem that hardly anyone took seriously. "To Lucifer, Star of the Morning" was a plea for the inversion of conventional morality, and beneath the surface facetiousness there ran a vein of heartfelt sentiment—as in the last six lines:

> *Teach us, all Powerful One, that Wrong is Right,*
> *And Virtue chief of Vices.*
>
> *Lead us astray, and tempt us as thou wilt;*
> *But when at last thou hast used us to thy ends,*
> *Let us arise and leave thee all the guilt—*
> *Parting, the best of friends.*[9]

One Bohemian Club member who did perceive what Stoddard meant in this poem—and who did not like it at all—was Ambrose Bierce. By the late 1870s, the two men had become "estranged," to use Bierce's term, and Stoddard hardly mentioned "Biercy" for the rest of his life. According to a staff member of the weekly *Argonaut*, to which both had begun contributing around this time, Stoddard "loathed Bierce, and Bierce detested him."[10] To a certain extent, the rift might be explained by their incompatible approaches to writing. "Bitter" Bierce was becoming increasingly scornful of the "Miss Nancys" of American literature (such as Henry James and W. D. Howells), who struck him as unbearably sunny, nice, and namby-pamby. To Bierce, Stoddard no doubt seemed another "Miss Nancy." But literary differences cannot completely explain their estrangement because the same differences, after all, had existed when the two men were friends. The real reason, as Bierce told Sterling after Stoddard's death, was that he could no longer abide Stoddard's homosexuality. "I did not care for him," Bierce wrote. "My objection to him was the same as yours—he was not content with the way that God had sexed him."[11]

While losing a friend in Bierce, Stoddard was gaining one in a writer who was soon to become more famous than either man. Although there is some confusion about when and where they met, it was during the winter of 1879–80 and, according to Robert Louis Stevenson, it was outside Stoddard's "Eyrie" on Rincon Hill. Stevenson had walked from his Bush Street lodgings to make some sketches of the bay:

> The first day I saw I was observed, out of the ground-floor window, by a youngish, good-looking fellow, prematurely bald, and with an expression both lively and engaging. The second, as we were still the only figures in the landscape, it was no more than natural that we should nod. The third, he came fairly out from his entrenchments, praised my sketch, and with the impromptu cordiality of artists carried me into his apartment; where I sat presently in the midst of a museum of strange objects,—paddles and battle-clubs and baskets, rough-hewn stone images, ornaments of threaded shell, cocoanut bowls, snowy cocoanut plumes—evidences and examples of another earth, another climate, another race, and another (if ruder) culture.

Stevenson recalled that it was in conversation with Stoddard that he "first fell under the spell" of the Islands.[12] At this time in his life, Stevenson was in even worse straits than Stoddard: more or less penniless, friendless, suffering from what seemed to be galloping consumption. Stoddard found him to be "unfleshly to the verge of emaciation," and while he was sympathetic, there was little he could do to help (*EE* 17).

The person in the Bay Area who did help Stevenson, however, was Mrs. Fanny Osbourne of Oakland. Through Joe Strong, Stoddard already knew Mrs. Osbourne, and he was fated to know her headstrong artistic daughter, Isobel, much better than he ever really wanted. Both Osbourne women ended up marrying their lovers at about this time. Isobel eloped with Joe Strong in the fall of 1879, and Fanny and Stevenson were wedded in the spring of 1880. As a general rule, Stoddard did not approve of marriage, particularly for his creative friends, and most particularly if they were foolish enough to marry each other. Nonetheless he gave his blessing to the Stevenson-Osbourne match, if only because everyone else in San Francisco believed that a motherly, resourceful woman was exactly what Stevenson needed if he were ever to regain his health. In the case of "Belle" and Joe, however, most everyone, including Fanny, felt it was an unwise match. Belle liked to drink and flirt as much as Joe did, and neither was especially prudent when it came to money. Stoddard may have sensed the trouble ahead for these two. As long as he did not have to see Belle too often, there were no problems, and they seemed to enjoy each other at first.

In 1880, the Strongs were living in a large studio on New Montgomery, near Market, in San Francisco; and, as Belle recalled, Stoddard frequently visited them, sitting for hours at the piano, singing "many strange airs and haunting melodies" or regaling them with "odd adventures in Tunis; or the night he lost his way in Constantinople; or the swimming party he joined at a pool in Tahiti." When Stoddard met her, "he held out both hands and said in that foolish but very genuine way of his, 'Belle, love Charley!' And I did from that moment to the end of his life."[13] In fact, however, Belle and Stoddard were later to become rivals in Hawaii, where they came to detest each other. Stoddard's relationship with Belle's mother, of whom he saw far less, was a happier one, and he wrote regularly to Stevenson until the latter's death in Samoa in 1894.

II

During his first two years back in San Francisco, Stoddard seemed to be relatively content. He enjoyed a brief moment in the limelight when he delivered a series of benefit lectures at Platt's Hall. Illustrated with "Stereoptic Views" flashed on the screen behind him, his talks about Europe and the Near East succeeded in "enchaining the interest of hearers to the very end."[14] Then there was the surprise visit to San Francisco of Kahéle, the lovable scamp who had guided Stoddard around Maui in 1871. The reunion was not quite what Stoddard hoped for, however; Kahéle had become a thoroughly heterosexual Romeo, and in a few days he deserted Stoddard to go to "Los Angel" with his new Mexican wife.

During the next two years, however, Stoddard grew increasingly depressed, frightened and helpless. He was subject to paranoia and "neurasthenia," complaining in his letters to Father Hudson that "the times are out of joint" and that "I am out of my element and shall ever be so."[15] Work dried up. By the end of 1879, the *Chronicle* editors decided they had no further use for Stoddard's warmed-over reminiscences of Europe, and during 1880 and 1881, he had no regular source of income. He began to pawn his precious souvenirs; finally he had to move out of the "Eyrie," cheap as it was. His sixty-seven-year-old father lost his job at the custom house, and his parents left for Hawaii, hoping to start a new life there with the assistance of their daughter, Sarah Makee. With no one to love and nothing to live for, Stoddard tried to commit suicide in February 1880. "I have been ill," he confessed to

Father Hudson. "I wanted to die and tried to, but failed. I have no wish to live and struggle on as it seems must ever be my fate."[16]

Whenever Stoddard found himself in desperate circumstances, his first impulse was always to escape. He would neither accept any responsibility for his plight nor try to extricate himself. It pleased him, rather, to cast the blame on the dreadful weather or unappreciative people or the poor job market or whatever and, having done that, to flee to a more congenial setting. However fond he was of New England, he did not wish to go back East. "I'm afraid of the East," he wrote John Hay in 1881, "where you are all such fighters."[17] Since the rest of his family was in Hawaii, he considered Honolulu—not so much with the idea of chumming with a savage (although he knew that he would probably fall in love with someone in the Islands, as he always did everywhere), but with the hope of finding a writing job and a vine-covered cottage.

While waiting, with characteristic passivity, for some turn of fortune, Stoddard received two pieces of heartening news in 1881. One was from D. Appleton and Company, which was planning to publish his *Chronicle* letters from Egypt as *Mashallah! A Flight into Egypt* in its new "Handy-Volume Series." There was no money in it, perhaps, but at least *Mashallah!* would keep him before the reading public. The other boost came when the good fathers of Santa Clara College invited him to deliver a poem at the Grand Annual Literary Entertainment, to be given in April by the Philhistorian Debating Society. In a "masterly manner," Stoddard read his poem, "Pedro de Alvarado, An Episode in the Early History of California," which ended on this obligatorily reflective note:

> *How oft, methinks, does thoughtless youth set forth*
> *With argosies, to sweep enchanted seas;*
> *How oft the student leaves the mother-house,*
> *Armed to achieve the conquest of a world!*
> *Yet for a cause—what cause oh! who shall say?*
> *Fast by the store, they wreck their hopes, and leave*
> *Their freighted fleets to rot upon the wave.*

According to an eyewitness from the *San Jose Herald*, Stoddard "received a perfect ovation at its finish, and bowed his acknowledgment amid a shower of bouquets."[18]

Then, finally, Stoddard's prayers were answered by an unexpected offer: to come to Hawaii to write editorials for the Honolulu *Saturday*

Press. "I hope to do some good work there and to do far more of it than I can do here or in your East," he wrote to Howells. "Perhaps it is all a dream but what of it so long as it pays me."[19]

When the *Australia* sailed into Honolulu harbor, all the bells in the town were ringing, a cannonade was set off, and the people ashore began cheering as the ship came into its berth. Colored lamps were hanging from the towers of the fire department and the Catholic cathedral, and amid the canopies and flags, some Chinese had erected a little kiosk that proclaimed, "Welcomed by the Children of the Flowery Land." However much Stoddard reveled in this elaborate show, it had not been planned for him. The town was giving a royal welcome to King Kalakaua, who was completing a goodwill tour of the world and whose presence on board must have occasioned an awkward moment or two for Stoddard; for, in a sense, he was being brought to Hawaii to join the enemy camp. He had been hired to write editorials that would indirectly attack the King by directly attacking Walter Murray Gibson, an unscrupulous ex-Mormon missionary, who was regarded by the *Saturday Press* as a wicked influence on Kalakaua. "This many-faceted Sandwich Island Rasputin," according to one source, had formed a "triumvirate with Kalakaua Rex and Claus Spreckels, 'the foreign interloper,' Gibson being considered kingpin in this so-called 'Unholy Three.' "[20]

Stoddard's editorials did nothing to deter King Kalakaua from appointing Gibson as Prime Minister the following May. The ineffectiveness of Stoddard's pieces is not surprising. First, Stoddard was not a political animal; and if he had any feelings at all about this conflict, they were sentimentally royalist. In reference to Kalakaua, Stoddard wrote some years later: "O what a King was he! Such a King as one reads of in nursery tales. He was all things to all men, a most companionable person."[21] Second, Stoddard's style was far from forceful enough to persuade readers to change their opinions, a point which has been well analyzed by Carl Stroven.[22] It appears that *Saturday Press* editor George W. Stewart soon sensed that Stoddard's talents lay elsewhere, and before long he was allowed to write on themes closer to his heart.[23] In "Birds of Passage," for instance, Stoddard deplored the fact that two famous opera singers stopping over in Honolulu had not been induced to give a series of concerts. In "Physical Culture," he exhorted the young men of Honolulu to use the town's gymnasium, citing the improvements to be expected if they would only follow Dr. Sargent's exercise program.

For a short time after arriving in Honolulu, Stoddard stayed at the imposing Royal Hawaiian Hotel on Beretania, but he soon moved into a "tumbledown old rookery" near the cemetery on Nuuannu Street. It was apparently as much of a Gothic ruin as the "Eyrie" had been, and Stoddard began calling his new home "Spook Hall." Its former owners had supposedly been murdered there, and the husband of its current owner, Mrs. Frank Harris ("Lady Spook"), had recently drowned. It all seemed somehow appropriate to Stoddard's mood. "I had but few acquaintances and cared but little to see them there," he recalled (*ITD* 117). He looked upon his last years in San Francisco as a soul-searing time, and "Spook Hall" seemed to provide a salutary seclusion.

Stoddard made some outings, of course. Every Sunday morning he went to mass at the cathedral; and if he wanted to watch the swimmers, he could go to Kapena Pool or Waikiki beach. Then there were Professor Berger's band concerts at Emma Square, where Stoddard could rub elbows with the highly decorative youths who strolled around in tennis suits. If he wanted to leave Honolulu altogether, he could always take the interisland steamer over to Maui and visit his family. Stoddard's parents ran the general store at Waihee, where Sarah's husband, Parker Makee, superintended the family sugarcane plantation.

The pleasure that suited Stoddard best was falling in love. Although some Honolulu gossips linked him to Mrs. Harris, the widow with whom he appeared to be living in sin, Stoddard's feelings were truly for Willie Lawler, a young man who lived at the hotel in Maui. To the best of his ability, this young man repaid Stoddard's attentions during their brief and furtive affair. One problem, however, was lack of privacy. Another was the "Kid"'s inexperience, which became evident when Stoddard took him to Waihee for a visit with Sarah and Parker. "Twice during our stay he had his own way with me," Stoddard wrote in his diary, "and had he been other than the immature youngster that he is, it would have reminded me of other days and other hours which were warmer than these in spite of the higher latitude" (D 5 Aug. 1882).[24]

Toward the end of the summer of 1882, Stoddard spotted clouds on the horizon that caused him, as usual, to throw up his hands in despair. The immediate problem was that Mrs. Harris was closing "Spook Hall" and leaving town in September. Then his contract with the *Press* was to expire on October 31, and it seemed doubtful that it would be renewed. Finally, the Lawlers were talking about going to Australia, and Stoddard hated the thought of losing Willie. What will become of me, he asked a friend in California, Theodore Dwight, who now held the prestigious and lucrative post of librarian for the State Department in Washington, D.C., and who tried to entice Stoddard into coming East and moving in with him. "I can house you so long as you will be housed. Coffee in thin porcelain shall be served to you at your bedside by the African Sphinx, James the black and speechless, called by some the 'Mind Reader.'. . . You shall have incitements to work and all the facilities of quills and paper. It is too happy a dream."[25] Dwight's offer was not tempting enough.

"I don't seem to care to return to the world," Stoddard had written to Father Hudson before going to Hawaii. He had conceded, however, that he had to go somewhere. "I do not yet know what I shall do but I try to rest content and trust that the way will be opened for me."[26] Once again the way was opened for Stoddard in a rather miraculous fashion. Further up on Nuuannu Street was a large, airy house, with a sweeping view of the town and the harbor, that was occupied by three fairly young and well-to-do bachelors who were looking for a fourth to help with housekeeping expenses. Since they all worked downtown during weekdays, Stoddard might have all the quiet he needed for his writing. In fact, life at "Bachelor's Bungalow" (or "Stag-Racket Bungalow," as he called it) solved Stoddard's major problem; for he found that his financial worries could be largely forgotten. Austin Whiting, the wealthy young lawyer who acted as head of the house, was willing to subsidize him from month to month, as an advance on his next book.

But loving companionship was lacking. As Stoddard wrote to Will Stuart, apparently in reply to some remark about Oscar Wilde: "Oscar Wilde! Shall I ever find him in this vague world? If you see him before I do, and of course you will, please say the unutterable things that stick in my throat—because here there is no one to spoon with, or to gush over, or to care a fig for and I am out of practice."[27] Nevertheless when Stoddard moved into his new home on September 2, he wrote in his diary that night: "Life is promiseful, and I thank God and the Saints that I am here at last" (D 1882).

It might seem odd that Stoddard felt he would fit comfortably at "Stag-Racket Bungalow," since he had so little in common with his housemates. Whereas he was a "prematurely gray, prematurely bald, sad-eyed, soft-hearted fellow," a forty-year-old, introverted, nervous homosexual, his fellows were much younger men who were "more or less wild," nonreligious, nonliterary, extroverted heterosexuals.[28] In addition to Whiting, there were William Sproull, who worked in Mac-Farlane's shipping office, and Charles Deering, who worked at the Bishop Bank. It was they and their friends who provided all the "stag-racket": poker parties, which usually included a great deal of yelling and drinking and swearing and which almost always ended with some-one doing a drunken hula-kai. Sometimes Stoddard would sit at the piano with his drink, plinking out a popular ditty and trying to get into the spirit of things. Other times he would escape to the darkness of the veranda, where he would smoke and brood and watch the merriment from afar, following his old childhood pattern. When it got very late, he would go into his bedroom, write in his diary, say his rosary, and try to go to sleep, praying that the din would soon die down.

But living at the Bungalow did have its compensations. One night when Stoddard and several of his new friends were threading through the potted palms at the hotel, he overheard someone mutter, appar-ently with some envy, "There goes the Bungalow Crowd now." There was, then, simply the sense of belonging. If Stoddard was never really "one of the boys," he was at least an honorary member of a set that was much in demand in Honolulu society. When the "boys" were invited somewhere for an evening or weekend, it appears that they were often urged to bring "Charley" along. Then, too, Stoddard enjoyed those "forbidden" thrills known only to homosexuals who find themselves living among high-spirited and ultramasculine heterosexuals. Since females were supposedly "forbidden the premises," everyone was free to run around naked, a house rule that delighted Stoddard more in his observing than his observance. Another rule was that overnight guests could share anyone's bed without much fanfare, with the result that Stoddard sometimes awoke to discover a naked young man sleeping next to him. Finally, in spite of what he had told Will Stuart, it appeared that there was going to be someone in the Bungalow to "gush over." He felt a strong attraction for the dark-eyed bank clerk, Charles Deering, and before long Stoddard decided that Deering was to be his new "Kid."

Stoddard began his "labor of love" by redecorating Deering's room with all manner of *objets d'art*, and he began to shower the young man with every sort of kindness. "O, this yearning," Stoddard wrote in his diary, "I thank God for it!" (D 12 Mar. 1883). For his part, Deering seemed genuinely pleased and flattered by the thoughtfulness of this middle-aged man, and he tried to express a reasonable gratitude. The problem was that Stoddard chose to interpret Deering's thanks as a sign of requited love. Stoddard became covert and ecstatic at the same time. "We don't wish to disturb the Bungalow Boys with a show of affection," he explained in his diary, "which would naturally leave them out in the cold. We feel thrice what we dare to say and know all the sweet caresses of secret love." In the same mood on another occasion, Stoddard asked his diary, "Will there be a consummation, I wonder? I long for it, and yet I fear it. Let us see!!" (D 19, 28 Mar. 1883).

Into this sanctum of quivering possibilities barged Belle Strong, who gradually began to assume the role—at least from Stoddard's point of view—of a seductive serpent. Belle had paved the way for her family's arrival in the Islands by sending "dear old Charley" a series of ingratiating letters, such as the one in which she compared Stoddard favorably to the young Oscar Wilde, who had visited the Strongs' San Francisco studio. "He was delightfully entertaining, and said that the only thing he regretted about California was that he had not seen the Yosemite Valley and Charley Stoddard. But you, Charley, are the real aesthete— he affects what to you is natural and he has not your languour, grace, or beautiful voice and so the general verdict is that we have a better aesthete at home than this fellow who came all these miles to 'show off.' "[29] Stoddard was disarmed by letters like this; and when the Strongs and their baby arrived during the fall of 1882, he was delighted at first to see them.

It was during the next spring that everything began to change. Before Stoddard's horrified eyes, young Deering fell in love with Belle, and she in turn welcomed his attentions. Joe, who had begun to loathe his wife and who hardly cared one way or another, would sometimes come up to the Bungalow to sleep overnight with Stoddard. Stoddard became intensely jealous of Belle, who took it upon herself to tear down the decorations that Stoddard had so lovingly arranged in the Kid's room and then to put up those of her own devising, having the nerve to ask Stoddard to entertain her all the while at the piano. When Stoddard demurred, she "pretended to be much hurt." One night when he had drunk too much, he told off this "heartless" and "stupid" woman to her "bulbous" face (D 13 Jan., Apr.–Sept. 1883).

A complicating factor, which sometimes reversed the polarities in the Stoddard-Deering-Belle "triangle," was the arrival in town of a shipload of good-looking naval officers. According to one source, sailors of many nationalities "longed for assignment to the Pacific" because they knew of the cordial welcome awaiting them from certain "hospitable residents" of Honolulu.[30] Belle aspired to be one of these. The visit of the USS *Essex* in 1883 serves to illustrate the two ways Stoddard benefited from Belle's kindness to these men. First, he had the pleasure of meeting some of them at her receptions. One June 26, for instance, he captured a "prize beauty" who "guyed" him, gave "taffy" in profusion, and was altogether "very agreeable" (D 18 Jul. 1883). Even more delightful was what happened after Belle fell in love with one of the *Essex* officers. Then it was Deering's turn to be jealous, and he looked to Stoddard for comfort during all-night tête-à-têtes that filled many an "exquisite hour, never to be forgotten." But when her sailor went back to sea, Belle gravitated once more to Deering, who then became oblivious of Stoddard, who in turn tried to be philosophical about his situation. Stoddard noted in his diary that "this will last till the next ship of war arrives and then the Strongs will be swamped and the Kid will be miserable and my duties as consoler and counselor will come in nicely. Patience my heart!"

One further complication in Stoddard's private affairs, though it did not diminish his idolatrous love for the Kid, was his secret relationship with a salesman named Leverette Doyle, whom he had met in February 1883 at the *Saturday Press* office. "Doylie" had begun making "unmistakable offers of fellowship," which Stoddard had found to be by "no means unwelcome" (D 26 Feb. 1883). During the following months, Stoddard occasionally slipped out of the Bungalow for a late assignation with Doyle, who, unlike Willie Lawler, proved to be "eminently satisfactory, yea, accomplished." On the night of Easter Sunday, for instance, they met in a little shanty and "made merry until moonrise" (D 25 Mar. 1883). Doyle was, in fact, an experienced and aggressive homosexual who did not hesitate to proposition good-looking men, a fact that soon became notorious in certain quarters of Honolulu. That June, in fact, Deering warned Stoddard that half the young fellows in town were wise to Doyle and that it was no longer safe to be seen in his company. In the case of "Lady Spook," Stoddard could afford to laugh at the local gossips, and he liked to boast that his indifference made him immune to the stings of the scandal mongers: "If an arrow flies this way, I receive it with the unction of a St. Sebastian."[31] But in the case of Doyle, the arrows were striking home, and Stoddard decided to end the relationship. "I am sorry for this," he wrote in his diary, "as he is alone in the world and seems a good sort of fellow" (D 22 Jun. 1883).[32]

III

During the upheavals of his first year at the Bungalow, writing offered Stoddard a welcome form of escape and emotional compensation. In addition to pieces for the *Saturday Press* and the *Overland Monthly* in San Francisco, he was also pursuing several projects for book publication. Of comparatively minor interest is the pamphlet he wrote for the Oceanic Steamship Company. *A Trip to Hawaii* (1885) consisted of brief essays on each of the islands that were calculated to lure tourists to the "Paradise of the Pacific." Somewhat more substantial were his "Lazy Letters from Low Latitudes," which began appearing in the *Overland Monthly* in 1885. Each letter described a different aspect of Honolulu life, subjects ranging from "By the Sea" to "A Poi-Feed" to "Among the Wreath-makers." Along with a few additional pieces, these were eventually published in 1894, under the title *Hawaiian Life, Being Lazy Letters from Low Latitudes.*

That summer of 1883, Stoddard also began his autobiographical San Francisco novel, which he had been pondering for at least ten years. The book was going to be misty and slightly wicked, and he felt that suitable titles might be *Summer Cloud* or *The Bohemian*. He began by interweaving his relationships with Eben Plympton and Julia ("Dudee") Fletcher, but the idea of telling the truth, however obliquely, was threatening. "A great fear comes over me," he wrote in his diary, "and I feel as if it were folly to attempt it" (D 26 Jul. 1883). The novel refused to go anywhere, and after writing a few chapters, Stoddard decided to drop it.

Of all that Stoddard wrote in 1883, nothing was more revealing than an offbeat story called "The Schism at St. Aidenn," which appeared in the *Overland Monthly* in April. In this tale, "compiled from the papers of Philemon, Superior of the Brothers of the Lily and the Rose," Stoddard joyously committed all of his favorite fantasies to paper. In projecting himself into the role of Philemon, he became a sort of abbot to a jolly band of young men.

The setting is a bucolic estate known as Saint Aidenn-down-dale (modeled on Santa Clara College), from which a "pastoral letter" is issued to the "wandering flock I [Philemon] so long to gather into this flowery fold." While most of this flock are artists of some sort (actors, painters, playwrights), several have been chosen to "ornament" the order simply by virtue of their beauty. The Brothers begin to arrive for their retreat; all are obliged to renounce their sweethearts and wives. For a while everything goes well enough. Everyone abides by the rules and engages in the prescribed activities, which include lawn tennis, bowls, baseball, lacrosse, gymnastics, and boating. Rather than trying to play tennis in their cumbersome robes, the young men, at Brother Festus's suggestion, wear nothing more than "simple bathing-suits"— an idea defended at length:

> How is it any more indelicate in a man to parade his natural outline upon the sod than upon the sand? Why may he not with equal propriety, so long as a spectator is as clear visioned in the one spot as in the other, pose in a drawing-room, with his figure, if he have one, set off to advantage in a seamless male jersey, such a garment as is affected by well-proportioned youths at watering places. The popular gymnasts and the chorus of the opera comique have accustomed the eye to lines of beauty: Brother Festus was right; the bathing suit is the proper suit for lawn tennis; I applaud his innovation.[33]

The tale ends on a strongly misogynic note, with females cast in the role of descending furies. (At the time of composition, Stoddard had begun to think of Belle Strong as an abductress, whose very presence in the Bungalow was a desecration and whose flirtation with Deering was unforgivable.) Sweethearts and wives rush through the gates, taking the Brothers "by storm" and leading them "away captive," thus perpetrating "the rape of St. Aidenn."

Although his writing gave Stoddard a diversion, it could not provide him with what he felt he needed most—love. Although Stoddard kept trying out different strategies to win back Deering's affection, their friendship was more or less moribund by the end of 1883. In December, Stoddard took to his bed with a case of "boohoo fever," a malady with no known cause or cure, characterized by depression and weeping.[34] Stoddard prayed that this "illness" would finally melt the Kid's chilling indifference, but everyone in the household became solicitous except the Kid. Whiting and a local priest prescribed a change of scene, and they obtained for Stoddard a pass from the steamship company that allowed him to spend three restorative months in San Francisco.

When he arrived back in Honolulu in March 1884, Stoddard found that Deering was still "distant" and "indifferent." Stoddard plied him with gifts—a Japanese lantern, a kimono, two Japanese fans, a painting, a pipe bowl, and a Japanese frieze—all to no avail. Deering gave the kimono to Belle, explaining, "She will appreciate it more than I do" (D

17 Mar. 1884).[35] Stoddard then reversed his tactics, pretending that he did not care if the Kid spoke to him or not. But, of course, he did care, and every precious utterance was duly recorded and evaluated in his diary. (Deering's "Well, good bye," for example, seemed somehow more significant than merely his "Good bye.") Stoddard concluded that it was Deering who was behaving in a peculiar fashion. In his diary he would ask, "What is the matter with him?" or comment, "What a strange Kid he is!" (D 10 Mar. 1884). Only rarely would he wonder if he himself might be out of step. "How strange this world is and how hateful," he wrote at the end of April, "or is it only I that am so?"

Maybe the Bible had some answers. Stoddard would close his eyes, open the Bible at random, and place his finger on what he hoped would be an instructive passage. "Thy place is not in this city," a verse told him one day that spring, and he wondered if he should spend a few months at Waihee again, however dull it would be. But then Stoddard had an inspiration: what if he were to slip out of Honolulu without "so much as a good bye to a living soul"? (D 27 Apr. 1884). His absence might become a cause for gratifying wonderment and concern. Surely, even the Kid would be obliged to feel some "compunctions of conscience." Stoddard sailed for Waihee early in May, leaving behind a note for Whiting that was carefully designed to set his scheme into motion: "I have absconded—with heavy heart as I can carry; will write particulars by return mail. Say 'Good Bye' to the Bungalow Boys for me—I have not the courage to say it" (D 5 May 1884).

In visiting his family at Waihee, Stoddard was simply exchanging one baleful and depressing atmosphere for another. In recent years the Stoddards had turned into a "sorry lot of worn out, impoverished disheartened folks." His father was making hardly any money at the store; his mother's health was declining; Fred had failed in business again and was back "home" with nothing to do; and Sarah, while not impoverished, seemed to be chronically ill and out of sorts. Never very close to his father, Stoddard felt a much greater affinity to his "poor" mother, whom he sometimes assisted in the garden. From time to time he escaped to Sarah's house, where he could play the piano, drink some claret, borrow a few books, and chat with "Sister" if she were well enough to sit up. It was with his younger brother Fred, however, that Stoddard seemed to have the most in common—too much, in fact, for his own peace of mind. During the ten weeks at Waihee, he and Fred had many a long talk at twilight on the veranda; after one of these,

Stoddard wrote in his diary: "What luck this poor fellow has had and what a range of *unpleasant* experiences—a photographer, a baker, a butcher, a house painter, a theatrical 'super,' a tramp, a house servant, a nurse, a hotel boy, a drudge—and I know not what else" (D 30 Jun. 1884). In addition to being a ne'er-do-well, Fred gave every appearance of being both alcoholic and homosexual as well. In Stoddard's eyes, Fred served as a living cautionary tale that told what he himself might become.

During the torrid and lackluster days at Waihee, Stoddard's spirits sank. The future was as "blank as a drab wall," and he would often "sit and mope and wonder if life is worth living." He even lost interest in the amorous game he thought he was playing with Charles Deering, who, in any case, had grown no fonder of Stoddard in his absence. He did try to do a little writing while he was on Maui, producing a series of eight local-color sketches of island villages for the Honolulu *Daily Hawaiian.* Other than that, almost nothing. He returned to the Bungalow in mid-July, his heart "marble."

I V

The only person who was giving Stoddard the comfort and encouragement he so desperately needed at this time was Father Hudson of Notre Dame. In addition to mailing him books, pictures, the *Ave Maria*, and a steady supply of religious objects, Father Hudson was also taking an interest in Stoddard's writing career. For some time the priest had been urging Stoddard to write the story of his conversion, with the idea that it could run in the *Ave Maria* and then be published as a book. Stoddard was now in the mood to start on this project, which proved to be a healthy distraction from the silly affairs of the Kid and Belle and Joe and everyone else. His confessions are especially interesting in the context of the woebegone life he was leading at the time of their composition.

What Stoddard wrote that summer appeared serially in the *Ave Maria* during the fall of 1884; *A Troubled Heart and How It was Comforted at Last*, the book version, was issued by a Notre Dame publisher the next year. Stoddard insisted on anonymity because the subject matter was "controversial" and because he felt he was "baring his soul." In this regard, his preface is of some interest:

> Let it amaze no one that I have at last chosen to unveil my heart to the possibly unsympathetic eye of the general reader.

> Again and again, and yet again, I have been curiously questioned by those who could not follow in the path which led me away from my kinsmen . . . and to whom the mysterious influences which I found irresistible were unknown. . . . What my lips dared scarcely utter . . . my pen in the serene solitude of my chamber has related unreservedly. (*TH* 7)

From this preface, which did not appear in the *Ave Maria* serial, the twentieth-century reader might easily suppose that Stoddard is on the verge of confessing not that he is a Catholic, but that he is a homosexual.

A Troubled Heart should be read in the context of the virulently anti-Catholic literature of the nineteenth century: anti-Popish novels (*The Female Jesuit; or, The Spy in the Family*); plays (*The Jesuit: A National Melodrama in Three Acts*); tracts (*Thoughts on Popery*); scurrilous "exposés" (*Open Convents; or, Nunneries and Popish Seminaries Dangerous to the Morals and Degrading to the Character of a Republican Community*). There were even anti-Catholic almanacs and gift books. According to George Shuster, the Catholic author was often placed in the position of having to refute the "astonishing charges that his priests have cloven feet and that his churches are stocked with ammunition."[36] "Coming out" as a Catholic *was* a bit risky; and Stoddard, neither a daring man nor a fiery controversialist at heart, had no desire to become a champion of the church. He did have some anti-Protestant points to make, however, and anonymous publication enabled him to make them while remaining safe from counterattack.

Much of *A Troubled Heart* is soft-spoken and deliberately vague. Stoddard is especially hazy in the first two-thirds of the book, in which he describes his childhood and conversion. New York, for instance, is never named as such; California is "a far country" (*TH* 25); and nearly all of the persons in the tale remain shadowy and disembodied, including the narrator-hero. Stoddard sketches his Protestant home life, his harrowing experience at the revival, his growing interest in Catholicism in San Francisco, and finally his first communion, during which invisible choirs chanted "Holy, holy, holy!" and he was filled "to overflowing with unspeakable peace" (*TH* 131). Taking an occasional swipe at Unitarians, Episcopalians and (especially) evangelical Methodists, Stoddard sometimes halts his narrative to attack the "childish and stupid" arguments of Protestant partisans: the "empty, vulgar and worthless" tirades of "infidels and fanatical writers" (*TH* 111). "Protestants may fortify themselves with the bulk of their best known treatises, and believe themselves secure; but let them read standard Catholic writers; these books will be volumes of revelation to them. Let them carefully compare all, and I venture to assert, if the readers be of sound judgment, they will soon lean joyfully toward the Mother Church" (*TH* 112).

The last part of *A Troubled Heart* was padded out with miscellaneous chapters about Stoddard's "pilgrimage" to Europe, the universal Catholic brotherhood, the significance of the Mass, the reality of miracles, and the comforting presence of his guardian angel. One chapter consists entirely of a prayer of praise and supplication to the Virgin Mary. The last chapter begins, "I do not know what hope the Protestant has in the future of the departed soul" (*TH* 185); and Stoddard goes on to say how much more satisfactory he finds "the death of the good Catholic" (*TH* 187).

When *A Troubled Heart* is placed beside Stoddard's diaries for 1884, certain discrepancies appear. His sincerity is not in question; he certainly cherished the church as a bulwark that gave his chaotic life some dignity, structure, and purpose. But the tone of serenity that pervades much of *A Troubled Heart* was far from an accurate reflection of how Stoddard was feeling at this time. Although he asserts with unwavering confidence that the church has an answer—often a rather marvelous and miraculous one—for every problem in life, Stoddard found himself to be overwhelmed by problems. In presenting an idealized picture of the church, he felt obliged to show that its faith, in contrast to that of the Protestants, was sufficient to every troubled heart. But despite the comfort of faith, his own heart was sorely troubled, to the extent that he was not at all certain that life was worth living. In the last few lines, Stoddard revealed his true state of mind: "Remember me who am still this side of the valley of the shadow, and in the midst of trials and tribulations. And you who have read these pages, written from the heart, after much sorrow and long suffering . . . I beseech you PRAY FOR ME!" (*TH* 192).

Father Hudson was not only kind enough to encourage Stoddard in his writing; he was also paving the way for Stoddard to come to Notre Dame. In one letter, Stoddard had casually mentioned that he would enjoy visiting the campus, but then the subject was dropped. South Bend, Indiana had little to recommend it compared with New England or California, where Stoddard felt he had some roots. At the same time, the dream of finding refuge behind the walls of some Catholic institution was becoming more and more appealing, especially in light of his enjoyable stay at Santa Clara. Indeed, in 1882 he had gone as far as to sketch out the sort of life he might lead if he were "called" to the Santa Clara campus: "I have some kind of class there and a small but regular salary. Hours my own, am permitted to go to Frisco on Friday night and stay till Monday morning when I please—once or twice a month, for instance—enjoy those dear to me or necessary to me—play, opera, Club. Live a good, wholesome, and regular life with them [the campus clergy] in their delightful atmosphere. I can think of nothing more suitable—I long for it" (D 24 Sept. 1882). About the same time he was finishing *A Troubled Heart*, he received word from Father Hudson that Notre Dame wished to institute a course of "Belles Lettres" devoted to the study of English and American authors. The course would begin in February of 1885, and Father Hudson wondered if Stoddard would be interested at all in joining the Notre Dame faculty.

He now had to grapple with a familiar dilemma for which he had never found an entirely satisfactory solution. While he was drawn to the otherworldly atmosphere of Catholic institutions and to the haven they offered, Stoddard knew he was so incorrigibly worldly that he could not easily make the renunciations that institutional life required. But perhaps Notre Dame would meet him half way. In a sixteen-page letter written that September, Stoddard asked a number of questions with this idea in mind. He had been a "free liver," he warned, and thus he wondered if the school would allow him to smoke, drink, write, and receive letters without their being inspected, visit his "literary and artistic friends" from time to time, and have a private room that he could transform into a "pretty and cozy retreat." In presenting his qualifications, Stoddard regarded his extraordinary interest in young men as an asset rather than a liability. "I am fond of the society of young men and lads: I can say, from long experience, that I nearly always win their confidence and attract them to a rather unusual degree."[37]

While waiting to hear if Notre Dame would accept him on his own terms, Stoddard decided to pay a brief visit to the leper colonies on Molokai. On October 6, accompanied by two physicians, he left for Kalawao. Stoddard was deeply touched by all that he saw during his brief stay, not only by the plight of the lepers, but also by the quiet heroism of the priests who cared for them. When Stoddard later learned that Father Damien had contracted leprosy, he was awed all the more by the willingness of this priest to become a modern-day martyr; and, as a result, it is Father Damien who dominates Stoddard's little book, *The*

Lepers of Molokai, which was written and published the following year.[38]

Stoddard arrived in Honolulu on October 11, believing that the final word from Notre Dame would be delivered by the next boat from the States. Back home in the Bungalow, but hopeful that he would soon be leaving the Islands forever, Stoddard found that Deering had warmed toward him again; and he began to have second thoughts about going to Notre Dame. On October 13, there was a dinner party during which everyone got so "*full*" that "penance all around" was required on the morrow. How "hollow and unsatisfactory this life is," Stoddard noted in his diary. The 17th was the Kid's twenty-fourth birthday, and Stoddard gave him another kimono, which he kept this time. On the 19th Stoddard stayed in bed all day, "dozing and dreaming of the Kid and others," longing "for one of the old fashioned times." On the night of the 20th, he and Deering went downtown to visit friends, returning to the Bungalow at eleven to sit on the veranda until one, "chatting cozily in the dark." On the 21st Stoddard knew that the mail would arrive the next day, a fact that left him "hoping, fearing in the same breath" that he would be called to Notre Dame. On the 22nd Stoddard finally read that Notre Dame did indeed want him to come, and he could bring as much bric-a-brac as he wished (D Aug.–Oct. 1884).

Although it is obvious why Stoddard was "hoping" to be called to Notre Dame, it is perhaps less obvious why he was fearing this news. To some extent, he did not want to leave the Bungalow now that he and his "Kid" were friends again, but there was more to it. Stoddard knew he was a butterfly, with a tendency to flit from place to place and a predisposition to escape rather than to endure. Notre Dame was no place for butterflies. By agreeing to go there, he was committing himself to a regimen of hard work; at this late date, he would need to show some signs of fortitude, self-discipline, and perhaps even self-sacrifice. It was the disparity between what was expected of him and what he knew of himself that made Stoddard wonder if he could measure up.

8

WHEN STODDARD arrived at Notre Dame in January 1885, he was relieved and perhaps a little startled to see that campus life was a good deal less regimented than he had expected. Some of the rules in the school catalog, for instance, did not appear to be taken very seriously—such as the prohibitions against smoking and drinking. Even the president of the student abstinence society once returned from a temperance meeting in South Bend with a flask of whiskey that he shared with Stoddard. And there were Saturday night socials during which the young men danced with each other rather than the young ladies from nearby Saint Mary's Academy. "Encouraged by the French background of the University," Arthur Hope has explained, "a training in politeness was part of the education which the University sought to bring to its students." According to the South Bend *Register,* the "Stag" dance at Notre Dame was "at once diversion and an exercise in physical grace, and the young gentlemen enter into the spirit of it with apparently as much ardor and enjoyment as though doing the graceful to the fairer sex."[1] Whether it was the French background or something else, Stoddard may have felt he was seeing Saint Aidenn-down-dale come to life.

Notre Dame had been founded by seven French members of the Congregation of the Holy Cross in 1842. By 1885, the school had a student body of about five hundred, and five faculties (arts, science, commerce, law, civil engineering) composed of about twenty-five members. The five-story Main Building, in which Stoddard lived, was the focal point of the campus, containing the junior and senior dormitories, refectories, armory, reception parlors, study halls, classrooms, school offices, library, museum, society rooms, and living quarters for other lay faculty. Brother Anselm (vocal music) lived in the tower, on top of which stood a large statue of the Virgin Mary. Stoddard's room faced south, affording him a view of the gym and the Music Hall, where plays and concerts were presented.

I

To their great credit, the staff and faculty went out of their way to make Stoddard feel at home during his first months at Notre Dame. Father Hudson may have warned everyone that the newcomer was something of a rare and sensitive tropical plant that would require careful nurturing. In any case, Stoddard was showered with acts of kindness. Father Thomas Walsh, the school's president, brought him some stationery, ordered a sofa for his room, and often dropped by for a friendly visit. They did not agree on Walt Whitman, however, as Father Walsh saw only the coarser side of the poet. Professor James Edwards, the librarian with a boyish face, brought him reference books he could keep in his room. Stoddard and Edwards had so much in common that they were probably bound to clash eventually; Stoddard came to regard him as very temperamental and fastidious, with a tendency toward preciousness. The law professor, "Colonel" William Hoynes, was a marvelously entertaining character. A hefty Irishman who had fought in the Civil War and had later been a reporter and a lawyer, Hoynes often brought Stoddard the Chicago papers or invitations to join him in his room for a nightcap. But it was Father Hudson who did the most to make him comfortable. Almost every evening he would rap lightly on Stoddard's door, enter with his arms full of things to read or eat, and then sit down for an hour's chat about people, books, and writers. "I have almost in one sitting converted him into a Walt Whitmanite," Stoddard wrote in his diary. "He is certainly a liberal man in his views of literature" (D

3 Feb. 1885).[2] Evidently, Stoddard was using the poet as a litmus test: if a new acquaintance warmed to Whitman, Stoddard had confidence that a friendship would develop.

While Stoddard was making a deliberate effort to like all the members of the faculty, he was aware as he looked around the campus that liking the students would require no effort at all. Many of them were Irish, with dark good looks and a playful love of blather. There was sweet, helpful, pious Charles Porter, whose family had homes in Chicago and Eau Claire, and who invited Stoddard for walks around the campus lake. There was the Idaho cowboy, Frank Hagenbarth, "a splendid bit of flesh and as bright as a new dollar." Charles Stubbs, a Texan with a "thin, smiling, intelligent face," was another "chum" that year. Particularly ingratiating was a "savage" innocent "whom strong men have wept over at parting." This was Dan Byrnes, who had a "magnificent physique," and who liked to "dance, drink, smoke, chop wood, drive logs, speak in public, be with brainy men." (He did not much care for girls [D 18 Feb.–4 Apr. 1885].) Then one night in the infirmary, Stoddard was much taken by the glance of an absolutely charming young man whose name he did not know. The boys were so delightful that Stoddard began the semester in a state of near euphoria.

After only two weeks, however, he had come to the sobering realization that he was failing in ways that left him particularly vulnerable. Stoddard was afraid that he was not teaching his courses in composition and literary criticism according to Notre Dame standards. "What would these good people say," he asked himself, "if they knew just how at ease I have been in my classes and how the miserable textbook has been thrown almost to the winds?" Discipline was the answer, to be sure, and discipline was also the answer to the other problem that was coming to the surface, that of his "ungovernable" emotions. He was strongly tempted to make over one of these appealing young men—Dan Byrnes, perhaps—into one of his "Kids." "I pray God and the Blessed Virgin and all the Saints to keep me within the necessary bounds so long as I am permitted to stop here," he wrote on February 17, "and if I *must* give way to nature may I be taken where I can *give* without hurting any living soul!" On that date he resolved to *"rub out and begin again!"* (D 1885).

In his teaching, Stoddard made no major changes as the term progressed. He was anecdotal in style, lax in discipline, and generally disorganized. He also courted students by giving them very high grades. No doubt when some of the boys looked into his sad blue eyes, they could see that he was pleading with them to like him. Many of them did, and Stoddard began to forget all about rubbing out and beginning again. But in giving way to his nature, he did try not to hurt any living soul.

By the time the lilacs and apple trees were in bloom—he often had overflowing bouquets of these flowers in his room—Stoddard had fallen gloriously in love with Charles Porter, who often came into his room to give him an affectionate "good night" (D 7–9 Apr. 1885). Somewhat embarrassed by his own fickleness, Stoddard discovered in April that he was falling out of love with Porter and into love with Tom Cleary, the charming junior from Kentucky whom he had noticed that night in the infirmary. Cleary came from Covington, Kentucky; his father was a judge, his brother an actor in New York, and his mother an occasional visitor to campus. Stoddard began calling Cleary "the Cub" and looking forward to his visits, which soon became too frequent to be overlooked.

Notre Dame had a Prefect of Discipline, Father Regan, and ten Holy Cross Brothers who served as Assistant Prefects. Perhaps Brother Lawrence, who was assigned to Cleary's class, said something to Father Regan, who then took Father Hudson aside. At any rate, Father Hudson cautioned Stoddard on May 3 about Cleary's visits. "Our intimacy is being noticed," Stoddard wrote in his diary that night, "and there will shortly be talk about it." At first he took this development sanguinely, but after a few weeks he began to feel aggrieved. By the middle of May, his diary entries show the prefects metamorphosing into adversaries. Perhaps Professor Edwards (thought Stoddard), consumed as he was with "jealousy," was goading them on. Stoddard was convinced that the prefects were saying things "to poison the minds of the lads" and that they had conspired to deny Cleary the first-class honors he had expected to receive.

Whenever Stoddard fell in love, his emotions overshadowed the rest of his life, but his first term at Notre Dame was not devoted entirely to courting students and criticizing prefects. There was writing to be done: sketches for the *Ave Maria* about his trip to Molokai. ("The Martyrs of Molokai" ran serially in the summer of 1885, and it appeared in book form that fall.)[3] There was also proof to read on *A Troubled Heart;* and when the book was published that spring, Father Hudson sent copies to dozens of his and Stoddard's friends all over the world.

Their reactions varied. Oddly enough, Stoddard's Presbyterian father seemed to like it, while a staunchly Protestant lady in San Francisco, not recognizing him as the author, wrote to say that she did not appreciate receiving Catholic propaganda. Mark Twain's response was especially interesting:

> You must not make the mistake of supposing that absolute peace of mind is obtainable only through some form of religious belief: no, on the contrary I have found that as perfect a peace is to be found in absolute unbelief. I look back with the same shuddering horror upon the days when I believed I believed, as you do upon the days when you were afraid you did not believe. Both of us are certain, now; and in certainty there is rest. Let us be content. . . .
>
> You have told your story eloquently, beautifully,—how well a gifted man *can* argue from false premises, false history, false everything![4]

Stoddard was also keeping up his voluminous correspondence. There were increasingly perfunctory letters to the Bungalow Boys and also letters of advice to Arthur MacKaye, who was about to marry, despite Stoddard's discouragement, the daughter of Joaquin and Minnie Myrtle Miller. Stoddard told Theodore Dwight that he had at last found a haven, and Dwight told of his life in Washington as an assistant to Henry Adams. Other correspondents included a convict in Sing Sing, a homosexual poet in Indianapolis, and his "poor" mother, to whom he tried to send a little money from time to time.

During the 1885 summer vacation, Stoddard was given a railroad pass to take a trip to Alaska in the company of Father John Zahm, the physical science instructor who doubled as the curator of the school's museum. Father Zahm wanted to collect Alaskan curios for his museum, and Stoddard hoped to make some money by writing up his adventures for the *San Francisco Chronicle*.[5] The two men toured Denver, Portland, Juneau, and Sitka; all the while Stoddard brooded over the situation at Notre Dame, especially the denial of first-class honors to Tom Cleary. As he wrote to Father Hudson on August 1, "I've been thinking much of Notre Dame . . . wondering if ever again I shall *love* it *as I have loved it!* Can one *love* without *trust*, is the question? Tom's treatment shook my faith in the justice of the powers that be to the foundations thereof. . . . I no longer hope anything in particular, nor expect anything in particular and I have lost faith in the impartial justice that should be there, and more than all and worse than all—I have lost faith in the Beads!"[6]

As the 1885–86 school year began, Stoddard was feeling depressed and secretive, telling himself in his diary, "I must brace up, or I am lost indeed!" He was cheered considerably, however, when Tom Cleary spent two hours with him every Sunday afternoon. These visits were variously described in the diary as droll, rollicking, cozy, charmed, affectionate, tropical, jolly, satisfactory, merry, and delicious. As Christmas approached, Mrs. Cleary invited Stoddard to Covington for the holidays, and he accepted at once. The twenty days he spent with the Clearys turned out to be blissfully indolent: "Generally Tom and I are not out of bed until toward noon."[7]

Back on campus in January, Stoddard grew increasingly uncomfortable. He was plagued by malarial fever and chills; he could not depend on the steam heat and electricity in his room; he felt that both he and his classes were disintegrating. Two deaths at school during that spring, one a suicide, convinced Stoddard that the Brothers were doing a disgraceful job of running the institution. Disposed to believe the worst, Stoddard swallowed the tales told him by Brother Polycarp, another unhappy soul, about witchcraft and demon possession among the clergy. "All this is uncanny," noted the gullible Stoddard, "and I like it not" (D 19 Apr. 1886). By the end of the term his only friend on the faculty was Colonel Hoynes. Father Hudson's nightly visits had ended, and Stoddard had long since stopped speaking to Professor Edwards and Father Regan.

Stoddard decided to quit. In submitting his official resignation to Father Walsh—who was, he suspected, also against him—he explained that the school physician had ordered his "immediate removal from the state" because of his malaria. To others, he added that he was leaving Notre Dame "full of disgust and malaria."[8] By the end of June 1886, both Stoddard and Cleary had removed themselves from the "unwholesome atmosphere" of Notre Dame to Covington.

The Indiana climate was "anything but kind," Father Hope writes in *Notre Dame: One Hundred Years*, noting also that Stoddard's "sensitive nature recoiled from the warning administered by Father Regan . . . that he must not give 'sigarettes' to the boys."[9] Carl Stroven attributes Stoddard's resignation to his dispute with the prefects over their denying honors to Cleary.[10] But neither malaria nor the honors imbroglio was the main reason. Stoddard blamed the Holy Cross Brothers for something he hesitated to articulate, for fear that any charges against the clergy would redound to himself.

The real issue for Stoddard at Notre Dame was the orthodox Catholic position on homosexuality. On the one hand, Stoddard was operating under these premises: (1) that God-given instincts must by their very nature be right; (2) that the expression of his affectionate feelings for other males, since they were the only ones he had, was therefore not wrong; and (3) that the Catholic church made allowances for those of his temperament in a way that the Protestant denominations did not. On the other hand, the Brothers of the Holy Cross viewed the physical expression of homosexual love as a sin, and they did not hesitate to say so. "There can be no intimate [male-male] friendships," one of the Brothers had warned Tom Cleary the year before, "without sin." Tom had retorted, "Then I will live in sin" (D 30 May 1885).

When Cleary had told him this news, Stoddard was enraged to the point of launching a counterattack in his diary. "How foul these brothers are," he wrote, "how prone to think evil and poison the minds of the lads." On this point he was adamant. He would give up almost anything else for the church—smoking, for instance, or drinking. But love? Never! The "palpable embodiment of . . . love," he had written during his first days at Notre Dame, was his "meat and drink," and he later vowed that nothing could persuade him "to foreswear these experiences" he had been having with Tom Cleary (D 15 Feb. 1885, 19 Jan. 1885).[11] Either the Brothers were wrong or he was wrong. Stoddard would not allow this difference of opinion to drive him out of the church, but it certainly was reason enough to leave Notre Dame.

II

That September Stoddard wrote to Father Damien that he was "once more a wanderer," asking the priest to pray that he might "find rest at last—somewhere."[12] For the next two years, somewhere was the Cleary home, where he was accepted merely as Tom's good friend, a charming conversationalist, a noted Catholic writer, and a disarming if slightly eccentric houseguest. For a while Stoddard was content to explore Covington, a bucolic suburb of Cincinnati. Eventually, he became part of a group of Bohemian artists in Cincinnati that revolved around Harry Farny, whom he had met in Munich during his stay with Joe Strong and Reggie Birch. By 1887, Stoddard had settled into a comfortable routine in his "Old Kentucky Home," dividing his time between writing letters and articles, reading books, collecting autographed pictures, taking rides in the countryside, and occasionally going into the city to chat with Farny or to see a play. One of the most heartening developments was the repair of his relationship with Father Hudson, who continued to solicit articles for the *Ave Maria*. Their correspondence was full of news about writers and books, both sacred and profane, and gossip about the beloved "boys" of Notre Dame. The priest also condoled with Stoddard after his mother's death in February 1887.

One of the books that Father Hudson forwarded to Stoddard that year was *A Look Round Literature* by the prolific Scottish writer Robert Buchanan. It was inscribed "To Charles Warren Stoddard. A token of sympathy & admiration from Robert Buchanan"—to which was added this bit of verse:

> *"I never bowed, but to superior work,*
> *Nor ever failed in my allegiance* there. *"*

YOUNG[13]

Buchanan had achieved notoriety in England by attacking D. G. Rossetti and "The Fleshly School of Poetry," but it was his views on American literature that endeared him to Stoddard. Buchanan held that Whitman was one of the greatest poets of the century. (By contrast, Howells and James were effeminate "man-milliners.") Buchanan also decried the American neglect of Melville and of Stoddard himself.

A more famous Scottish writer that Stoddard and Father Hudson discussed in their letters was Robert Louis Stevenson, who was soon to arrive in America en route to the South Pacific. "He is the fashion, the rage just now," Stoddard opined. "Fashions change and rages exhaust themselves. Presently there will be a reaction and he will be underrated in the same proportion that he is over rated now."[14] No doubt Stoddard kept such opinions to himself when he met Fanny Stevenson during her visit to Covington and Cincinnati in October 1887. Fanny told Stoddard about her plans to spend the winter—along with her husband, son, and mother-in-law—in the Adirondack Mountains in northern New York, where the bracing air of Saranac Lake was thought to be ideal for consumptives. Stoddard was invited to join them.[15]

When malaria struck him again during the winter of 1887–88, however, Stoddard was too seriously ill to think of traveling all the way to New York. As usual, the Clearys were extremely solicitous, providing around-the-clock care while he was bedfast. By the first week of February 1888, Stoddard was looking and feeling much better, and he decided to go East after all—not to the Adirondacks, which the Stevensons were in the process of leaving, but to New England.

Although born in New York, Stoddard liked to think of himself as a child of New England; and when he received an invitation from his friend Theodore Vail to come to Boston Highlands for the summer, he accepted at once. Vail was the president of the Metropolitan Telephone and Telegraph Company of New York, a wealthy Presbyterian with a wife and a son recently graduated from Phillips Exeter Academy. Vail also enjoyed collecting books, paintings, and interesting people, and he promised Stoddard that there would be plenty of yachting that summer up and down the New England coast. For the next several months, Stoddard accompanied the Vails and their wealthy friends aboard the *Norma* as it sailed up Long Island Sound and over to Provincetown and along the Maine coast as far as Bar Harbor. Mrs. Vail and young Davis were planning a trip to Europe, and Stoddard was asked to be their traveling companion—all expenses paid. He could hardly refuse so generous an offer, even though he had come to regard Davis as "bloated, overgrown, ungainly, uninteresting and spoiled utterly."[16]

Before the mid-August sailing date, Stoddard was able to visit a great number of people in Boston, and he was especially delighted to meet someone to whom he had been writing for years. W. D. Howells was spending the summer with his family at Little Nahant in hopes that the salt air might restore the health of his daughter, Winifred, who was to die the next year. Wearing a new pair of his host's "Wigwam" slippers, which he was urged to keep as a souvenir,[17] Stoddard basked contentedly as Howells urged him to work on the San Francisco novel he had laid aside in Hawaii. This book should not be quite so airy as *South-Sea Idyls*, Howells advised. Stoddard should depict characters and settings drawn from ordinary life. But that was a problem for Stoddard. How acceptable, after all, would be the truth about a young man whose emotional life consisted of falling in love, time after time, with other young men? Nevertheless, Stoddard decided to sit down to work, and for a few days in August he wrote several pages every morning. But there was no completed manuscript for Howells to read until 1896, and the novel itself did not appear until 1903.[18]

The other person Stoddard wanted to see in Boston that summer was his old San Francisco friend, Theodore Dwight, who was now cataloguing papers for the Adams family in Quincy. Both men had been dropping hints in their letters for some time. Most recently, Stoddard had written of his great fondness for Tom Cleary, and Dwight had replied that he wished some similar relationship might brighten his own life. Stoddard and Dwight met several times, mainly in restaurants, where they dined on lobster, drank claret, and gossiped for hours. It is likely that Stoddard brought Dwight up-to-date on all of his "Kids," one of whom, Willie Woodworth, was soon to become a good friend of Dwight. (Woodworth was graduating that summer from Harvard, where he would stay on to do graduate work in zoology under the direction of the famed Louis Agassiz.) Dwight perhaps told Stoddard about his circle of homosexual friends in Boston, each of whom was cultivating the friendship of some promising and discreet young man. Dwight himself had a special interest in photographing good-looking bathers at the seashore, and he had gained some expertise at developing his own prints.

III

After spending a "glorious day" in New York, Stoddard joined Mrs. Vail and Davis aboard a German steamship bound for Bremen. Once in Germany, Stoddard began to think he had made a mistake. The Vails were all too proper and conventional, and he began to chafe at the "tediously polite bondage" to which he had submitted himself. He complained to Howells that "respectability bores me horribly" and to Father Hudson that he was not going to be allowed to enjoy Europe in the "good old Bohemian fashion."[19] But he did his best to adjust and to behave, having little choice in the matter. He let Mrs. Vail take his good arm when they went into first-class hotel restaurants, and he tried to establish some rapport with Davis, whose chief aspiration, once he got to Harvard, was to row on the varsity crew. In Munich, where they settled for the winter, all three signed up for daily German lessons— something that was not Stoddard's idea. He would much rather have spent his time visiting the old haunts, carousing with the Munich artists he had met in the 1870s and, through them, meeting the new crop of art students from America.

Obliged to behave circumspectly, Stoddard decided to write up his mild "adventures" for the *Ave Maria*. In contrast to his *Chronicle* pieces of the 1870s, the tone of these "Letters from Over the Sea" is relentlessly pious; a reader might get the impression that Stoddard did little else in Europe but visit cathedrals. Of course he *was* visiting cathedrals, and he knew that *Ave Maria* readers wanted a Catholic slant on Europe. But there was, perhaps, a more subtle motivation for his scrupulously devout manner. In the back of his mind Stoddard kept rehearsing his battles with Father Walsh and Father Regan, never convinced that he had succeeded in discrediting them while exonerating himself.[20] Thus the "Letters from Over the Sea" might help to counteract any anti-Stoddard rumors that were still being circulated by his various "enemies" at Notre Dame.

The highlight of Stoddard's stay in Europe came in March 1889, when he and the Vails went to Italy. Its sensuous beauty was especially welcome after the cold, dull winter in Germany, and Stoddard was apparently able to break free from the Vails much of the time during his trip. A few precious days were spent in Venice, where Stoddard lolled about in gondolas. In Florence, he was granted an audience with "Ouida" (Marie Louise de La Ramée), whose popular novels he had treasured for years. In Rome he visited the Vatican, spending many hours at the American College in search of old and new friends. He was also received at the Palace Barbarini by William Wetmore Story, an elderly American poet and sculptor who had been living in Rome since 1856. Story knew many of the "better" people on both sides of the Atlantic, and he may have said something to Stoddard about his friend, Henry James, who by that time had been living in London for some years. At any rate, James became one of the people that Stoddard decided he must meet before he sailed home to America.

The most important thing that happened to Stoddard in Rome was his meeting an Irish-American priest named John J. Keane, the former Bishop of Richmond who had resigned his see in 1887 to become rector of the new Catholic University of America. Keane had come to Rome to obtain papal sanction for the school, which was scheduled to open in the fall in Washington, D.C. He was also interviewing potential faculty members, all of whom were to be "professors with proven ability and outstanding reputations for scholarship": such men as Henri Hyvernat, the eminent Egyptologist, for Old Testament; Joseph Pohle, then teaching at the seminary at Fulda, for Thomistic philosophy; Joseph Schroeder, the brilliant linguist and writer, for dogma.[21] There was also to be a chair of English literature, and, surprisingly, Keane offered it to Stoddard, who promptly accepted.

Stoddard certainly had no reputation for scholarship, and it is debatable whether he had demonstrated any teaching ability at Notre Dame. Furthermore, he had no regular college training and no advanced degree. But Keane was under pressure to secure several Americans for his faculty, and he apparently believed that his literature professor need not have a degree if he had some reputation as a man of letters. If not Stoddard, who else was available in the field of Catholic American literature? Orestes Brownson was dead by this time, and neither Father John Bannister Tabb nor Maurice Francis Egan was apparently available. Stoddard was becoming well known in the *Ave Maria*—*A Troubled Heart* and *The Lepers of Molokai* had been praised by Catholics across the country—and he had a distinguished air that would lend a certain dignity to the chair of English literature.

In view of his unhappy experience at Notre Dame, it may seem unaccountable that Stoddard should have accepted this position. But the rector convinced him that his teaching in Washington would be much easier than it had been in South Bend. In a letter to Father Hudson, Stoddard explained that he would give only several lectures a week: "There will be no text book; no essays to correct; the students will listen to my talk, take what notes they can, and then—at suitable intervals—I can call upon one or another to relate what he may remember."[22] More important, the school's head was going to be on his side. In showing Stoddard a sketch of Caldwell Hall, which was to contain both private quarters and classrooms during the first few years, Bishop Keane offered him free choice of his rooms. The nation's capital would be a more stimulating atmosphere than the dreary midwestern countryside. There would be a generous salary, and money was important just then for a variety of family reasons. Finally, what alternatives lay before Stoddard as he thought of returning to America? Although Howells had suggested that he settle in Manhattan and try to write salable fiction, Stoddard was not at all confident he could do so. Catholic University offered a far more secure situation.

With an exciting and definite future to plan, Stoddard was more discontented than ever as he tagged along after the Vails on sightseeing trips during the next few months. As spring turned to summer, he grew increasingly impatient to return to Covington, where he would prepare for the fall. A departure date in early August was agreed upon, much to Stoddard's relief; he and the Vails would be spending their last two weeks in England before sailing from Liverpool.

The person Stoddard most wanted to see in England was Frank

Millet, who by 1889 had been married for ten years. With his wife and three children, he was living in an artists' colony at Broadway, a picturesque, almost medieval hamlet in the green hills of Worcestershire. "There are to be athletic sports in the field back of our house on Wednesday," Millet's invitation had promised.[23] Stoddard was less interested in the sports than in seeing Frank again and in meeting Edwin Abbey and the other artists who lived nearby.

Broadway had recently been described, in the June issue of *Harper's*, by Henry James, whom Stoddard had hoped to meet in England.[24] He had admired *The Portrait of a Lady* when he read it in Hawaii; and, in addition to Millet, the two writers had many other friends in common, such as Story, Howells, Stevenson, Eugene Benson, and "Dudee" Fletcher. The question that remained unanswered, as Stoddard arrived in England, was whether or not James had any desire to meet *him*. Sharply aware of everyone's credentials, James was no doubt persuaded that, from both a social and a literary point of view, Stoddard was his inferior. At any rate, they did not meet that summer; and when they did some years later, it was to be under the most peculiar circumstances.

After sailing with the Vails to New York, Stoddard went immediately to Covington, where he began work on his lectures. The university was not to open until November—the construction of Caldwell Hall was still in progress—and so Stoddard had some extra time. Father Hudson, kind and generous as always, was sending him a great number of books from the Notre Dame library. "I must read or own a hundred such volumes," Stoddard wrote. "I must know the minds of the best men on the topics I shall have to talk about."[25] This time Stoddard was determined to succeed, if for no other reason than that, should he fail, he had no idea where he would go or what he would do.

9

Aᴌᴛʜᴏᴜɢʜ ᴄᴏɴᴠɪɴᴄᴇᴅ that its night air was malarial, Stoddard found Washington to be at least tolerable and sometimes quite pleasant. Its snowy winters were "majestic" and its spring foliage "enchanting," with the magnolias "glorifying all the beautiful squares."[1] Stoddard soon discovered some special haunts: the "Log Cabin," where he could eat lunch for twenty-five cents; Brentano's, where he was always buying books; the theaters and music halls, where he saw most of the production companies that passed through town. He also established a small circle of friends in Washington: people who tended to be wealthy, literary, and overwhelmingly hospitable. As usual, he cared little for politics, even though he was frequently meeting congressmen and prominent government officials. On 8 November 1892, he did note in his diary that it was Election Day, but then he added, "Thank God we know little of it here—save from the chatter at the table. I'll be glad when the whole thing is over."

In those days the Catholic University, three miles north of downtown, was in the countryside, the tiny campus perched on a hillside across from the sprawling grounds of the Soldier's Home. Situated so loftily, Stoddard's corner windows in Caldwell Hall commanded a sweeping view. His rooms, the very ones that Bishop Keane had promised him in Rome, were soon converted into a "cozy den," where everything was exotically atmospheric and artistically arranged. The curtains at his double west window were Turkish, those at the south window were Madras grass cloth, and those in his bedroom were "Damascene"—all overhung by several large East Indian fans, some of them perfumed. Then there were his books (hundreds of them), his piano, his precious statuette of Saint Anthony, his rocking chair, and lots of ferns, palms, and Japanese lily bulbs, along with fresh flowers in season. Autographed pictures of actors and writers, friends and relations were strategically placed, with special prominence given to one of Tom Cleary. Before long Stoddard's quarters became legendary. Guests touring the building would often knock on his door for a peek at the curios of this unusual professor who was becoming something of a curio himself. Everyone else at the university, including both the other faculty members and the young men who were studying for graduate degrees in theology, was a priest. Surrounded by men in cassocks and birettas, Stoddard stood out with his dandified wardrobe and his neatly trimmed mustache and beard.

I

During his first several years at Catholic University, Stoddard managed to get along fairly well with his colleagues. Bishop Keane remained a dependable friend, and in 1892 he gave Stoddard an eight-hundred-dollar raise, bringing his yearly salary to well over two thousand dollars. Almost every night after supper, Stoddard would join the other instructors in the billiard room (although he did not care to play himself), and listen to them exclaiming in Latin, Italian, and French. The small faculty was united in the face of all the troubles that were threatening their school; for it soon became obvious that not all Catholics in America wished this university well.

The Jesuits at Georgetown were a little troubled and suspicious, having heard rumors that Bishop Keane wanted to appropriate their medical and law schools. More important, the new university was caught in the cross fire between the opposing camps of American Catholicism.[2] On one side were the "liberals," many of them Irish, who believed in Americanizing the church, in cooperating to some extent with Protestants, and in abstaining totally from drink. Bishop Keane was a "liberal." On the other side were the "conservatives," many of them German, who, under the banner of Cahenslyism, argued vociferously that the German-American parishes should remain Germanic and that, while the Irish might not be able to hold their whiskey, the Germans were quite able to hold their beer. The conservatives opposed Keane and his university, and a split developed on the staff when Professors Schroeder and Pohle sided with the Cahenslyists. A "liberal" insofar as he was loyal to Bishop Keane, Stoddard otherwise did not take sides in the controversy. On 6 October 1892, he noted that the "German element" was being forced out of the house, commenting: "This would have scandalized me once; now, thank God, it has little or no effect on me." He remembered from Notre Dame how petty some Catholic officials could be, and he was relieved to think that, in this particular battle, he might remain uninvolved and unscathed.

At first Stoddard felt slightly intimidated by his students, these intense, serious young priests, all of whom had a better formal education than he. "I do not hope for the responsiveness I found in the young hearts at Notre Dame!" he wrote in November 1889. "Here I must work alone and for a company of priests who have already been in the pulpit and who have no doubt been looked up to as instructors by their several flocks."[3] Some of his students had actually been college professors themselves, and Stoddard worked hard to keep ahead of them. By the end of the first year, he felt his efforts were beginning to be appreciated. His lectures, which former students remembered as "beautiful and distinguished," sometimes evoked appreciative laughter and hearty applause.[4] Outside the classroom, however, most of the students remained comparatively reserved. They did not drop by his room at all hours for a smoke or a shot of whiskey, as the "boys" had done at Notre Dame. Their distance did not prevent Stoddard from falling in love, of course, but it did seem to prevent him from being loved in return. There was apparently to be no Tom Cleary for him at Caldwell Hall.

Stoddard often brooded about lacking a "Kid," and he prayed daily that God would send someone to his rescue. For a time he enjoyed the close companionship of "Davy" O'Hearn of Milwaukee; but after Father O'Hearn left Washington in 1892, Stoddard felt more alone than ever. Stoddard behaved himself so well at Caldwell Hall that, as he lamented, "How can one find anything to confess in the life we lead here?" (D 23 Dec. 1892). He concluded that if he were ever going to find a "Kid," it was not going to be at the university. In downtown Washington, the good-looking young men, not having taken vows of chastity, were more approachable. "The town is full of attractions," he sighed. "I never go into it but my heart yearns now and again."

Representative of Stoddard's state of mind and of his characteristic behavior is his diary entry for Tuesday, 22 November 1892. That day he had lectured on Margaret Fuller—not well, he feared—and he was feeling lonely. "If Davy O'Hearn were only here," he thought, "what a blessing it would be!" At about seven o'clock he took the streetcar downtown. He was carrying his opera glass because he was going to Metzerott's Music Hall to hear Master Cyril Tyler, "The Wonderful Boy Soprano." After a bite of hash at the "Log Cabin," he arrived at the concert hall, found his seat in the gallery, and began observing the audience. A young man rushed to greet another young man, who turned out to be someone he knew. It was Frank Blodgett, a strangely magnetic homosexual who was studying for the priesthood in Maryland, and who owed Stoddard five dollars. "What is it," Stoddard wondered, "in this extremely plain, vain,—to me disagreeable—person that casts a spell over lads who come under his influence? . . . He has a head, face and expression such as one would . . . usually expect to see in an Insane Asylum." Stoddard was relieved to turn his attention to Master Tyler as the curtain went up. Great things were expected of this twelve-year-old prodigy, whom the program notes compared to Jenny Lind and Mme Patti.[5] But Stoddard thought the boy's voice was "rather thin" and that he squealed on the high notes. Nevertheless he purchased a photograph of the singer during intermission to add to his collection. After the concert, another purchase was made—a flask of whiskey, which was a regular part of an evening in town. Taking the ten o'clock streetcar, he enjoyed the ride out to the university, cold as it was. By the time the car got to Brookland, all the lights were out in Caldwell Hall. In his room he opened the flask and drank alone. He had seen enough that night to make his heart yearn again, and the whiskey was "consolation," as he called it, "for the darkness of the house." By midnight he was in bed.

II

Fortunately, there were attractions of another sort in town that did not leave Stoddard so wistful and despairing. These were the friends he had made: interesting, wealthy, accomplished persons, whose invitations to lunch or tea or supper helped to stimulate him. One of them was Henry Adams, whom he met through Theodore Dwight his second day in town. Through Adams, Stoddard met John Hay, his next-door neighbor on Lafayette Square, the artist John LaFarge, and Theodore Roosevelt, whom Stoddard did not care for. Then, too, there were William Phillips and Tom Lee who, along with Stoddard, were regarded by Adams as his "three lunatics." These two loved "fishing, hunting, and tramping about in strange woods"; and although Adams sometimes joined them on these outings, Stoddard either was not invited or did not care to engage in the strenuous life.[6] Stoddard did enjoy the afternoon when Phillips took him to Adams's house to meet "Prince" Tati Salmon of Tahiti. When he happened to be in town, Adams often wrote Stoddard oddly worded, brittle notes—invitations to dine, usually—and he seemed to enjoy Stoddard's company. Both men were often overwhelmed, for different reasons, by a sense of *fin de siècle* gloom, and they discovered that in their lunatic moods they were able to cheer each other up.

Other friends in Washington at this time included five women, three of them writers of some renown. The oldest was Mrs. E. D. E. N. Southworth, who had been churning out melodramatic novels since Stoddard's childhood. He had always been fond of her books, and he grew to be fond of her as well. "Why have you never married?" she once asked him. The explanation that he snored did not satisfy her. "But why should you be lonely," she persisted, "when so many warm-hearted men and— what is better still—so many sweet women love you so truly and so purely?"[7] Stoddard also called on Mrs. Frances Hodgson Burnett in her stately home on Massachusetts Avenue. He was struck by her handsome son, Vivian, whom Reginald Birch had used as his model when he illustrated *Little Lord Fauntleroy* (1886). Stoddard's other writer friend in Washington, Kate Field, was quite as androgynous as he, but she was his opposite in nearly every other respect. She edited *Kate Field's Washington*, in which she crusaded for feminism, cremation, anti-Mormonism, and a number of other causes. Aware of her own sexual makeup, she apparently understood Stoddard's too; and from her suite in the Shoreham Hotel, she often wrote him notes of crisp advice. "Too bad you are still unwell," read one of them. "If you lived more in harmony with your nature, you'd be better, but it's useless to wrestle with such a distorted being as you are. . . . Eat beef and drink a pint of hot water one hour before every meal. Stop smoking cigarettes and limit yourself to three cigars a day after meals. Of course you won't."[8]

Compared to these women writers, Mrs. Bellamy Storer and Mrs. "Laddie" Mitchell were a bit more conventional. He had known Mrs. Storer (née Maria Longworth) for several years, having met her during his Covington-Cincinnati years. This artistic, wealthy, and generous woman, then in the process of converting to Catholicism, was in Washington because her husband was serving as a congressman. Although not quite so socially prominent as Mrs. Storer, Mrs. Mitchell was almost as rich. When Stoddard stayed with the Mitchells, he slept in a fabulous bed that once had belonged to the Empress Eugénie. These women were especially kind to Stoddard, always asking him to join their family circle on holidays.

As much as Stoddard enjoyed escaping from Caldwell Hall into the salons, parlors, and breakfast nooks of these friends, he took greater joy in escaping Washington altogether on trips to New York and Massachusetts during the summers and the university recesses. In Manhattan, he was usually the guest of old California friends, but his favorite host was his seemingly evergreen "Kid," Reginald Birch, whose heart he found unchanged after fourteen years. In Massachusetts, Stoddard visited Eben Plympton's country estate, "The Grange," on the shores of Silver Lake in Plymouth County. Eben's temperament, as well as his male houseguests, continued to be unpredictable. In Cambridge and Maine, Stoddard's host was "that darling Willie-Boy" Woodworth, who was still an instructor in the zoology department at Harvard. During these years, however, Stoddard seemed to rely most of all on the devoted friendship of that singularly entertaining adventurer, Theodore Dwight.

Not long after introducing Stoddard to Washington society in 1889, Dwight moved to Boston, where he continued his work for the Adams family. He had a marvelous zest for living: he was trying to get Mrs. Charles Francis Adams and her daughters to share his enthusiasm for the Boston baseball team; he was often seen in the company of Mrs. Jack Gardner, the indefatigable art collector; he was much in demand as a dinner companion to William Woodworth, George Santayana, and other men from Harvard; he loved dressing up in costume for the Tavern Club carnival nights. Dwight had become a good friend of the maverick Brahmin-turned-Buddhist, William Sturgis Bigelow, whose island retreat off Nantucket Stoddard would one day come to cherish. With the help of his connections, Dwight was chosen as the head of the Boston Public Library in March 1892.

Dwight's private library was well stocked with pictures of naked young men, both those he had taken himself and those he was smuggling through customs. In 1890, he told Stoddard of his adventures in claiming some Neapolitan photographs he had ordered from Pluschow, the notorious purveyor of erotica.

> The contest is over and I have won! The 83 photos are safe in my bureau upstairs—safe, tho somewhat the worse for much handling and crumpling. It would almost seem they had passed through the hands of every official in both Post Office & Custom House. . . .
> I was shown the pictures and to my surprise and pain they were too, too proper—only 35 had been impeached—among them some of yours but there are others truly exquisite. After much babble the Deputy took me with great kindness to the Collector & acted as my advocate. The Collector's Secretary had formerly been Secretary Folger's & knew me—all was civility & kindness. The Collector like a Solomon said he would submit the question to two men in the room—two lawyers, who withdrew, examined the package & reported that if nudity was obscenity, some of these prints were obscene. Then we were taken to a mild, elderly deputy collector on whose opinion the Collector depended as a finality, & he quietly glanced at them & as quietly remarked—these are artists models! . . . I had nothing to do but look unconcerned. I paid $2.08 duties, pocketed my photos, took an affectionate leave of the amiable officials and came home at 1:30 to lunch.[9]

While touring Europe with Mrs. Gardner during the summer of 1892, Dwight purchased some additional material that he planned to share with Stoddard. In Munich he bought 121 photographs from the Pluschow and von Gloeden collections, buying 216 more in London. (The Sicilians, he wrote Stoddard, "are dreams.") Even more suavity was required when he went through customs this time. "The photos were never discovered or their place of concealment examined," he wrote Stoddard, thus allowing Dwight to escape "confiscation and imprisonment." He added, "When you see my spoils you will comprehend my dangers."[10] Dwight was also taking pictures of naked young men in Boston—and, if possible, going to bed with them. Sometimes his models were Irish, but more often they were Italians who had been procured for him by his barber. After he began earning five thousand dollars a year from the library, he usually had one of these models living with him as his "valet."

Thus when Stoddard went to stay with Dwight, as he did every summer, he found himself in the midst of a homosexual milieu well beyond anything he knew in Washington. According to a turn-of-the-century report, "Boston, this good old Puritan city, has them [homosexuals] by the hundreds . . . throughout all classes, from the slums of the North End to the highly fashionable Back Bay. Reliable homosexuals have told me names that reach into the highest circles of Boston, New York, and Washington, D.C., names which have left me speechless with astonishment."[11] Several members of Dwight's circle were fairly well-known writers, and it was during this time that Stoddard got to know Thomas Russell Sullivan and Meredith Nicholson.

Sullivan was a bachelor in his forties who wrote plays and novels and who went through anguished affairs of the heart. In December of 1891, for instance, Sullivan was having "a time" with a "would-be protégé" named Belknap, while Dwight was going through similar difficulties with Rudolph von Holcomb, an untrustworthy young man who lived in New York and who was also involved somehow with a young Indiana writer named Meredith Nicholson. A bachelor in his late twenties, Nicholson was writing for the Indianapolis News. He had also published a volume of poems, and he was a "dear" friend of James Whitcomb Riley. In getting acquainted with Nicholson, Stoddard became increasingly interested in the famous Hoosier Poet, whose "dialect" verses were enormously popular. Stoddard decided not only to begin writing to Riley but also to bare his soul to this man with whom he seemed to have so much in common.

What had led Stoddard to believe that Riley might be sympathetic? We do not know what Nicholson may have told him because Nicholson's many letters to Stoddard have not survived.[12] It is possible, however, that Nicholson knew of Riley's stormy relationship with Charles Phillips, a young Kokomo newspaperman. In 1879, Riley had written a note to Phillips apologizing for an "insane burst of affection," but then holding his ground. "I am what I am," he argued, "God made me so."[13] Or perhaps Stoddard had merely read several of Riley's poems that glorify the "youthful friendship" of young men. Nicholson may also have told Stoddard about Riley's periods of "dejection, loneliness and self-suspicion," and about his drinking.[14] In any case, Stoddard liked to presume that others had undergone calvaries that were very much like his own; on 17 December 1890, he wrote to Riley, hoping to establish some common bond.

In this first letter, Stoddard declared that the other poet he had gotten "close to" was Walt Whitman and that he could not be "natural" at Caldwell Hall: "I am in a 'Holy House' where every heart wears a coat of mail. I cannot get near these fellows and it is out of the question for me to blossom in such an atmosphere."[15] In replying, Riley expressed no interest in Stoddard's plight and made no response to the mention of Whitman, a poet he regarded as a humbug. Stoddard tried again, quoting one of Riley's poems ("He Is My Friend") that sentimentalizes male friendship, professing that it meant a great deal to him, and expressing the wish that he "were a savage."[16] This time Riley replied in a Sunday-school vein, exhorting Stoddard to bear his burden like a good Christian: " 'Every back is fitted for its burden' and every burden is the best thing that ever happened to the back of mortal man! Them's my views, doggies!"[17] Still Stoddard persisted, saying in another letter that he regarded himself as "despised and rejected of men," and insisting in yet another that "I love my friends dearly and nobody shall stop me!"[18] Finally, on 9 March 1891, Riley ventured to touch on the subject that was obviously so vital to his new correspondent. "Indeed, I like a good man," Riley confessed, "if he's temperate about it." Even more pointedly, Riley added, "And don't think God has much affection for the other brand."[19]

Stoddard might logically have concluded that he and "Whitcomb" were never going to establish rapport after all. But then on 2 April 1892, the two men apparently met in Washington. Perhaps Stoddard was in one of his lachrymose moods; Riley quoted in his autograph album, "There! little girl, don't cry."[20] After 1893 however, their correspondence dwindled, and Stoddard was disappointed. "I started out by saying that silence doesn't matter," he wrote. "It does matter when a man writes such letters as you do: I can feel the life–blood pulsing in them. I wonder if you write many? Some day they will show to the world a side of your nature which even your exquisite poems do not betray. May *that* day be long distant."[21]

III

During these years Stoddard earned about fifty dollars a month for his stream of contributions to the *Ave Maria*, some of which were travel sketches recycled from the *Chronicle* series of the 1870s. During the summer of 1892, he finally completed the autobiographical novel he had begun in Hawaii. It took him only seven weeks to write most of its seventy thousand words; but as the writing flowed, he lacked the courage to look back and rewrite or even reread. "I'm not to look at it . . . until my next summer vacation," he told Russell Sullivan, "and then I'll see if it be fish, flesh or fowl."[22]

The best literary news of these years was that Scribner's was issuing a new edition of *South-Sea Idyls*.[23] It is not clear who arranged the republication. It may have been Edward L. Burlingame, editor of *Scribner's Magazine*, or Howells, who wrote the laudatory preface. At any rate, the book appeared in the fall of 1892 and received generally good reviews, "most of them extremely flattering." Stoddard noted that "Herman Melville, Kinglake (in his *Eothan*) and Pierre Loti . . . have been my despair. To all of these have I been compared and in some cases the palm has been given to me" (D 6 Oct. 1892). *The Dial*, for instance, ranked Stoddard with Stevenson, Loti, and Melville, calling *South-Sea Idyls* a "classic": "In their happy combination of humor and poetic feeling, in their graceful style, and in their simple human sympathy, the sketches are so satisfactory that we cannot imagine the thing being better done."[24] The *Catholic World* was "at a loss to recall an English equivalent" for Stoddard's "charm of diction, power of picturesque suggestion, and other purely literary qualities." The reviewer added that a "rigid censor" might find Stoddard "too hospitable . . . of some of the lights and shades"—referring here, perhaps, to his pagan sensuality and chumminess with the savages—but he concluded that "the whole spirit of the book is as pure as it is poetic."[25]

Stoddard also received batches of congratulatory letters from the literati. From Harvard, Charles Eliot Norton wrote that the idyls had "kept me up to a late hour night before last, and wrapt me from the harsh chill of our rough winter into the Elysium of the soft airs of summer seas." Norton believed that the book could have been written only by an American, for it shows "the fineness of American nerves, the characteristic American conflict between temperament and conscience—the shiness [sic] of the betrayal of emotion displaying itself by the vail [sic] of pretended cynicism."[26] Rudyard Kipling, living in Vermont, told Stoddard that reading *South-Sea Idyls* had given him "as bad an attack of 'go-fever' as I've had for a long time past. . . . Your book is highly improper, and I doubt not immoral . . . it is sinful beyond telling that a man should wear no clothes."[27]

In terms of literary success, then, these early years at the Catholic University were not unrewarding. Stoddard was written up in the newspapers; Robert Buchanan dedicated a volume of poetry to him; and a group of Catholic ladies in Salem, Massachusetts constituted themselves as the "Charles Warren Stoddard Reading Circle." But alone in his room at Caldwell Hall he found that praise was no substitute for close companionship, and he often felt unbearably lonely.

Then one fall Saturday afternoon in 1892, while he was reading the playbills downtown, he heard someone say, "How do you do, Mr. Stoddard?" (D 15 Oct. 1892). He turned around and recognized a dark-haired youth who had used to come out to the university to visit Frank Blodgett. When together, they had struck Stoddard as "Beauty and the Beast." The youth's name was Kenneth O'Connor, and he came from a "commonplace" Irish family on 9th Street. Kenneth walked Stoddard to the streetcar, and back at Caldwell Hall that night he prayed, "O, if only such a Kid were to fall to my lot!"

10

F ALLING IN love with Kenneth O'Connor and moving with him into a house on M Street were the most important events in Stoddard's life during the mid-1890s. The first obviously led to the second, although Stoddard had been growing tired of Caldwell Hall in any case. Kenneth did visit him on campus during the day, but this was no more satisfactory than the alternative of Stoddard's going to the O'Connor house at 815 9th Street, where he occasionally slept with Kenneth overnight. Stoddard was crazy with love, and he wanted his new Kid always within arm's reach.

I

Aged fifteen in 1895, Kenneth O'Connor weighed one hundred and fifty pounds and stood (taller than Stoddard) at five feet, six-and-a-half inches. Abandoned some years before by her husband, Mrs. O'Connor had raised her six children—four others had died—as best she could. Kenneth, the youngest, complained of being "picked on" at home, but in many ways he seemed able to hold his own. In fact, having dropped out of school, he was turning into something of a street-corner

"tough"—Stoddard preferred the term "waif"—who smoked cigarettes, drank whiskey, and "knew the score." While he sometimes dated
girls, he also had sex with other boys. (During the fall of 1895, his own
"Kid" was an Italian youth named Tony.) Kenneth loved show business,
and he idolized a brother who performed with his trick dog in the Mabel
Page theatrical troupe. In the eyes of other people, certainly the members of his own family, he did not seem very remarkable. But to Stoddard the Kid was the most wonderful creature on earth. "He loves me,"
Stoddard told Father Hudson.[1]

Kenneth had many reasons to be fond of this kindly old man who was
always giving him nice things. One Saturday during October 1895,
Stoddard bought him "a pair of shoes; 4 pairs of stockings, 2 pairs of
drawers, 2 undershirts, 1 white shirt, 6 collars, 4 pairs of cuffs, a suit of
clothes—coat, vest & pants, a cravat and a hat" (D 13 Oct. 1895). On
other occasions Stoddard would give him money for theater tickets or
carfare, baskets of fruit, cigarettes, or "Kiss Me" chewing gum. They
were fond of oyster dinners, and "Dad" always paid the bill. Stoddard's
reward was that he felt needed by this "tender-hearted, sympathetic,
loyal" young man. He was most supremely happy when they slept in
each others' arms at night, so happy sometimes that he preferred to lie
awake. Once in the middle of the night Kenneth asked him, "Are you
happy now?" Stoddard assured him that he was (D 2 Nov. 1895).

At first glance, it might seem surprising that Stoddard's friends on
campus and in town did not disapprove of this relationship. On the
contrary, nearly everyone appeared to regard Stoddard's interest in the
youth as altogether admirable. How can this be explained? First of all,
Stoddard was never secretive about his fondness for Kenneth. As his
love grew, so did his chattering about the Kid to anyone who was willing
to listen. His students and colleagues grew weary enough of hearing
about Kenneth that some of them began "chaffing" and teasing Stoddard about his marvelous youth, just for the fun of watching him
explode. (On this subject, as on many others, Stoddard had no sense of
humor.) His friends may have reasoned that any relationship so widely
broadcast was perfectly innocuous. But Stoddard also practiced a bit of
deviousness. Especially after he planned to live with the Kid, he sought
to allay any suspicion by casting himself as a savior rather than a
seducer. Thus he stressed the "inhumane" treatment Ken had been
receiving at home. Before long he was able to convince himself and
perhaps others that the Kid's home life had been something out of

Dickens. To Father Hudson, Stoddard charged that the O'Connors were cruel people. "I pittied [sic] him and championed his cause in defiance of his whole family. . . . I hope to save him from the dismal fate that threatened him."[2] To Father Richards of Georgetown, where Stoddard managed to get Kenneth a prep-school scholarship, a similar background was sketched: "When I became intimate with the family and saw his unfortunate predicament . . . my sympathy was aroused and I took up his defense."[3] At any rate, all the Washington people, from Henry Adams to Bishop Keane, seemed to give their blessing to Stoddard's and Kenneth's living together in their new home.

The day for taking possession of the house at 300 M Street was Saturday, 9 November 1895. Ken, wearing his blue and gray jersey, spent the day in class at Georgetown. Stoddard ate lunch at the university and "flew" into town to see the matinee performance of *Nancy Lee*. He dined at the "Log Cabin," chatted with the actor Arthur Mayo, and then came home to the "Bungalow." For a while he talked with Jules, a middle-aged Frenchman, formerly employed as a janitor at the university, who was to be his cook, "man-servant," and factotum. (The other permanent resident was Stoddard's dog, Mexique.) Stoddard was in a decidedly honeymoon mood when he went up to the bed "chamber," where the twin beds had been made up with new sheets, which he thought of as "virgin." But midnight came, and Kenneth was nowhere in sight. Stoddard dozed, awoke, fretted, tried to read. It was after 2:30, when up the stairs came Ken and his show-business brother, Eddie, and finally Eddie's show dog. The dog had muddy paws, and its first trick was to jump into bed with Stoddard and desecrate the "virgin" sheets. Then Eddie decided to stay the night! The crestfallen Stoddard knew, however, that there would be many other nights. The next morning Jules served them all a hearty breakfast of cornmeal mush, beefsteak, creamed potatoes, rolls, and coffee. The breakfast table was especially pretty with its scarlet cloth and napkins. Stoddard "said grace, being quite in the mood." He felt "grateful and happy" (D 9 Nov. 1895).

Stoddard continued to be delighted with his new life in the "Bungalow" (sometimes called "Saint Anthony's Rest"), which was, after all, the first home he could truly call his own since leaving San Francisco. On the outside, the house was just another narrow, two-story red brick building, indistinguishable from all the others along the street except that its corner location afforded an eastward view from the ivy-covered side windows. But inside, the house soon reflected Stoddard's personality, which expressed itself in all of the exotic trappings he had been carting around for years. Many friends helped with the furnishings. Mrs. O'Connor herself went with Stoddard to pick out kitchen things. (This woman had given Kenneth to him " 'Body and Bones,' as she said,"[4] and thus the Kid had become his quasi-"adopted" son.) The Storers contributed velvet Morris chairs; Henry Adams sent over three Persian pillows; Father Hudson mailed surprise packages; the ladies of the Charles Warren Stoddard Reading Circle proffered a cut-glass punch bowl.

Soon after moving in, Stoddard began to send glowing reports to Father Hudson: "We three are happier than I can tell you. Our life is almost ideal. . . . This is a rare house—a house of love. We all love each other here and Jules is devoted to Kenneth."[5] But the euphoria could not last forever. Visitors to the "Bungalow" observed that Stoddard was, indeed, deeply troubled and depressed. A reporter noticed that his eyes were "blue and melancholy," that he was in a "most terrible fit of the blues," and that he loathed having to go to the university on lecture days.[6] Of his teaching, Stoddard told Hamlin Garland, "I do it only because I *must* pay my board." Garland felt that all of the religious statuary in the house "did not lighten his gloom," that Stoddard resembled an "aged lion muttering behind his bars, patient but breaking forth now and again in growls of pain."[7] Stoddard, in fact, did have a number of concerns. Would there be money enough to pay for everything? Could he sell some articles to the New York magazines or place his novel? Was Kenneth, who was more "clever" than "studious," playing hooky from Georgetown? Was he being influenced by low companions? Was he staying away from women? High on this list of worries was the situation at the university.

II

On 15 September 1896, the Pope dismissed Bishop Keane in a move generally hailed as a victory for the Cahenslyists. The new rector was Dr. Thomas Conaty, a nominally "conservative" priest from Massachusetts. Caught by surprise, the liberals were staggered. The Archbishop of Saint Paul wrote to a friend: "Something is to be done to stop this dreadful and diabolical conspiracy. . . . The university is dead: nothing can revive it. The Jesuits have triumphed there for good."[8] Stoddard's assessment of the situation was equally dark. "This university scandal is

killing me," he wrote in November 1896. "It is killing the institution."
About a year later he commented, "All is chaos out at the CU of A; never
was there anything more disheartening."9

Adding to Stoddard's insecurity was the appearance of a rival: Maurice Francis Egan, the new professor of English. During Egan's first
year on campus (1895–96), Stoddard tried not to pay this "fauning [sic]
flattering fool" the "slightest heed."10 Of course, he was not unaware of
Egan's many accomplishments. Although ten years younger than Stoddard, Egan could boast of degrees from four universities, a number of
published works, a wife and three children, and a growing acquaintance with the cream of Washington society. Egan *did* boast of these
things, but at the outset Stoddard liked to think he still had the upper
hand.11 The university, after all, had just granted him an honorary
Doctorate of Letters. He was Professor of English Literature; Egan
merely his associate. Even before the departure of Bishop Keane, however, Stoddard regarded Egan as "frivolous, superficial, treacherous,
untrustworthy in all things; a living lie."12

Egan gloated about all the courses he was offering. While Stoddard
continued with his History of English Literature (three hours a week),
his rival was teaching Anglo-Saxon, Chaucer, Shakespeare, Philology
of Tudor English, History of English Journalism, The Art of Versifica-
tion, and ever so much more. In his autobiography, Egan characterized
Stoddard as an incompetent and childish colleague whose ignorance—
"he would spell Carlyle 'Carlisle'"—and casual approach to teaching
had been a "thorn" in his side.13 Worst of all, perhaps, the university
was facing a financial crisis that made it likely that one or the other
would soon be asked to resign. Stoddard could not depend on the new
rector's favor as he had depended on Bishop Keane's.

The pattern of Stoddard's social life changed somewhat after he had
set up housekeeping, and it was modified further when the storm clouds
began to drift over the university. Throughout 1893, 1894, and 1895, he
seemed to be in a comparatively carefree mood, busy with his Washington friends when he was not on vacation with far-flung acquaintances: Willie Woodworth in Maine, Frank Millet and Joe Strong at the
Chicago Exposition in 1893, his colleague Father Pace on a trip to
Florida in 1894. During the summer of 1895, he visited relatives and
old Bohemian Club members in San Francisco. As usual, he spent
many of his holidays in Massachusetts. In Auburndale he met the
Catholic poet Louise Imogen Guiney, who shared with him an interest

in the trappings of medievalism and in the career of the young poet Bliss Carman. He continued to see Theodore Dwight until the winter of 1893–94, when Dwight suddenly and mysteriously left the Boston Public Library because of "poor health," languished for a while at home, and then, to the surprise of nearly everyone, married a sympathetic woman with whom he left for a honeymoon in Europe.[14]

After moving into the "Bungalow," Stoddard did less traveling. Household expenses consumed most of his salary, and, besides, he now had Kenneth for company during vacations. During the summer of 1897, he did go to Nahant as the guest of Henry Cabot Lodge, and he also stopped in New Jersey to visit the retired actress Lotta Crabtree. But Stoddard generally stayed in Washington, where he would sometimes take the Kid to call on wealthy friends. "My Ken has always had an ambition to see something of Washington society," Stoddard wrote to Father Hudson, and this ambition was gratified in the salons of Mrs. Burnett and the Storers. "With the little experience he has had," Stoddard proudly reported, "his ease and self-possession are remarkable."[15]

By the mid-1890s, a great variety of people were leaving their calling cards at 300 M Street. There were newspaper reporters, actors and artists, former students, deposed Hawaiian royalty, famous Catholics, aspiring young writers, friends of friends with notes of introduction. If he was in the right mood, Stoddard "received" with a certain theatrical flair. After presenting their cards to Jules, visitors would be escorted into the reception room to find their host enthroned in his Calcutta chair, often wearing one of his Hawaiian kimonos. Three men who called at the "Bungalow" during these years are of particular interest.

Although he was only in his thirties, Hamlin Garland knew as many literary personalities as Stoddard, to whom he brought a note of introduction from Howells. Since his brother was an actor, Garland also knew about show business, which was one of Stoddard's favorite topics of conversation. Garland gave his "electrical grip" (said to bring good luck) to Stoddard, who found his guest to be "like a breeze from the Prairies."[16] Best of all, Garland was an appreciative audience, and Stoddard, forgetting his aches and worries, his eyes brightening and his voice deepening, became dramatic. He acted out the story of an impaled fly and some ants to the rich satisfaction of them both. When asked to autograph his latest book, Garland had the grace to write: "To Chas. Warren Stoddard, who has the courage of his artistic perceptions."[17]

If Garland was sympathetic, the poet Bliss Carman was *simpatico*. A tall, thin Canadian, whose unconventional appearance Stoddard found wonderfully picturesque, Carman wore his hair long and favored full flowing cravats, heavy tweeds, sandals, and jewelry. Carman's public persona was that of a footloose Bohemian who had fallen in love with the Open Road—an image created by his two books of poems, *Songs of Vagabondia* (1894) and *More Songs from Vagabondia* (1896), which he had written with his Harvard friend, Richard Hovey. Carman was truly a vagabond only in the sense that he wished to escape the restraints of society, a desire with which Stoddard could always identify himself. In addition, Carman apparently shared Stoddard's appreciation of good-looking young men, although this part of his personality was generally masked during his lifetime and denied after his death. In any case, Carman often visited the "Bungalow" during these years, and the poet looked up to Stoddard as a "Vagabondus" of the older generation, someone whose "unfailing friendship through beautiful Washington days" he would always remember with love.

In a book that he presented to Stoddard, Rudyard Kipling wrote, "Men's insides is made so Comical, God help 'em."[18] This was an apt inscription for a man whose peculiar psychological "imbalance" was a source of mild amusement to many of his more conventional friends. But Kipling too had his intense devotion to young men, such as the late Wolcott Balestier, the American writer and publisher, whose sister he had recently married. In London during the early 1890s, Kipling and Balestier had become more than just "jolly friends"; they had loved each other "almost at first sight," according to Leon Edel.[19] "Perhaps there never was a more beautiful fellowship than theirs," Stoddard wrote, "or a sadder one."[20] Kipling seemed attracted to athletic and manly chaps, whether they were British "hearties" in the barracks or American adventurers in the Wild West. In Stoddard he found a Westerner different from the type he had admired in reading Bret Harte and Mark Twain, but they nevertheless became "the best of friends."

During an 1895 visit to "Naulakha," Kipling's country estate in Vermont, Stoddard received some good advice about his San Francisco novel. Its working title then was *So Pleased to Have Met You*, which Kipling convinced him to change to *For the Pleasure of His Company*. In fact, Kipling urged him to change the whole novel, which he thought was a "rummy, queer, original, fascinating" story that needed a "closer-knit" shape.[21] Over the next few years, Kipling took a proprietary interest in the novel, exhorting Stoddard to send him revised chapters on a regular basis.

Meanwhile, the *Ave Maria* continued to publish Stoddard's articles, and Father Hudson managed to get two of his books into print: a new edition of *The Lepers of Molokai* in 1893, and, three years later, Stoddard's life of his beloved Saint Anthony, *The Wonder Worker of Padua*. But Stoddard gained neither money nor national attention from these books. They were advertised only in Catholic periodicals and available only in Catholic bookstores. Nor did he profit when, in 1894, a disreputable Chicago firm published a cheap paperback edition of *Hawaiian Life, Being Lazy Letters from Low Latitudes*.

His other late books, which were based primarily on old material from the magazines, reinforced the impression that Stoddard was merely a chronicler of bygone days. *A Cruise under the Crescent* (1898) recalled his trip to Egypt and the Holy Land. *Over the Rocky Mountains to Alaska* (1899) was based on the summer he spent in the Northwest during his unhappy Notre Dame period. *In the Footprints of the Padres* (1902) contained youthful memories of colorful spots in Northern California. *Exits and Entrances* (1903) interwove personality sketches (of Bret Harte, Mark Twain, and Robert Louis Stevenson) with picturesque travelogue. *A Troubled Heart* was republished in 1900, with Stoddard's name on the title page. None of these books sold very well, but publication did give Stoddard some personal satisfaction. He felt that his life had been interesting; and although he conceded that "the half has not been told" in his writings, he was content to share the part that could be told with the readers of America.

III

If his literary career was not bringing him everything he might have wished, Stoddard's position in society provided him with a constant round of pleasant experiences. In Washington, he continued to see much of Henry Adams, and he started visiting back and forth with the unfortunate ex-Queen of Hawaii, Lillilukalani. When Mrs. Burnett was in town, she and Stoddard shared gossip. He became reacquainted with old California friends: Fanny Stevenson, now a widow; Belle Strong, now a "grass widow"; and Joaquin Miller, as much of a humbug as ever. Invitations to visit came from friends up and down the East Coast. Stoddard spent some time with Father Joe Kirlin in Philadelphia, where he met an interesting art student named Ned McGeorge. Another new friend from Philadelphia was DeWitt Miller, a middle-aged lyceum lecturer, who collected books and young men. As usual, Stoddard gravitated to Massachusetts, where his hosts included the Theodore Dwights at Kendal Green, the Henry Cabot Lodges at East Point on Nahant, and the architect-poet Edgar Newcombe at North Scituate.

It was during these years that Stoddard was introduced to Nantucket and Tuckernuck, two islands south of Cape Cod. While he found Nantucket charming, he fell in love with Tuckernuck, which seemed the closest thing to paradise he had ever seen in America. "Tuckanuck," a rambling house that dominated the sparsely populated island, belonged to William Sturgis Bigelow, the rich Bostonian eccentric who had given up medicine to dabble in Buddhism. Only the "elect"—and only men—were invited to Bigelow's estate, which Russell Sullivan recalled as sitting "on a high bluff, or sand dune, overlooking the water, with meadowland stretching inward to the south. The Gulf Stream, making in here, gives this place a mild climate of its own, to which the pleasant, traditional *dolce far niente* life conforms. As there are only male servants, pajamas, or less, are the only wear."[22] As Stoddard remembered, it was usually "or less."

Outdoors, Bigelow encouraged his guests to do as they pleased, whether golf, tennis, tetherball, or swimming. Inside the house, with its smart, all-white sleeping rooms upstairs and a lovely veranda for alfresco dining, Bigelow provided the last word in luxury. There was a sunken Japanese bathtub with a firebox under it, and in the white washroom "a row of white china wash bowls, one for each guest, set at a convenient height for shaving, and a little shelf above with a row of soap dishes containing Pears' soap, also bottles of Pears' Lavender Water, French shampoos and other lotions and shaving creams."[23] Stoddard was so fascinated with "Tuckanuck" that he wrote a series of four articles about it for the *Ave Maria*, in which he took care to gloss over the pagan and homoerotic aspects and to stress the unearthly beauty of the setting.[24]

Stoddard would also cast his eyes upon the beautifully bronzed physique of a young man whose presence added immeasurably to the enchantment of "Tuckanuck." This was George Cabot Lodge—or "Bay," as he was called—the son of Senator Lodge, who worked in his father's office by day and wrote poetry by night, and who was considered to be extraordinary by nearly everyone who knew him. Edith Wharton, for one, recalled that "he lived every moment to the full, and the first impression he made was of a joyous physical life. His sweet smile, his easy strength, his deep eyes full of laughter and visions,—these struck one even before his look of intellectual power."[25] A British diplomat remembered "the immense joy [Bay] had in jumping into the water, and then lying out in the sun till he was all browned—as strong and healthy a creature as I have ever seen, and exulting in his life."[26] At "Tuckanuck," Lodge's first loyalty was to Bigelow (whose influence over him Mrs. Wharton deplored). But he also had time for Stoddard, who shared with him (albeit somewhat vicariously) a delight in playing the role of a naked savage.

Walt Whitman's poetry provided another bond between the two men, despite the fact that Lodge was more interested in the rhythms of *Leaves of Grass* than in its celebration of comradely love. When Lodge tried writing Whitmanesque verse of his own, Stoddard was happy to offer advice, but he did not really understand "Bay" 's literary philosophy, "Conservative Christian Anarchism." Perhaps he never quite understood Lodge himself, but he certainly loved the young poet and told him so.

In 1903, for instance, Stoddard wrote a rambling letter to Bay, pouring out his heart and expressing fears about his health, his writing, and his future. "I wonder why I write all this today," he concluded. "Perhaps it's because I happen to be deuced blue—yet why I know not, unless it's because I love you and would be so glad to see you."[27] Stoddard never had the audacity to claim Bay as one of his "Kids"; there was something majestical about George Cabot Lodge that set him above all the Kenneth O'Connors of the world. But Bay was most certainly his special friend.

The other young poet whose friendship meant a great deal to Stoddard was Yone Noguchi, who had been born in Japan in 1875. About the same age, Noguchi and Lodge were otherwise complete opposites, at least as Stoddard viewed them. While Bay was placed on a pedestal and admired for his rock-hard manliness, Yone seemed as delicate and moody and vulnerable as Stoddard himself. In 1897, Noguchi had started sending letters from "The Hights," Joaquin Miller's residence near Oakland. It was the "Poet of the Sierras" who had commended Stoddard to Noguchi, and the young Japanese, struggling to establish himself as a writer in the Bay Area, became interested in Miller's picturesque friend. In 1900, he paid him a call at the "Bungalow."

Although disappointed that Yone was not wearing a kimono, Stoddard found him to be "sweet, serious, often sad—sometimes in tears, he knows not why. We are sympathetic to the last degree" (D 27 Sept. 1900). Yone, in fact, sometimes slept with Stoddard, according to an article he wrote about the "Bungalow" for the *National Magazine*. In doing so, however, he was trying mainly to comfort his sighing, sad-eyed host: "How he hates to be constrained! He wishes to be perfectly free. After all, he is nothing but a spoiled child. 'I am even a baby,' he will proclaim off-hand."[28]

In 1903, Noguchi went off to London to win fame with *From the Eastern Sea*, a book of poems dedicated to Stoddard. Later he was to talk of marrying their mutual friend, the young reporter Ethel Armes. Stoddard opposed this marriage vociferously. In his heart of hearts, he wanted to keep Yone as one of his "Kids," one who would somehow never grow into sober, preoccupied manhood and thus out of his reach. He seemed to feel the same way about Bay Lodge, who married in 1900, but to whom Stoddard continued to cling with nearly pathetic desperation. Even Kenneth O'Connor had begun to slip away from Stoddard, who was forced to stand by helplessly and watch the disintegration of their "ideal" home life.

IV

Anyone could have predicted that Stoddard's relationship with Kenneth would change as the Kid developed a need for adult independence. But Stoddard wished to possess and protect Kenneth as if he were the Kid's lover, big brother, and mother rolled into one. Kenneth had never been all that dependent on his new "Dad." During the early "Bungalow" years, the young man relied on Stoddard for money, but he never forgot he had a family home to which he could always return. Not a gerontophile, the Kid must have tired of this fat old man's love of cuddling. The Spanish-American War gave Kenneth a chance to escape such smothering affection, and later it gave Stoddard something to blame for all of the deplorable "changes" in his Kid.

Stoddard's reaction to Kenneth's enlistment illustrates how essential the Kid had become to him during their three years together. "Ken is begging leave to enlist," Stoddard wrote Father Hudson in April 1898. "I would not object did I not fear that the worry would drive me mad."[29] Stoddard no doubt did object, but Kenneth enlisted anyway. With other

"District Volunteers," he was given a "rousing sendoff" at the train station in mid-May. Too rousing, in fact. The Kid was "kissed by scores of women and girls," Stoddard complained with fierce resentment, "most of whom were unknown of him."[30] Stoddard sank into "a state verging on madness" after Kenneth left him. "I am almost in despair," he told DeWitt Miller.[31]

The "splendid little war" was over by August, and in September Kenneth returned to Stoddard, who spent a few weeks with him in Atlantic City at the Hotel Ruscombe. The war had made "wrecks" of them both, he told Father Hudson, but in the healthy sunshine and salt air they were "picking up together." Back in the "Bungalow," however, they were soon falling apart. Kenneth began—or, more accurately, continued—to drink, carouse, and squander "Dad"'s money. Soon, all of Kenneth's "short-comings of character," as Carl Stroven has noted, were blamed on "the boy's experiences in the army."[32]

But Stoddard himself really knew better. In 1901, when the Kid turned twenty-one, Stoddard confessed to DeWitt Miller that "Kenneth has outgrown me and is running with a set that I have nothing to do with. . . . I need a great deal of cuddling and I don't get it nowadays."[33] It was this "outgrowing" process that must have hurt Stoddard more than anything else, but there was nothing he could do about it. Just as painful was Kenneth's turning for sex to a type of person that Stoddard would have nothing to do with.

While little is known of Kenneth's "fast" group of friends, some contextual facts suggest what the Kid may have been doing when he thought no one was looking. First, Lafayette Square provided a popular cruising ground that was not too far from the "Bungalow." According to one report, both black and white "moral hermaphrodites" had been arrested *in flagrante delicto* under "the very shadow of the White House"[34]—not to mention the very shadow of Henry Adams's house. Second, whether Kenneth found his partners in the park or on the street, he sometimes brought them home to the "Bungalow." One December dawn in 1901, Kenneth slept "with someone whom he brought in from the streets . . . at four or five o'clock." Stoddard was in Providence Hospital at the time, but Yone Noguchi, then a houseguest, told him all. Stoddard showed no astonishment, a fact suggesting that Kenneth did this sort of thing from time to time. But Stoddard hoped, as he wrote in his diary, that the Kid's stranger "took only his possessions with him." Stoddard was not so old that he could not remember what it was like to be young, impulsive, and sexually adventurous. "Heaven knows what he did last night," he wrote of Kenneth a week later. "Perhaps I used to do it myself."[35]

During the years after his return to Washington, Kenneth also continued to have relationships with younger "Kids" of his own. From about 1900 through 1903, Will Combs, who lived with his mother on G Street, was especially devoted to Kenneth. In fact, Will worshiped Kenneth, and he sometimes would accompany his idol to work just to spend the day in his company. (After being discharged from the army, Kenneth did manual labor for a railroad and later worked in Senator Lodge's office.) Stoddard had not objected to Tony, Kenneth's previous "Kid," and he actually became fond of Will, who was "handsomest when least clothed," as Stoddard confided to DeWitt Miller, adding that the youth "strips like a Roman gladiator and is an artist in the sexual line."[36] Sometimes the matter of who belonged to whom became ambiguous at the "Bungalow," and in later years Stoddard spoke of Will as one of *his* "Kids."

How much the officials of Catholic University knew about Stoddard's life at the "Bungalow" cannot be known for sure. Certainly, everyone on campus must have been aware of Stoddard's continuing love for Kenneth. After the Kid had joined the army, for instance, Stoddard found the empty house so unbearable that he moved into the college dormitory for several weeks. As far as official records go, there is little evidence to show that Rector Conaty was distressed by Stoddard's sexual "irregularity."

Other aspects of Stoddard's last years at the university, however, are a matter of public, or at least private, record. In Stoddard's opinion—and, perhaps, in fact—Maurice Egan continued to conspire against him. While professing to be his friend, Egan may well have maneuvered to have Stoddard's classes declared elective after 1897, while his own remained compulsory. The enrollment in Stoddard's course dwindled in any case, sometimes leaving him with only two or three students to lecture. Furthermore, Stoddard was often unable to meet his classes because of illness. During these years he was in and out of Providence Hospital, suffering from symptoms of malaria or the grippe.

Finally the university, troubled by declining enrollments and shaky finances, decided to fire Stoddard. His diary entry for Wednesday, 13 November 1901, records the event:

Today having lectured on Hazlitt to a class of one—Rector Conaty met me in the Corridor of McMahan Hall and asked me to his room. He did not invite me to be seated. He said bluntly:—"Are you aware that the Faculty of Philosophy and the Senate have decided that your services are no longer required in this University?" A strange little flutter of joy quickened my sad heart. I said without change of countenance, I was not. He continued that "such was the case. You have been ill and absent so often. Have not attended the faculty meetings regularly, etc. No one has spoken unkindly of you; all spoke warmly and even affectionately, etc."

Well, I went home and was glad. My day of deliverance is at hand! Thank God!![37]

Stoddard's sense of deliverance was soon followed, however, by acute apprehension about the future. On New Year's Day of 1902, he wrote to Father Hudson: "Now we begin to dismantle the Bungalow. It is heartbreaking. Perhaps when I am settled in my new quarters I shall feel more at ease. Now, at intervals, as I think of the future, I am positively sick with fear."[38] The new quarters turned out to be the upper-story rooms in Mrs. O'Connor's house on 9th Street. It is to Kenneth's credit that, although his relationship with Stoddard had changed, he remained willing to help his "Dad" at his moment of crisis. The move was made in February, and Stoddard never felt at home during the year he stayed with the O'Connors, which became "one of hellish torture."[39] Overwhelmed by a sense of "Paradise Lost," he grew increasingly wistful about the "dear old Bungalow" days.

In truth, the "paradise" had been lost for some time, a fact he had to face every day in his dealings with Kenneth. It was not just that their quarters were cramped in contrast to the spaciousness they had enjoyed in the "Bungalow." What was really "hellish" was that the Kid was now under no obligation to obey him. Not that he had been especially compliant during the last few years at the "Bungalow," but there at least Stoddard had been in a position to lay down the law. Now if the Kid wanted to drink and carouse all night, Stoddard was powerless to object. As soon as the school year was over—Stoddard was allowed to work until then—he left town in a hurry.

He wanted to be with people who appreciated him and still loved him. The first part of the summer of 1902 he spent with a former student, Ned Crowley, in North Adams, Massachusetts. Crowley, who lived in a "cozy little nest" with his widowed mother, was studying for the priesthood in Montreal. Avoiding Nahant because the hyperactive Theodore

Roosevelt was there, Stoddard went next to Nantucket, where he was a guest of Charles Webb. From there he left for "Tuckanuck" to spend some glorious Indian summer days in the delightful company of Sturgis Bigelow and Bay Lodge. "I dread the thought," he wrote Father Hudson, "of returning to Washington at all."[40] Nevertheless he went back to his rooms at the O'Connor house in October and tried to pick up his life as best he could.

V

Stoddard had little to cheer him. Even though a San Francisco publisher had agreed to publish *For the Pleasure of His Company*, he continued to have mixed feelings about the novel. "I am glad it will appear out yonder," he said, "where no one will see it." From an artistic point of view, *For the Pleasure of His Company: An Affair of the Misty City: Thrice Told* warrants little attention. Robert Gale judges accurately that this book "must rank as one of the strangest novels ever written."[41] *For the Pleasure of His Company* is so strange, in fact, that it seems as if Stoddard set out to write an "antinovel" or a "metafiction" long before anyone had ever heard of these genres. Nor is the book especially useful from a biographical point of view. Stoddard so thoroughly jumbled up people and events from the late 1860s, 1870s, and early 1880s that the novel gives only a refracted and confusing picture of Stoddard's life. Whatever its other deficiencies, however, *For the Pleasure of His Company* does not lack "love interest," as Gale charges. While there is no heterosexual romance, there is a thread of homoerotic "love interest," and it is on this basis that the book merits at least brief examination.

Even as a rudimentary "homosexual novel," it must be said, *For the Pleasure of His Company* is a failure, mainly because of its obliquity. But Stoddard had little choice but to write as he did. At the turn of the century, any American writer who chose to touch on homoerotic themes was obliged to be vague in order to be published. Realism, after all, had its limits. When Stephen Crane started reading a tale of homosexual low-life to Hamlin Garland, this champion of realism was "horrified and begged him to stop."[42] Novels that dealt directly with homosexuality, such as *Teleny* or *Imre*, usually had to be privately printed abroad and circulated underground. Even had Stoddard felt free to do so, the fact remains that he was incapable of writing a novel in the realistic or naturalistic mode. *For the Pleasure of His Company* was cast in the genteel style Stoddard had been refining since the 1860s, a style modeled in turn on the example of early nineteenth-century authors. To be sure, it was the very obliqueness of this style that had always allowed him to tell the truth, but tell it slant. In the novel, however, the evasive fancy prose leaves readers so bewildered that they can hardly recognize the truth, even when it has been told.

In the first of the three "books" into which the novel is divided, Paul Clitheroe is introduced as a hapless "heathenized-christian" newspaper columnist, who loves living in his (Rincon Hill) "Eyrie" (*FPHC* 20). By the third chapter, some of his Arcadia (Oakland) friends introduce him to the mysterious, fascinating Foxlair (Wylde Hardinge). Foxlair is so magnetic that when he asks Paul to spend the night with him, the youth agrees to do so "without a moment's hesitation" (*FPHC* 23). For the next week they are inseparable. It is possible that Hardinge was bisexual; in the novel, at least, Stoddard suggests that Foxlair loves Paul as much as the "lad" loves him. Indeed, in the fourth chapter, it might be said that Foxlair proposes to Clitheroe:

> "Look here, Paul Clitheroe," cried Foxlair, turning suddenly upon the youth who was seated in his deep, sleepy-hollow chair. "I love you better than any fellow I ever met. You understand me; these brutes about us are incapable of it." He came and sat on the arm of Paul's chair, facing him, his two hands resting on Paul's shoulders, and resumed: "Let's leave this cursed land. Let us sail into the South Seas. You love them and so do I. . . . If we can't get money in advance to pay our way in the cabin, I'll go before the mast. I can do it—have done it before. Once on the other side of the sea we are all right, no one can touch us there!" (*FPHC* 40–41)

Paul is tempted to yield to Foxlair's "subtle charm," but he hesitates about leaving the Misty City (San Francisco). Shortly after this scene, Foxlair is exposed as the "Prince of Frauds," and he vanishes, taking with him Paul's ring, scarf pin, vest, trousers, cane, and mackintosh. Nevertheless, Paul is never able to think of Foxlair "without the tenderest regret" (*FPHC* 42–43). At the end of each of the three sections, Paul rushes off in search of some form of refuge. In "Balm of Hurt Wounds," the chapter that concludes this first book, Paul has gone on retreat with some local priests.

In the second book, a major character is Miss Juno or Jack, a young woman modeled on Julia ("Dudee") Fletcher, whom Stoddard had known in Italy. Her function in the novel is to talk with Paul about such matters as androgyny, love, and the purpose of fiction. Since Jack is at the very least a tomboy, she is ideally suited to discuss girls who want to be boys and boys who want to be girls. Paul mentions what is apparently one of his pet peeves: that sissies are ridiculed in America, while tomboys are indulged and even admired. "But why is it," he asks, "that girl-boys are so unpleasant while tom-boys are delightful?" (*FPHC* 98). Jack hardly knows. With his new pal, Paul also discusses love and its ideal role in fiction. "What is true love? It is bosom-friendship," he asserts (*FPHC* 106). The purpose of the novelist is to prettify, not revolutionize. Revolutionary approaches, Paul insists, "only soil the water": "I'd beautify the banks of the stream, and round the sharp turns in it, and weed it out, and sow water-lilies" (*FPHC* 105).

At the end of this section, Jack has taken Paul's advice and written a novel, one based on her theories, not his. She has thus become a success. From Italy she writes to a friend that during a recent visit to San Francisco del Deserto, she remarked that one of the friars was "none other than Paul Clitheroe!" (*FPHC* 114). Thus Paul has supposedly found refuge in the bosom of a monastery, a lifelong fantasy for Stoddard that was not without its homoerotic appeal.

The last section, "Little Mama," focuses on another female character—which should not lead the reader to expect that *For the Pleasure of His Company* becomes any more heterosexual. Somehow back in the Misty City after all, Paul is no more romantically interested in Little Mama than he was in Miss Juno. Indeed, Little Mama (based on Jenny MacKaye Johns Peet) is there mainly to introduce likely young men to each other. This apparently naive and dimwitted panderess introduces Paul to the actor Grattan Field (Eben Plympton) with the following speech: "There, you are to be brothers, and love one another with brotherly love! . . . I arranged this meeting; I chose to bring you two together; my boys must always meet; and they must always let me plot for them" (*FPHC* 133–34). They are quite able, however, to plot for themselves as they start to sense a "bond of intimacy that knit them closer and closer every hour" (*FPHC* 143). Paul spends the night with Field, and for a while everyone is happy—including Little Mama, who exclaims, "These are my Jewels!" (*FPHC* 143). Later she asks Paul if he would like to join her Order of Young Knighthood, which very much resembles the all-male utopia of Stoddard's story about Saint Aidenn-down-dale. Paul thinks not. His interest in life has ebbed to a low point.

He has become weary of Grattan, of "Bohemianizing," and, in fact, of Little Mama.

At the end of the novel Paul has escaped the Misty City by going on a summer cruise with some hedonistic friends—a rather long cruise, apparently, because one night Paul sees three naked islanders approaching the yacht in their canoe. Lonely, unloved, and bored with his traveling companions, Paul motions for the islanders to approach. Since the three young chiefs turn out to be friends from his past, he jumps into their canoe and greets them passionately. With this scene, the novel ends, having touched on most of the themes so dear to Stoddard: his love for other males; his blasted hopes of finding a lasting refuge in the church; his dream of escaping into some kind of secular, all-male utopia; and the fantasy of returning to the South Seas, where he might be "natural" in a way that was proscribed in America.

As might be expected, most reviewers in 1903 seemed no more aware of the homoeroticism in *For the Pleasure of His Company* than they had been thirty years before in *South-Sea Idyls*. Kipling's prediction that Stoddard would be "misunderstood" if this novel were published did not come true.[43] What the reviewers did notice was the novel's lack of structure and its airy unreality. Kinder critics gave Stoddard the benefit of the doubt: "The book, for all its rambling and inconsequent manner, is a piece of charming literature, the expression of a spirit unfettered by the conventions, freely disporting itself in its own native element of imagination and fantasy."[44] Others saw an unfortunate lack of purpose: "There is no ease of diction nor is there a convincing excuse for telling the tale at all. The action is tedious, lagging, it does not give the impression of inevitableness, nor of sincerity."[45]

The reaction of friends who recognized themselves in the novel was in some cases extremely negative. Ina Coolbrith did not much care for Elaine, the sad, drooping minor poetess whom Stoddard dubs "Our Lady of Pain." "As his dear friend for many years," her biographers have written, "she must have resented Paul Clitheroe's obvious preference for two other females in the book."[46] The model for "Little Mama" was furious at Stoddard's portrayal of her as an unwed mother who needed to claim "a father for her children." Mrs. Jenny Johns Peet charged that since Stoddard's novel had exposed her reputation to "utter ruin," he must never reveal the characters' identities.[47]

Stoddard liked to pretend that such reactions did not hurt. It was a "jolly experience," he told Howells, "to be called every bad name in the dictionary."[48] He had published the novel, he explained to others, only to get it off his mind. Yet he continued to feel embarrassed that the tale had ever appeared in print. Rather than insincere, as the *Overland Monthly* charged, he felt he had been all too painfully honest. In the final analysis, the real cause for shame was not that he had written a *roman à clef*, but that he had written it so badly.

Professor Charles Warren Stoddard during the 1890s

Stoddard's grave, Monterey, California

11

For much of the winter of 1902–03, Stoddard was stricken with inflammatory rheumatism, and he had to enter the Georgetown University Hospital for treatment. After his release, he decided to put everything in storage and to leave Washington forever. He was planning to throw himself upon the hospitality of friends in the North. In early April 1903, the Kid and Will Combs saw him off at Penn Station, where they kissed him good-bye and "left with much suppressed emotion." Stoddard later wrote in his diary:

> I caught a glimpse of them as they stood on the platform under the car window—my heart flew into my throat, my eyes grew misty—I felt myself breaking down—with a gesture I waved them away and they vanished on the instant!
> So ends the experience of my life, when for fourteen years I have been the champion, protector, lover of one who needed me and all I could do for him. (D 6 Apr. 1903)[1]

If there was to be another "Kid" for Stoddard, he would have a different role in his life. Stoddard recognized that he was regressing into a helpless second childhood; he was becoming "more of a lad than ever," as he told a friend. What he needed now was a "Kid" who would provide for him, rather than the other way around. On his sixtieth birthday in 1903, he wrote: "How I need a guide, philosopher, and friend—in fact a Kid—to care for me in these sad times" (D 7 Aug. 1903).

I

For a few weeks after leaving Washington, Stoddard was the guest of Ned McGeorge, the art student and potential "Kid" he had met in Philadelphia. He felt "more normal" during his stay with McGeorge's family in Atlantic City, and he began to long for Ned when he was not in sight. They took the train to New York, where the young man was studying at the Art League. In his diary Stoddard noted that Ned was "beginning to depend somewhat" on him, but he must have concluded that he could not, finally, depend on Ned (D 17 Apr. 1903). In a few days Stoddard moved out of McGeorge's apartment up to 87th Street, where Mrs. Burnett had a lovely room waiting for him.

During the following month, Stoddard toyed with the idea of establishing himself as a professional writer in New York. Both "Fluffy" and Vivian Burnett urged him to get started on his next novel, *Taboo*, which was to be a "naked romance of the South Seas." In this never-to-be-written sequel to *For the Pleasure of His Company*, Stoddard was to tell what happens to Paul Clitheroe after he meets the three young chiefs in their canoe. But there were too many distractions at the Burnett's. The "enchanting" Kitty Hall was a guest. Belle Strong and her son came to call, and visits back and forth with Fanny Stevenson were in order. Special dinners were planned, including a memorable one at a rooftop restaurant at which Richard LeGallienne and Gelett Burgess were among the guests. Invitations to the theater came from Bliss Carman, Yone Noguchi, and Percy MacKaye.

Determined to settle down to work, Stoddard moved into a "quaint" flat, furnished it with Belle Strong's bric-a-brac, and faced the blank page. But he was unnerved by the "appalling noise, rush, and vulgarity" of Manhattan, and he was afraid to stay in his apartment by himself. In June, Stoddard finally collapsed into "nervous prostration," and Willie Woodworth came to the rescue, taking him home to Cambridge.[2]

By this time, Dr. William McMichael Woodworth had become something of a minor legend at Harvard. His home on Brattle Street, the historic Riedesel House, was famous for its splendid array of exotic furnishings. As the keeper of the Museum of Comparative Zoology, Woodworth had accompanied Louis Agassiz on collecting trips to Samoa, Australia, Africa, and South America, bringing back curios for his house as well as for the museum. Woodworth also collected a wide variety of seemingly disparate people. In his library on Sunday afternoons, one might find the colonel of marines from the Charleston Navy Yard and an English army captain rubbing elbows with Charles Macomb Flandrau, author of *Harvard Episodes*, and Pierre LaRose, author of *Harvard Celebrities*.[3] It was into this house and this circle that Stoddard was welcomed, and it is not surprising that he immediately felt at home. Woodworth, who oversaw Stoddard's convalescence with the help of two servants, was exactly the sort of "Kid" he needed.

But Stoddard still was not content at 149 Brattle Street. A great believer in the spirit world, he had concluded that the house was haunted, perhaps by the ghost of Lafayette. There was also some friction with his host, who resembled him in so many ways that personality clashes and petty jealousies were perhaps inevitable. By the fall of 1903, Stoddard had moved into separate lodgings at nearby Prescott Hall.

Here disaster struck. One winter morning he was found unconscious and rushed to Cambridge Hospital, where his condition was diagnosed as "brain congestion." Stoddard remained gravely ill for several weeks, and it was generally assumed that he was dying. Relatives were alerted; friends came to pay last respects; a priest administered the last rites; newspapers and magazines prepared and even began to publish eulogies.[4] The *Overland Monthly*, for instance, reported that "Chas. Warren Stoddard, the author of many of the sweetest poems in the language, is dying. It is said that, though he should recover, his mind will remain a blank." He was remembered as being "delicate and sensitive as a girl, in his nature almost feminine—never effeminate—worshipped by his friends, a rare, sweet soul."[5]

By February 1904, however, Stoddard was rallying. "I know how awkward it is," he wrote in a later issue of the *Overland Monthly*, "for one to re-appear upon the stage when one's friends have said their last adieus," and he went on to insist that his mind was no more of a blank than it had ever been.[6] Back in Woodworth's house to convalesce, Stoddard soon came to take a fresh and vital interest in the future. The *National Magazine* in Boston invited him to write monthly personality sketches—fifty dollars each for only five pages—and he embarked on this project with relish. From the West Coast came word that the *Sunset* was willing to commission a six-months' series of feature articles on the old missions of California, and Mrs. Storer wrote to say that he was to be the beneficiary of a fifty dollar per month stipend for the rest of his life. Stoddard wrote to Father Hudson, "I really feel as if I had at last succeeded in tacking around a bend in the stream of life where I have been struggling against the current for so many years."[7]

In the fall of 1904, *The Island of Tranquil Delights*, a collection of South-Sea tales, was published. In the older material, which he had written years before, Stoddard's hints of homoeroticism were characteristically veiled. But in several recently written sketches, Stoddard was comparatively outspoken. The last paragraph of "Kane-Aloha" provides a good example. After recounting his experiences with this youth, who was "well named the Loving Man," Stoddard concludes by explaining why he had to write this story: "I cannot forget it nor refrain from recounting it since it once touched me to the quick." Warming to his theme and coming as close as he ever would to declaring himself an apologist for "Unnatural Love," he concludes: "It does not matter if in my calmer moments reason cautions me to beware—my head and my heart don't hitch—they never did—and so I have written as I have written; and I shall not have written in vain if I, for a few moments only, have afforded interest or pleasure to the careful student of the Unnatural History of Civilization" (*ITD* 276).

One impetus to Stoddard's candor was probably the reading he had been doing on homosexual themes for the last few years. In 1901, DeWitt Miller had sent him John Addington Symonds's *A Problem in Modern Ethics*, and Miller was to continue sending him similarly provocative books for the rest of his life. Perhaps he had also been having conversations with Woodworth and others about what was "natural" and "unnatural" among various species. From an entry in his notebook, it is clear that he was thinking about a piece to be called "The Confessions of an Unnaturalist." With the publication of *The Island of Tranquil Delights*, the careful reader could see that Stoddard no longer cared very much what people might think of his unorthodox emotional life.

It was in this comparatively assertive mood that Stoddard began making travel plans for California in order to visit the old missions and to write them up for the *Sunset*. He would make his headquarters in Santa Barbara, perhaps, or Monterey. He would bask in the warm California sunshine and then, when he was rejuvenated, would return to New England where he "belonged." With Woodworth for a traveling companion, he left Boston in late March, arriving in San Francisco on 3 April 1905.

II

The city had changed, of course, and not for the better in Stoddard's view. Like the unbearable Teddy Roosevelt, San Francisco had become noisy and strenuous: "I had suddenly dropped into a whirl of excitement that seemed to me breathless after the comparative repose of my later years. Many of the old companions had gone forever. I was constantly meeting new faces, and hearing voices pitched in an unfamiliar key. It was beginning to tell upon me: the restless, strenuous life."[8] For a few weeks Stoddard stayed with his sister Sarah on Baker Street, not far from Golden Gate Park. There was a quiet family reunion. Stoddard's father and brother Fred were both ailing; for that matter, he was not feeling so well himself. Stoddard was bothered by the fog, and he wanted to flee the city for some warmer clime to the south. But first he meant to enjoy the "Welcome Home" dinner in his honor that the old-timers at the Bohemian Club were planning for April 13. Woodworth would still be there to escort him, and other notable visitors, including Enrico Caruso and Henry James, would be attending as well.

James was rounding out his tour of America after an absence of twenty-one years. He was, in fact, seeing the Far West for the first time, and the sights were not altogether pleasant. In San Francisco, as he later wrote, he detected "a poverty of aspect and quality."[9] It is possible that James attended the dinner under the misapprehension that *he* was to be the guest of honor. In *Henry James, The Master*, Leon Edel remarks that James "enjoyed being feted by the Bohemian Club, where he talked with Charles Warren Stoddard, author of books and sketches about Hawaii and Tahiti."[10] But the *Annals of the Bohemian Club* record merely that James was one of the speakers that night.[11] Perhaps he rose to thank the club for giving him a painting; perhaps he said nothing in praise of Stoddard, whom he had never met, after all. But "Charley" Stoddard was affectionately well known by the others.

"We have killed the fatted calf," intoned the poet Lucius Harwood Foote, a former ambassador to Korea, "and are glad to welcome back the prodigal son to the haunts of his youth." In his tribute, one of many "efforts at oratorical pyrotechnics" to be heard throughout the evening,

Foote recalled the Golden Age of California literature, placing Stoddard in the pantheon beside Bret Harte and Joaquin Miller. "While Hua Manu no longer stands watching for his friend where the long Pacific surges break on the strand of his island home," Foote concluded, "the printed page will continue to tell the tale, and the art of the master is eternal."[12]

That Foote should have called Stoddard "the master" in the presence of James may seem ironic now, when Stoddard seems not to have been "the master" of anything, especially of his literary generation. James himself, as he watched the honored guest that night, is unlikely to have perceived any distinction to rival his own. On the surface the two men did, in fact, resemble each other in several striking ways. Exactly the same age, they were equally short and stout and balding, and both had remarkable blue eyes—James's were hard, piercing, and omniscient, while Stoddard's were soft, liquid, and beseeching. Above all, each man had the dignity and the stage presence of a personage; each projected the aura of an urbane, courtly, slightly fastidious grand old man of letters. But there, James may well have told himself as the toasts and the tributes dragged on, the resemblance ended.

Yet in one important way, perhaps, Stoddard was more of a master than James. "Live all you can," the latter had recently written, "it's a mistake not to."[13] To be sure, James had formed several emotional attachments to good-looking young men. There was a Norwegian-American sculptor, Hendrik Andersen, a few years back, and home in England there was now a lovely Irishman, Dudley Jocelyn Persse, with whom he was having such an "exquisite relation."[14] But Stoddard could claim that he had always lived as if Lambert Strether's famous advice in *The Ambassadors* had been his life's motto.

By mid-May Stoddard had decided to go down the peninsula to Atherton to spend some weeks at the magnificent home of his former "sweetheart," Fred Henshaw. A forty-eight-year-old state Supreme Court justice who had married a millionaire's daughter, Henshaw was able to provide Stoddard with every comfort at "El Nido." Of course, the relationship between the two men was hardly the same as it had been during the blissful summer of 1873, just before Stoddard left for Europe. But Fred was extremely kind to Stoddard, whom he kept supplied with notebooks, fountain pens, purple ink, books, and even some dashing new clothes.

Such things fell short, however, of meeting Stoddard's deepest needs.

Most of all he wanted to find a cozy bungalow by the sea and a "Kid" with whom to share it. During the next couple of years, he would be on the lookout for both. Few seaside cottages escaped his notice if there was something picturesque about them, and few young men escaped his inviting looks as he embarked on a search for a West Coast "Kid." He might make a fool of himself, he realized. "I know that with all my experience I have gained no practical knowledge," he told himself, "nothing that shall save me from other follies." It would be worth it all if he could have "friendship, fellowship, intimacy" (D 6 Jun. 1905, 7 Sept. 1905).[15]

Stoddard saw such promise in a twenty-three-year-old day laborer at "El Nido." Edwin McKenzie had a "shapely figure," "kindly blue eyes," and "brown hair clustering in curls." Guests should not mingle with the servants, Stoddard knew, but he could not resist a pleasant chat with McKenzie, who blurted out the story of his life. He had run away from home, had been a stowaway and a tramp; he loved the books of Jack London, and he had a brother at Santa Clara who was working his way through college by teaching swimming. Falling in love on the spot, Stoddard soon began to plan out the life that he and McKenzie would share in some storybook cottage. There would be a "big bedroom," a "bathroom where he can help me to bathe," and "our little breakfasts together"; it was to be understood that Edwin would "spend his evenings at home" (D 13–17 Jun. 1905). After a few days, however, the youth's work was finished, and with great reluctance Stoddard said good-bye.

After a short visit to San Francisco in the middle of June, Stoddard decided to admit himself to a sanitarium run by the Sisters of Charity in San Jose. He was not feeling well, at least not well enough to write all of the articles he had promised to the *Sunset* and the *National.* The sanitarium had been recommended by Father Harry Stark, a young priest who had been Stoddard's student at the Catholic University of America. Now assigned to a San Francisco parish, Father Stark had become remarkably and irresistibly solicitous toward his former professor. As with Edwin McKenzie, Stoddard began to fantasy a "Dad/Kid" relationship with Harry, one he imagined as "the most perfect I have known in a life of sixty-two years—and a very loving and liberal life at that" (D 28 Jun. 1905). But, in fact, Stoddard was not deterred from moving on to Monterey after his cure at Saint Joseph's Sanitarium.

It had been twenty-seven years since he had been there, and much had changed. But the weather was heavenly, the people were kind, and simple pleasures abounded. Stoddard felt as if he had been transported back to Italy. He rented a bright apartment, in a house near the water he called "Casa Verde," and set about writing his overdue articles. Occasionally the distractions outside his window made it difficult for him to concentrate. Italian fishermen in hip boots were drying their nets; sailors from foreign vessels were coming ashore; young people in bathing suits were trooping to the beach; young soldiers in "almost skin-tight trousers" were strolling by. Some of these soldiers, noticing that Stoddard was eyeing them, began to lift their hats in salutation. He purchased some curtains of a material heavy enough to hide him from view but gauzy enough to allow him to continue to espy everyone passing by.[16]

Some nights Stoddard would walk to the Monterey Hotel for a nightcap, and at the bar he regularly encountered his new friend, Captain Conrad. This career army officer seemed to have a decided taste for alcohol and the company of good-looking young men, and before long Stoddard was addressing him as "Camerado." On other nights, when there was nowhere to go and no one to see, Stoddard might bring home a bottle of "soft Zinfandelle" to keep him company and make him feel drowsy. He chose to do this, for instance, on Wednesday night, 13 September 1905. The last "bugle cry" had sounded at the Presidio; people were settling down for the night; the only sounds he could hear were the rising and the falling of the surf. Stoddard was lonely. Like a character out of E. A. Robinson's "Tilbury Town," he sipped the wine in his rocking chair and gazed out the window at the moonlit harbor. "If only my Kid were with me!" he mused in his diary, as the wine began to tell. But which one? "I know not," he wrote. And then, "I would have them all—one after another" (D 13 Sept. 1905).

Monterey provided him with almost everything he desired except a "Kid." It was not for lack of trying. Stoddard felt out almost every likely young man he came across, from bootblack to cannery worker to bellboy; but they were not, alas, "responsive" (D 10 Oct. 1905ff.). Stoddard turned his gaze toward the slightly older Bohemians who were starting to move into Carmel, especially toward George Sterling.

Sterling was a troubled man, unhappily married, who had always needed a hero to admire and to please. In his home town in New York, he had developed an adolescent crush on a prize-fighter named Pete M'Coy. When he moved to the Bay Area in 1890, Sterling fell under the spell of Ambrose Bierce, who began molding him into a poet. Writing verse within the narrow confines of what Bierce regarded as the "great tradition," Sterling was eventually rewarded by extravagant praise from his mentor. Sterling would become one day, Bierce predicted, "the poet of the skies, the prophet of the suns."[17] By 1905, however, Sterling had found a new idol in Jack London. Comfortable in the role of hero-worshiper, Sterling was taken off guard when Stoddard worshiped *his* heroic proportions in an obsequious poem in the *Sunset*.[18] Although he assured Stoddard that "To George Sterling" had been "a joy" to read, he had to wonder what Stoddard meant by "love." There was only one kind that Sterling thought proper between men, and that was the manly affection he felt for his "darling Wolf." He gradually concluded that Stoddard's love was not in this category. As he wrote to Bierce in 1908, Stoddard's was a "case of inversion of sex," and Sterling found that merely being in the old man's presence gave him the "jims." If he was not careful, the "old devil" might wind up "compromising" him.[19]

At the same time he was reporting his horror to Bierce, Sterling was continuing to visit Stoddard and to send him affectionate notes and letters. What was the truth about Sterling's feelings toward Stoddard? At this point, we can only guess. Whatever they were, Stoddard never seemed to perceive any chill upon his friendship with Sterling. Perhaps Sterling disguised his revulsion so well that Stoddard never detected it. Or perhaps Sterling was never, in fact, as scandalized by Stoddard's "affectionate manner toward others of his own sex" as he wanted Bierce to believe.[20] If so, then it may be that Sterling was deflecting upon Stoddard any suspicion about his own fondness for London, whose influence over him Bierce had bitterly resented for years.

Compared with Sterling, Jack London was a model of suave imperturbability on the subject of sexual inversion. He was, in his own words, "no spring chicken in the ways of the world." As a "sailor and a tramp and a prisoner," a recent biographer asserts, London had come "to be tolerant" of men who loved other men.[21] He was, in fact, fascinated by the idea of homosexuality. "I have for years specialized on sex," London wrote to Edward Carpenter.[22] To another homosexual correspondent, Maurice Magnus, he boasted of reading "the whole literature and all the authorities of the 'curious ways.'" He knew about homosexuality "fairly thoroughly and scientifically," but, of course, he was "a lover of women."[23]

Everyone agrees that London was a narcissist; he loved his own body, as long as it was muscular, and he loved being photographed wearing as few clothes as possible. Moreover he never bothered to hide that he was tantalized by the physiques of other young men who were equally well built. London apparently found the muscles as well as the mussels delectable at George Sterling's beach parties at Carmel. "Gee!" he once wrote to "Greek," as he called Sterling, "I'd like to be out with you one day for a muscle-feed."[24]

Thus when London began receiving amorous letters from Stoddard—the two men had apparently been put in touch by London's friend, Cloudesley Johns—he was more intrigued than appalled. Stoddard presented himself as a harmless old man who wanted to love London from afar. Stoddard wrote in August 1903:

> I am very old, very tender-hearted and very faithful: my heart is faithful, tender and true, if there ever was one. I suppose Cloudesley thinks me foolishly sentimental. I cannot help that. I am what I was when I was born. . . .
> My God! How you have lived as with a heart of fire. I have felt the warmth of it even out here, when re-reading your books and your letters. Even when thinking of you there comes a glow upon my cheek and a warmth in my heart. . . .
> That is because you are my own Jack and I am your very Dad. . . .
> Does all this seem like nonsense?[25]

Whether it did or not, London continued to respond to Stoddard in a way that was not only cordial but affectionate. After Stoddard sent him a copy of *South-Sea Idyls,* London mailed the "Love Man" a copy of *The Son of the Wolf* with this inscription: "To Charles Warren Stoddard. O, you Singer of the South Seas! How can I write aught else just now, to you who know? There is neither time nor space for love—yet, I can only repeat, O you Singer! P.S. I have just finished your 'Idyls' and come back to earth."[26]

As it happened, there was little time for love between London and Stoddard, even after the latter had come to California. When they met each other, Stoddard felt drawn to London more powerfully than he ever had been to Sterling. "I wish you knew Jack London," Stoddard wrote to Horace Traubel, Whitman's companion. "His love is inspiring and gives as much as it takes. He has wonderfully magnetic eyes. When he looks at me, I feel as if a fairy cobweb were waving in my face."[27] But London was extraordinarily preoccupied at the time of Stoddard's arrival in California; and as far as love was concerned, he had found his "boy-girl" sidekick and comrade, Charmian Kittredge, whom he married in 1905. Stoddard contented himself with the occasional receipt of a photograph or a letter or a new book from "his" Jack. Stoddard especially prized a revealing snapshot and the novel about a beautifully built prize-fighter, *The Game*. "A superbly fleshly story," he commented, adding, "Jack is a boy after my own heart."[28]

III

During the fall of his first year back in California, Stoddard found himself becoming restless, as well as chilled, in foggy, rainy Monterey. He was happy to accept Joaquin Miller's invitation to come to "The Hights" for an indefinite stay. At Miller's famous home, high above Fruitvale in the Piedmont hills, he could absorb all the background color he needed for the article he was writing on "The Byron of the Rockies" for the *National*. On 28 October 1905, Stoddard wrote in his diary: "After long years it has come to pass. I am at the Heights [*sic*] . . . where many strange and curious things have happened and are probably yet to happen."

Since their days together in New York, Miller had continued to enjoy a private life that was, in its own fashion, even more strange and curious than Stoddard's. As fond of young females as Stoddard was of young males, Miller bedded as many women as he could, in total disregard of his marriage vows. While his first wife was still alive, he had carried on an affair with Mrs. Frank Leslie and then, apparently without benefit of divorce, had married the New York hotel heiress, Abigail Leland. Estranged from Abigail after their daughter was born, Miller returned to California and established "The Hights" as a lovers' hideaway. The women who came to the mountain included voluptuous divorcees, first-rate and honky-tonk actresses, and a sixteen-year-old "half-breed" who bore him several illegitimate sons. Smitten by George Sterling's sister, Miller put on his long black coat and went courting at the Sterling home on Sunday afternoons, even though the young lady was only fourteen.

Miller's concupiscence was no obstacle to his establishing himself as a respected poet and sage. "From the turn of the century until he died," Miller's biographer has noted, "Joaquin Miller was a Very Important Person. He was especially important in California, where he was regarded as a state jewel, a landmark, a combination of Homer, Shakespeare, Keats and Edwin Markham."[29] Oakland schoolchildren, who knew his "Columbus" poem by heart, trooped to "The Hights" to pay homage and plant trees. Reporters dropped by for interviews, while autograph hounds came for a drink of whiskey and a chance to witness Miller's "miraculous" rain dance.

Stoddard was an old hand at prettifying everything he wrote about, but it must have been a formidable challenge to present a rosy view of "The Hights" for his *National* readers. His diary reveals that he was disheartened by the shabby, ramshackle aspects of Miller's residence, where everything seemed to be as coarse as Joaquin himself. In his bleak room, Stoddard found faded magazine pictures "tacked about indiscriminately" on the walls, miscellaneous objects hanging from nails, and everything "more or less cramped and of the very cheapest description" (D 28–31 Oct. 1905).

Stoddard was also disappointed when he met the two Japanese youths who were living on the estate; they did not measure up to his memory of Yone Noguchi. One of them was immediately rejected when Stoddard learned that he had become, of all things, an evangelical Protestant. The other one, Issio Kuge, was more poetic and pagan, but he did not seem to be "in the least fleshly." Issio might provide "spiritual nourishment," Stoddard decided, but he needed someone else, preferably a "simple bucolic" who "should bring me my mail and my daily paper; keep my fires going. Make my bed and me comfortable—and cook. Yes, to make it perfect—cook!" (D 30 Oct. 1905). More idle dreaming, of course, and Stoddard knew it. He was leaving "The Hights"; and when he got back to Monterey, he had neither the money nor the room that another "Kid" would require.

After spending most of the winter of 1905–06 in Monterey, Stoddard decided to travel northeast again, this time to visit the old missions at San Juan Bautista, San Jose, and Santa Clara. He needed to get the "feel" of these places for the *Sunset* articles he had finally started to write. Going to San Jose in February, he stayed at the sanitarium for a while and later moved into a boarding house in suburban Saratoga. The mission articles began appearing in the *Sunset* in June. Meanwhile, his personality sketches for the *National* were bringing him "more enthusiastic letters from unknown readers than anything I have ever published."[30] Away from the coastal fogs, Stoddard felt himself to be "at peace with all the world."[31] Even the great San Francisco earthquake of 18 April 1906 did not seem to rattle him. Of course, Stoddard was apprehensive about aftershocks, but he felt fortunate not to be among the refugees who were fleeing south.

During this time, Stoddard was, as usual, falling in love continually. At the sanitarium he fell for his masseur, a good-looking ex-cowboy with "velvet" hands. Later he became infatuated with an appendicitis patient, a "well developed" lad with beautiful eyelashes.[32] Then there was a youth he spotted one day on the campus of Santa Clara College. Stoddard was in the company of two professors when this student approached them and paused. Before one of the priests could introduce him, Stoddard cried, "You are McKenzie." He was right; this was Edwin McKenzie's younger brother, Harry, the crack swimmer. Stoddard had instantly felt "the same magnetism" that had drawn him to Edwin at Fred Henshaw's home the previous year.[33] Although they were together for "a moment only," Stoddard began to miss "his presence"; and when Harry later sent him a letter, saying "I could not help writing you for I took to you on sight," Stoddard replied in an effusive and vaguely seductive way, blessing the young man "for those words" and treasuring the pricelessness of passionate friendship between males.[34] But when Stoddard moved back to Monterey that fall, he had to accept the likelihood that there would be no "Kid" to comfort him in his old age.

IV

Now the pace of Stoddard's life slowed. Bouts of the grippe, rheumatism in his legs, concern about his dying father in Berkeley, his own financial insecurity—these troubles deprived him of the childlike joy he had felt in Monterey during the summer of 1905. When his spirits and the weather were good, he continued to wander the streets in the old way. Sunday always found him in his pew at mass, and there were visits to the artists' colony at Carmel. George and Carrie Sterling set aside a big chair for his special use in their cabin, and Mary Austin, who wrote "Indian" stories and novels up in her tree house, welcomed him as a living bridge from "the Bret Harte period to ours."[35] But Stoddard was not enthusiastic about the struggling art colony. "Carmel does not interest me," he told Ina Coolbrith in 1907, "though some of its people do."[36] The Carmelite atmosphere was altogether too active—in a political way, as well—for someone of his age and disposition. Stoddard was always glad to retreat to his den in Monterey.

It was in "Casa Verde" that Stoddard preferred to do most of his visiting; and regardless of who called, he invariably gave what might be called a command performance. A single question would trigger a dramatic monologue that might go on for hours. With his den as a stage and his bric-a-brack as props, Stoddard slipped effortlessly into the role of a storytelling actor. His repertoire was vast; he could reenact scenes, complete with running commentary, that involved a variety of famous or notorious people from many parts of the world.

George Wharton James recalled one such performance in an account of his first visit to Stoddard:

> I climbed up the stairs to the room which his landlady had denoted to me, and knocked. Almost instantly he opened it, and without a word placed one arm around me, taking my right hand in his, and drew me to him into the room, and kissed me, while tears rolled down his cheeks. His desk stood in a square "bay," with windows on three sides, and still without speaking, he gently led me behind the desk, pushed the curtains aside and began to talk. And for fully half an hour I stood there, silent, listening to one of the sweetest, most poetic, pathetic, tender pourings out of heart I have ever heard.

After Stoddard had exhausted himself on the subject of living in Monterey, James asked him a question about Mark Twain, whose autobiography was then running serially in the *North American Review.* Twain had written of his days with Stoddard in London, suggesting that his secretary-companion had not been awake very often. "That's very funny," Stoddard said, proceeding to tell James his side of the story at great length.[37] At night Stoddard often repeated such stories to himself in bed, as a means of quieting his nerves and easing himself to sleep.

During the Monterey years, much of Stoddard's "visiting" was done by correspondence, to which he often devoted many hours a day. Magazine articles came first in his writing schedule, but after 1907 there were fewer and fewer of these to be written.[38] During an average month he wrote about a hundred letters, nearly all of them in the purple ink that had become his trademark; and he would mail them in envelopes bearing the initials "S.A.G." (Saint Anthony, Guide). To Ina Coolbrith, Stoddard gossiped that Joaquin was planning to run for a Senate seat in Oregon, and that, if he only had a "Kid," he would not mind moving into an empty cottage at "The Hights." To Robert Ballard of London, with whom he had spent one night in Honolulu in 1882, Stoddard complained that the West Coast was too strenuous, that he felt lost, and that there was no time for deep affection. To his sister in Europe, he described his meeting with the famous actress Nance O'Neill, and from his brother in Berkeley he received increasingly gloomy reports about their father's health. Yone Noguchi, now a university professor in Japan, wrote to urge him to come to Tokyo and become the new Lafcadio Hearn. To Jack London, Stoddard confided that he found George Sterling rather too "spirituel" for a Bohemian, and he offered Jack, who was planning his epic voyage, some letters of introduction to people in Hawaii and Tahiti. To Booth Tarkington, he advised that thin ham and iced figs was the proper breakfast order on Capri, and to his old drinking companion, Captain Conrad, now in the Philippines, he sent his love.[39]

To Horace Traubel he rued that he was beginning to grow dull and sad because he lacked the rejuvenating companionship of young men. About Walt Whitman, whom Traubel had befriended during the final years in Camden, Stoddard added: "Do you know what life means to me? It means everything that Walt Whitman has ever said or sung. . . . He breathed the breath of life into me." Herbert Peet, one of "Little Mama's" many sons, wrote to say how much he had enjoyed rereading *South-Sea Idyls*, now that he was old enough to grasp its full beauty. From Washington, Corinne O'Connor reported that her brother Kenneth was continuing to slide downhill. Now an unemployed vaudeville actor, using the stage name of "Kenneth Stoddard," he had sworn to his family that he would never touch another drop of alcohol. But "he is such a liar," Corinne added, "and we haven't any way of ascertaining the truth of what he says." When Stoddard told his old English friend Iza Hardy that Jack London was now one of his "Kids," Miss Hardy wrote back to exclaim, "What a long line of Kids you have! . . . They 'stretch out to crack of doom'!"[40]

To Father Hudson, still at Notre Dame, Stoddard wrote to say that Father Harry Stark was as dear to him as Kenneth had ever been, and to predict that Teddy Roosevelt, a "victim of progressive insanity," would end up in a "madhouse." He often wrote of religious matters to Father Hudson, sometimes hinting he would like to end his days in a monastery, perhaps at Santa Barbara, "if they would only take me as a lay brother." All of DeWitt Miller's questions, so full of sexual curiosity, were answered. Stoddard described Reginald Birch in the nude, claimed that he had never "spooned" with the actor Harry Woodruff, and insisted that Joaquin Miller was not "so." To Mark Twain he wrote to solicit a donation for Ina Coolbrith, whose home had been destroyed in the earthquake; and he also commented on the London episode in the *Autobiography:* "I feel as if I were almost famous. Everybody wants to shake hands with me and it is becoming a little embarrassing. I thank you for what you have written, dear Mark. All the past comes back to me touched with a vein of sadness." To Benton Gifford, the young man who had nearly become his "Kid" in Monterey, he wrote of his loneliness: "I need a Kid right by me and someone who would be sure to be here at night when I am most lonely."[41]

The plaint common to many of Stoddard's letters was his need for comfort and consolation, but he sometimes reciprocated. He did his best to cheer Ethel Armes, whom Yone Noguchi had jilted in favor of the dreadful woman who had borne his child. "Do nothing rash," Stoddard wrote to another young friend, who was perhaps thinking of suicide. "There is so much to live for if you only take life in the right spirit." When a Bostonian wrote to say that his "inseparable companion" of eleven years, Ned, was engaged to be married, Stoddard replied: "Shall I go into mourning for our dearest Ned? I could very easily. Yes, I know what it means. . . . I've had it torn up by the roots and God! How it hurt; then I began to grow numb, and so, finally, I became indifferent."[42]

As always, Stoddard continued to "beguile the hours" by reading; and since he stayed home more often now, books became more and more important as a substitute, however inadequate, for human companionship. His taste in books was as catholic as his taste in friends: a week's reading in Monterey might include the latest Jack London novel, a California history, a collection of short stories by H. C. Bunner, something by Mary Austin, and an adventure tale for boys, such as *Sky Pilot.* The books sent to him by DeWitt Miller were of special interest because they allowed him to see how others in his situation had coped with life. Thanks to Miller, Stoddard was able to read *The Satyricon* of Petronius Arbiter, a lesbian novel by Mary MacLane, and several books about Oscar Wilde's life and trial. In January 1907, Stoddard asked Miller to send him Adolf Wilbrandt's *Fridolin's Mystical Marriage,* the story of a bisexual German professor who finds love in the arms of a handsome young man. "It is a book that appeals to me strongly," Stoddard later wrote, "and I like to look into it once in a while."[43]

Of all such books that came into his hands during these years, the one that argued most movingly for love between males was a novel called

Imre. Privately printed in Italy in 1906, this extraordinary love story had been written by a middle-aged American, Edward Prime-Stevenson, under the pseudonym "Xavier Mayne."[44] It may have been sent to Stoddard by the author himself, or by their mutual friend in America, George Woodberry, or perhaps by Miller. At any rate, Stoddard must have read *Imre* with mixed feelings. How pale and timid his adventures of Paul Clitheroe seemed by contrast to this passionate story—one that must have aroused wistful memories of his own youthful intrigues. "The silences of intimacy stand for the most perfect mutuality": Stoddard copied this sentence into his notebook.[45]

During the last months of his life, Stoddard lived mostly in silence, sustained by memories of past intimacies that had all too rarely brought perfect mutuality. By January 1909, crippled by rheumatism, feeling too worn to write any more, Stoddard sensed that his life was ending. During the months that followed, he often stayed in bed all day. It was heart disease, the doctor told him. A new will was prepared; brief notes were written in a trembling hand to such old friends such as Ina Coolbrith and Father Hudson. On Friday, 23 April, Stoddard suffered a heart attack and died.

During services the next Monday, the eulogy was delivered by Father Stark, and Stoddard was buried in the Catholic cemetery in Monterey. Some time after the funeral, Ina Coolbrith returned to Monterey in search of any stray manuscripts that might be included in the memorial volume of Stoddard's poems she was trying to assemble.[46] On his deathbed, however, he had gone through his personal effects, papers, and manuscripts, and, with his housekeeper standing by to help, he had consigned many to the fireplace.[47] Ina Coolbrith was slightly shocked to discover this conflagration, but she should not have been. Stoddard must have reasoned that some things would have to be destroyed in order not to bewilder or hurt the many good people he was leaving behind.

In 1909, the world was not ready to accept the type of person he was and had always been, and Stoddard knew it. As the author of *Imre* had said, sympathy for men who loved other men was "not yet in the common air."[48]

Notes

EDITOR'S PREFACE

1. "The Education of George Cabot Lodge: A Literary Biography" was submitted in 1970 as my doctoral dissertation at Indiana University; a revised version appeared as *George Cabot Lodge* (Boston: Twayne, 1976).

2. *Playing the Game: The Homosexual Novel in America* (Indianapolis: Bobbs-Merrill, 1977), issued simultaneously in hard and soft covers, sold several thousand copies.

3. *The Black Heart's Truth: The Early Career of W. D. Howells* (Chapel Hill: University of North Carolina Press, 1985).

4. Roger's original surname, I have inferred, was Asselstine. Why or when he changed it I do not know, but a comment in one of his letters leads me to believe that he renamed himself in honor of Jane Austen.

5. Stroven, long retired from the University of Hawaii, was extremely helpful to Roger (as he has been to me), generously opening his own files on Stoddard. His letter of 31 May 1981 offered a warm appreciation of Roger's accomplishment from a singularly informed perspective.

6. Austen probably learned about the incident from a footnote in Jonathan Katz's *Gay American History: Lesbians and Gay Men in the U.S.A.* (New York: Crowell, 1976), p. 579, n. 74.

7. The other scholar was the historian Lawrence R. Murphy, whose book on

the Newport scandal has appeared as *Perverts by Official Order: The Campaign against Homosexuals by the United States Navy* (New York: Haworth Press, 1988). In his preface, Murphy writes: "Roger Austen shared his insights into the scandal at an early stage in my research; his death preceded completion of a fictionalized account of the Newport scandal" (p. 4). Roger's book, which *was* completed, might be described as a nonfiction historical novel. Although he was pleased that his "rival" was both gay and generous—Murphy offered to exchange findings with Austen—Roger nevertheless hoped to beat him into print. It is sadly ironic that Murphy's book hit the same stone wall that *Boomerang* did. Russell Len Griffin notes that "the manuscript was finished in 1983, but Larry could not find a publisher willing or able to accept it" (p. xiii). *Perverts by Official Order* was finally published posthumously as a monographic supplement to the *Journal of Homosexuality*. For an excellent brief study of the Newport incident, see George Chauncey, Jr., "Christian Brotherhood or Sexual Perversion?: Homosexual Identities and the Construction of Sexual Boundaries in the World War One Era," *Journal of Social History* 19 (Winter 1985), 189–211.

8. In response to Roger's letter to *The Nation* (see below), Vidal himself later quoted the offending passage: "A correspondent writes: 'You are represented in Roger Austen's depressing catalogue, *Playing the Game*, only by *The City and the Pillar*—if you hadn't written that book someone would have had to invent it.' I answered: 'Austen is dull; I think he's not had much of a life and the fag ghetto is a grim place to spend a life. I have an allergy to fag-novels; most of the books he mentions are unknown to me or known by reputation like [James Baldwin's] *Giovanni's Room*, which I couldn't get through." "Exchange," *Nation*, 2–9 January 1982, 18–19. See also *Views from a Window: Conversations with Gore Vidal*, ed. Robert J. Stanton (Secaucus, N.J.: Lyle Stuart, 1980), pp. 89–90.

9.   *The Heart asks Pleasure—first—*
            And then—Excuse from Pain—
            And then—those little Anodynes
            That deaden suffering—

            And then—to go to sleep—
            And then—if it should be
            The will of its Inquisitor
            The privilege to die—

The Complete Poems of Emily Dickinson, ed. Thomas H. Johnson (Boston: Little, Brown, 1960), p. 262.

10. Gore Vidal, "*Some* Jews & *The* Gays," *Nation*, 14 November 1981. Several responses to the essay, including Roger's, appeared along with Vidal's rebuttals in "Exchange," *Nation*, 2–9 January 1982, 2, 18–19.

11. Generally favorable reviews *did* appear in the *San Francisco Examiner*, the *Washington Post, Village Voice, Gai Sabre, Journal of Homosexuality*, and elsewhere. Vidal's point is accurate, however, insofar as *Playing the Game* was ignored by the most prominent and influential reviewing media.

12. These papers include a monograph (150 pages) on "Masochism, Homo-

sexuality, and Revenge" in D. H. Lawrence, a long essay (50 pages) on the "double lives" of Lawrence and Jack London, and another long essay (50 pages) on the relationship of Lawrence and Maurice Magnus, to whose *Memoirs of the Foreign Legion* (New York: Knopf, 1925) Lawrence wrote a curiously ambivalent introduction.

13. I have inserted and revised portions of "Stoddard's Little Tricks in *South Sea Idyls,*" *Journal of Homosexuality* 8 (Spring/Summer 1983), 73–81.

14. The labor of re-creating the notes to *Genteel Pagan* has been shared by Eve Crandall, my research assistant during the summer of 1990. In turn we have relied heavily on two invaluable sources: Carl G. Stroven, "A Life of Charles Warren Stoddard" (Ph.D. diss., Duke University, 1939); Ray C. Longton, *Three Writers of the Far West: A Reference Guide* (Boston: G. K. Hall, 1980).

15. "Exchange," *Nation*, 2–9 January 1982, 2. In his response, Vidal asserts his belief that "*everyone* is bisexual" and that homosexuals will exist as a category only "as long as the Judeo-Christian majority insists that those who practice same-sexual activities are illegal or abominable or mentally ill" (p. 19). Like some "women writers" who resist this label, Vidal rejects the category of "homosexual novelist" as unduly restrictive and reductive.

16. "The Feminist Critical Revolution," in *The New Feminist Criticism: Essays on Women, Literature, and Theory,* ed. Elaine Showalter (New York: Pantheon, 1985), p. 6.

EDITOR'S INTRODUCTION

1. "The modern terms *homosexuality* and *heterosexuality* do not apply to an era that had not yet articulated these distinctions. Only in the late nineteenth century did European and American medical writers apply these categories and stigmatize some same-sex relationships as a form of sexual perversion." John D'Emilio and Estelle B. Freedman, *Intimate Matters: A History of Sexuality in America* (New York: Harper & Row, 1988), p. 121. See also Carroll Smith-Rosenberg, "The New Woman as Androgyne: Social Disorder and Gender Crisis, 1870–1936," in *Disorderly Conduct: Visions of Gender in Victorian America* (New York: Oxford University Press, 1986).

The new-historicist commonplaces that "doctors created and defined the identities of 'inverts' and 'homosexuals' at the turn of the century" and that "people uncritically internalized the new medical models" have been resisted by George Chauncey, Jr., who argues: "Such assumptions attribute inordinate power to ideology as an autonomous social force; they oversimplify the complex dialectic between social conditions, ideology, and consciousness which produced gay identities, and they belie the evidence of preexisting subcultures and identities contained in the [medical] literature itself." "From Sexual Inversion to Homosexuality: Medicine and the Changing Conceptualization of Female Deviance," *Salmagundi*, nos. 58–59 (Fall 1982–Winter 1983), 115.

2. Thomas Yingling, review of Charles Warren Stoddard, *For the Pleasure of His Company* and *Cruising the South Seas, American Literary Realism* 21 (Spring 1989), 91–92.

3. M. E. Grenander, "Ambrose Bierce and Charles Warren Stoddard: Some Unpublished Correspondence," *Huntington Library Quarterly* 23 (May 1960), 290–92.

4. Stoddard to Jack London, 13 August 1903, letter copied in Stoddard's Notebook (Charles Warren Stoddard Papers, The Bancroft Library, University of California, Berkeley).

5. The term "homosexual panic" has been used by Eve Kosofsky Sedgwick to describe one characteristic of the "homophobia" that developed in counterpoint to "homosexuality": the way the loathing of "homosexual" men by some "heterosexual" men—hatred that is a defense against their own gender uncertainties—redounds upon them, inciting fear lest their own "homosocial" inclinations might too be perceived as, or truly be, "perverse." See Sedgwick, *Between Men: English Literature and Male Homosocial Desire* (New York: Columbia University Press, 1985), pp. 88–90; "The Beast in the Closet: James and the Writing of Homosexual Panic," in *Sex, Politics, and Science in the Nineteenth-Century Novel: Selected Papers from the English Institute, 1983–84*, ed. Ruth Bernard Yeazell (Baltimore: Johns Hopkins University Press, 1986), pp. 148–86.

6. *Imre: A Memorandum* (Naples, Italy: The English Book-Press: R. Rispoli, 1906) was the work of Edward I. Prime-Stevenson, who was born in New Jersey in 1868, but who subsequently settled in Europe. In 1908, he published—again under his pseudonym and in a small, private edition—*The Intersexes: A History of Similisexualism as a Problem in Social Life*, in which Stoddard's *South-Sea Idyls* was cited as an example of "American Philarrhenic Literature." See Roger Austen, *Playing the Game: The Homosexual Novel in America* (Indianapolis: Bobbs-Merrill, 1977), pp. 20–27.

7. Peter Gay, *The Tender Passion* (New York: Oxford University Press, 1986), p. 202.

8. *Cruising the South Seas: Stories by Charles Warren Stoddard*, ed. Winston Leyland (San Francisco: Gay Sunshine Press, 1987), p. 5. Henceforth *CSS*.

9. Roger Austen, "Stoddard's Little Tricks in *South Sea Idyls*," *Journal of Homosexuality* 8 (Spring/Summer 1983), 73–81. See also chapter 5.

10. *Nation* 17 (18 December 1873), 411.

11. "Recent Literature," *Atlantic Monthly* 32 (December 1873), 746.

12. Ibid., p. 741.

13. "Editor's Easy Chair," *Harper's Monthly* 136 (December 1917), 149.

14. See my essay, "Howells, Stoddard, and Male Homosocial Attachment," in *The Mask of Fiction: Essays on W. D. Howells* (Amherst: University of Massachusetts Press, 1989).

15. Sedgwick, *Between Men*, pp. 28, 206.

16. Letter in the Stoddard Papers (Bancroft Library).

17. Horace Traubel, *With Walt Whitman in Camden*, vol. 4 (Philadelphia: University of Pennsylvania Press, 1953), pp. 267–69.

18. *Walt Whitman: The Correspondence*, ed. Edwin Haviland Miller (New York: New York University Press, 1961–69), 2:81–82.

19. Horace Traubel, *With Walt Whitman in Camden*, vol. 3 (Philadelphia: University of Pennsylvania Press, 1961), pp. 444–45.

20. *Walt Whitman: The Correspondence*, 2:97.

21. Michael Lynch, " 'Here Is Adhesiveness': From Friendship to Homosexuality," *Victorian Studies* 29 (Autumn 1985), 90.

22. On nineteenth-century racism, see Jacques Barzun, *Race: A Study in Superstition*, revised edition (New York: Harper & Row, 1965), especially chapters 6–8; Stow Persons, *American Minds: A History of Ideas* (New York: Holt, Rinehart & Winston, 1958), pp. 276–97.

23. Ambrose Bierce to Stoddard, 29 December 1872 (HM 10102, The Huntington Library, San Marino, California).

24. Theodore Dwight to Stoddard, 7 July 1882 (STO, University of Notre Dame Archives).

25. *The Island of Tranquil Delights: A South Sea Idyl and Others* (Boston: Herbert B. Turner, 1904), p. 27. Henceforh *ITD*.

26. Quoted in Charles Phillips, "Charles Warren Stoddard," *Overland Monthly*, n.s. 51 (February 1908), 139.

27. The portrait is reproduced in Franklin Walker, *San Francisco's Literary Frontier* (New York: Knopf, 1939), p. 347.

28. T. J. Jackson Lears, *No Place of Grace: Antimodernism and the Transformation of American Culture 1880–1920* (New York: Pantheon, 1981), p. 184.

29. Walker, *San Francisco's Literary Frontier*, pp. 232–33.

30. *Mashallah! A Flight into Egypt* (New York: Appleton, 1881), p. 254. Henceforth *M*.

31. Lears, *No Place of Grace*, p. 223.

32. Ibid., p. 278.

33. Stoddard to Jeanne Carr, 30 March 1874 (CA 167, The Huntington Library); quoted in Carl G. Stroven, "A Life of Charles Warren Stoddard," (Ph.D. diss., Duke University, 1939), p. 182.

34. Stoddard to James Whitcomb Riley, 8 April 1891 (Lilly Library, Indiana University).

35. See chapter 7.

36. Characterizing Rolfe as "sexually abnormal . . . one of those unlucky men in whom the impulses of passion are misdirected," A. J. A. Symons, his first biographer, was dismayed and disgusted by this phase of his life: "That a man of education, ideas, something near genius, should have enjoyed without remorse the destruction of the innocence of youth; that he should have been willing for a price to traffic in his knowledge of the dark byways of that Italian city; that he could have pursued the paths of lust with such frenzied tenacity: these things shocked me into anger and pity." *The Quest for Corvo: An Experiment in Biography* (1934; rpt. New York: Penguin, 1979), pp. 257, 27.

37. A. O. J. Cockshut, "A. J. A. Symons' *The Quest for Corvo*," in *The Biographer's Art: New Essays*, ed. Jeffrey Meyers (New York: New Amsterdam, 1989), p. 96.

38. Quoted in Symons, *The Quest for Corvo*, p. 168.

39. Cockshut, in *The Biographer's Art*, p. 101.

40. George Chauncey, Jr., "Christian Brotherhood or Sexual Perversion?:

Homosexual Identities and the Construction of Sexual Boundaries in the World War One Era," *Journal of Social History* 19 (Winter 1985), 199, 202.

41. Ibid., p. 202.

42. Diary, 15 February 1885. Henceforth D. The University of Notre Dame Archives houses the diaries for the period between January and April 1885.

43. Chauncey, "Christian Brotherhood," p. 201.

44. Diaries for the period between late June and early October 1905 are collected in Robert Louis Stevenson House, State of California, Department of Parks and Recreation, Monterey District.

45. *In the Footprints of the Padres*, revised edition (San Francisco: A. M. Robertson, 1912), pp. 214–15, 217. Henceforth *IFPr*.

46. Sedgwick, *Between Men*, pp. 208, 210. See also *The Memoirs of John Addington Symonds*, ed. Phyllis Grosskurth (New York: Random House, 1984), pp. 271–83.

47. Michael Moon has shown "how Alger's reformulation of domestic fiction as a particular brand of male homoerotic romance functions as a support for capitalism." See " 'The Gentle Boy from the Dangerous Classes': Pederasty, Domesticity, and Capitalism in Horatio Alger," *Representations*, no. 19 (Summer 1987), 88–89. Before writing his popular tales, Alger had been expelled from his Unitarian ministry in Brewster, Massachusetts, for seducing boys.

48. Stoddard to Daniel Hudson, 9 December 1895 (CHUD, University of Notre Dame Archives).

49. After he left Washington to serve in the Spanish-American War, O'Connor never fully came home again to Stoddard, who grew more and more disconsolate over his "Kid" 's errant ways and diminishing love. In 1903, after loyally helping his "Dad" through the difficult period that followed his dismissal from Catholic University, O'Connor drifted off on his own, falling into alcoholic ruin after failing in a vaudeville career in which he had assumed the stage name of "Kenneth Stoddard."

50. Lynch, " 'Here Is Adhesiveness,' " pp. 92, 93.

51. "Roaming Poet Buys a Home," *Washington Post*, clipping enclosed with a letter from Stoddard to George Cabot Lodge, 4 December 1897 (Massachusetts Historical Society, Boston).

52. See 2 Samuel 1:26: "I am distressed for thee, my brother Jonathan: very pleasant hast thou been unto me: thy love to me was wonderful, passing the love of women." Lillian Faderman has played on this phrase for the title of her informative book about female same-sexuality: *Surpassing the Love of Men: Romantic Friendship and Love between Women from the Renaissance to the Present* (New York: Morrow, 1981). On "romantic friendship," see also Carroll Smith-Rosenberg, "The Female World of Love and Ritual: Relations Between Women in Nineteenth-Century America," in *Disorderly Conduct*, pp. 53–76.

53. Michael Moon points out that Horatio Alger's novels are "not only homoerotic romances but also represent a genuine reformulation of popular domestic fiction" in their depicting the transformation of the street urchin into the "gentle boy": "As long as he remains a poor boy on the streets, the Alger

hero's behavior remains fairly conventionally gender bound. But once the 'gentle boy' is removed from the street and street occupations and is placed in a private, at least minimally genteel domestic setting, he and his boy friends begin to differentiate themselves along (for boys of Alger's day, or of our own) highly unconventional gender-role lines." Running their household as if in accord with Catharine Beecher's principles of "scientific" domesticity, Alger's boys also begin to assume the customary roles, with the more "dominant" type often playing the maternal one. "'The Gentle Boy from the Dangerous Classes,'" pp. 97, 99.

54. "Roaming Poet Buys a Home."

55. Ibid.

56. W. D. Howells, "Editor's Easy Chair," *Harper's Monthly* 136 (December 1917), 148–49.

57. Kevin Starr, *Americans and the California Dream, 1850–1915* (New York: Oxford University Press, 1973), p. 242.

58. Ibid., p. 248.

59. Isobel Strong Field to Stoddard, [? March] 1882 (HM 37963, The Huntington Library).

60. Theodore Roosevelt, whose gender ideal of "the strenuous life" was antithetical to Stoddard's aestheticism, was speaking for popular American opinion when he remarked to George Cabot Lodge: "How remarkably Oscar Wilde has vindicated Nordhouse's judgement [Max Nordau, in *Degeneration* (1895)]. I took some pleasure in explaining to John Hay the other day, who is a champion of the Yellow Book, that the writers and illustrators of that pleasing periodical were on the high road to precisely the same kind of fate that overtook Oscar Wilde, [Wilde, in fact, was never published in *The Yellow Book*.] Unhealthiness, hysteria, morbid criminality, and absence of wholesome regard for what is pure and decent and truthful and brave, bring about mere rottenness in the end." Letter of 10 April 1895; quoted in John W. Crowley, "'Dear Bay': Theodore Roosevelt's Letters to George Cabot Lodge," *New York History* 53 (April 1972), 183. Stoddard considered Roosevelt to be a madman, better suited to an asylum than the White House. Reacting to the new strenuosity of San Francisco at the turn of the century, Stoddard wrote to a friend that he was "homesick for the life which is not Teddyfied, as all life on this coast today is—Cursed be the name of Roseveldt [*sic*]!" Stoddard to Jenny Johns Peet, 29 May 1907; quoted in Stroven, "A Life," p. 310.

61. Stoddard to Will Stuart, 23 September 1882 (location unknown).

62. Sedgwick, *Between Men*, pp. 216–17.

Chapter 1

1. Stoddard to Harry Van Dyke, 8 September 1903; letter copied in Stoddard's Notebook (The Bancroft Library, University of California, Berkeley).

2. Rochester *Democrat*, 6 November 1849; quoted in Carl G. Stroven, "A Life of Charles Warren Stoddard," (Ph.D. diss., Duke University, 1939), pp. 7–8.

3. See Rossiter Johnson, *The Grandest Playground in the World* (Rochester, N.Y.: The Rochester Historical Society, 1918), pp. 79–80.

4. "About Everything," *Golden Era* 17 (3 October 1869), 4; quoted in Stroven, "A Life," p. 6.

5. Stoddard, *A Troubled Heart and How It Was Comforted at Last* (Notre Dame, Ind.: *Ave Maria* Press, 1885), pp. 11–12. Henceforth *TH*.

6. "Autobiography, Book First" (rough draft in the effects of Josephine Makee-Crawford); quoted in Stroven, "A Life," p. 15.

7. *In the Footprints of the Padres* (San Francisco: A. M. Robertson, 1902), p. 4. Henceforth *IFP*.

8. Franklin Walker, *San Francisco's Literary Frontier* (New York: Knopf, 1939), p. 31.

9. "Confessions of a Reformed Poet" (Bancroft Library). Henceforth CRP.

10. Benjamin Estelle Lloyd, *Lights and Shades of San Francisco* (1876); quoted in Herbert Asbury, *The Barbary Coast: An Informal History of the San Francisco Underworld* (Garden City, N.Y.: Garden City Publishing Co., 1933), p. 101.

11. The quotation about the lewd pictures is taken from *IFP*r.

12. Stoddard described this voyage in "The Survivor's Story," *Ave Maria* 49 (23 December 1899), 810–14.

13. Ibid.

14. "A Couple of Cubs," *Ave Maria* 51 (3 November 1900), 554–57.

15. "Vacation Vagaries," *Ave Maria* 51 (24 November 1900), 656.

16. "Little Valley," *Ave Maria* 51 (10 November 1900), 577.

17. "The Two Randolphs," *Ave Maria* 51 (17 November 1900), 617–21.

18. "Little Valley," p. 577.

19. Ibid., p. 578.

20. "Hearts of Oak," *Overland Monthly* 6 (April 1871), 358–59. Quotations that follow are documented in the text.

21. Blake McKelvey, *Rochester: The Flower City* (Cambridge: Harvard University Press, 1949), p. 44.

22. Charles G. Finney, *Charles G. Finney: An Autobiography* (1876; rpt. Westwood, N.J.: Fleming Revell, 1908), p. 438.

23. "Home Again" *Ave Maria* 51 (22 December 1900), 778–79.

Chapter 2

1. Will Irwin, "The City That Was," rpt. in *Writing of Today*, ed. J. W. Cunliffe and G. R. Lomer (New York: Century, 1915), p. 23.

2. See the summaries of newspaper items for 1859–60 in *California Historical Society Quarterly* 38 (March 1959), 25–29; (December 1959), 329–40.

3. Philip Rahv, *Image and Idea: Twenty Essays on Literary Themes*, revised edition (Norfolk, Ct.: New Directions, 1957), p. 2.

4. Franklin Walker, *San Francisco's Literary Frontier* (New York: Knopf, 1939), p. 124.

5. Ina Coolbrith to Stoddard, 9 November 1874 (HM 38437, The Huntington Library, San Marino, California).

6. George Wharton James, "Charles Warren Stoddard," *National Magazine* 34 (August 1911), 659.

7. George R. Stewart, Jr., *Bret Harte, Argonaut and Exile* (Boston: Houghton Mifflin, 1931), pp. 16, 89.

8. Margaret Duckett, *Mark Twain and Bret Harte* (Norman: University of Oklahoma Press, 1964), pp. 20–21.

9. *Mark Twain's Autobiography*, ed. Albert Bigelow Paine (New York: Harper, 1924), 1:140; Richard O'Connor, *Ambrose Bierce: A Biography* (Boston: Little, Brown, 1967), p. 75.

10. *Selected Letters of W. D. Howells*, ed. George Arms et al. (Boston: Twayne, 1979–83), 4:30.

11. Stoddard to W. D. Howells, 30 November 1892, copy in Stoddard's 1904 Notebook (The Bancroft Library, University of California, Berkeley). See also John W. Crowley, "Howells, Stoddard, and Male Homosocial Attachment," in *The Mask of Fiction: Essays on W. D. Howells* (Amherst: University of Massachusetts Press, 1989).

12. *The Complete Poems of Emily Dickinson*, ed. Thomas H. Johnson (Boston: Little, Brown, 1960), p. 115.

13. "Island Heights," section 39, December 1866 (Bancroft Library). Henceforth IH.

14. See Edward Carpenter, *Intermediate Types among Primitive Folk: A Study in Social Evolution* (New York: Mitchell Kennerley, 1914).

CHAPTER 3

1. Isabella L. Bird, *Six Months in the Sandwich Islands* (1873; rpt. Honolulu: University of Hawaii Press, 1964), pp. 16, 14–15.

2. Ibid., p. 41.

3. "Hearts of Oak," *Overland Monthly* 6 (May 1871), 428.

4. Louis A. Sigaud, *Belle Boyd, Confederate Spy* (Richmond, Va.: Dietz Press, 1944), p. 156.

5. *For the Pleasure of His Company* (1903; rpt. San Francisco: Gay Sunshine Press, 1987), pp. 28, 34. Henceforth *FPHC*.

6. The reviews are quoted in Carl G. Stroven, "A Life of Charles Warren Stoddard," (Ph.D. diss., Duke University, 1939), pp. 88–89.

7. George R. Stewart, Jr., *Bret Harte, Argonaut and Exile* (Boston: Houghton Mifflin, 1931), p. 135.

8. Franklin Walker, *San Francisco's Literary Frontier* (New York: Knopf, 1939), pp. 214, 216.

9. Both poems are quoted from a copy of Stoddard's letter to John Ruskin, 19 February 1867 (Charles Warren Stoddard Collection [#8533], Clifton Waller Barrett Library, Manuscripts Division, Special Collections Department, University of Virginia Library).

10. *The Letters of Herman Melville,* ed. Merrill R. Davis and William H. Gilman (New Haven: Yale University Press, 1960), pp. 227–28.

11. All the responses to Stoddard's poems are quoted in CRP.

12. The reviews and Stoddard's own afterthoughts are quoted from CRP. Perhaps the most positive "Eastern" reviewer was Bret Harte, writing under his initials on 12 October 1867 in the *Springfield Republican,* who rhapsodized upon Stoddard's untainted lyricism: "How he has kept alive this sacred vestal flame, how he has remained faithful to this one shrine where there are so many altars, how he has kept his wings unsoiled, and his singing robes clean in contact with the dust and dirt of this fast community, and how he has preserved the serene repose of the true poet amid all this twitter, whirl and excitement, are secrets that even the frank confession of his verse leaves untold." *Bret Harte's California: Letters to the* Springfield Republican *and* Christian Register, *1866–67,* ed. Gary Scharnhorst (Albuquerque: University of New Mexico Press, 1990), p. 142.

13. Clara Barrus, *Whitman and Burroughs, Comrades* (Boston: Houghton Mifflin, 1931), p. 48.

14. Kevin Starr, *Americans and the California Dream, 1850–1915* (New York: Oxford University Press, 1973), p. 377.

15. Walker, *San Francisco's Literary Frontier,* pp. 232–33.

16. Stoddard to James Whitcomb Riley, 8 April 1891 (Lilly Library, Indiana University).

17. Walker, *San Francisco's Literary Frontier,* p. 233.

18. The review, published on 14 March 1868, is quoted in Stroven, "A Life," p. 111.

19. Richard O'Connor, *Ambrose Bierce: A Biography* (Boston: Little, Brown, 1967), p. 75.

20. Ibid.

21. Joaquin Miller's letters of 30 August 1869 and 2 February 1870 (The Huntington Library, San Marino, California) are quoted in Stroven, "A Life," pp. 133, 135.

22. Stoddard to Walt Whitman, 2 March 1869, in Horace Traubel, *With Walt Whitman in Camden,* vol. 4 (Philadelphia: University of Pennsylvania Press, 1953), p. 267.

Chapter 4

1. Horace Traubel, *With Walt Whitman in Camden,* vol. 4 (Philadelphia: University of Pennsylvania Press, 1953), pp. 267–69.

2. *Walt Whitman; The Correspondence,* ed. Edwin Haviland Miller (New York: New York University Press, 1961–69), 2:81–82.

3. "A South Sea Idyl," *Overland Monthly* 3 (September 1869), 257–64. A revised and expanded version appeared as "Chumming with a Savage" in *South-Sea Idyls* (Boston: J. R. Osgood, 1873). Henceforth *SSI.*

4. "Joe of Lahaina," *Overland Monthly* 5 (July 1870), 20–25; the tale also appeared in *SSI.*

5. Stoddard said that Joe had "seemed inclined that way" in a letter to DeWitt Miller, 15 October 1901 (HM 38383, The Huntington Library, San Marino, California). Miller had asked whether any of Stoddard's island companions had been "Greek"—in the sense meant by John Addington Symonds in *A Problem in Modern Ethics: Being an Inquiry into the Phenomenon of Sexual Inversion* (1891), which Miller had sent to Stoddard.

6. Harte quoted in CRP.

7. The quotations that follow are taken from columns published in the *Golden Era* between 19 September 1869 and 29 May 1870.

8. "The Pet of the Circus," *Golden Era* 17 (3 October 1869), 4–5. Carl G. Stroven, overlooking Stoddard's comic exaggeration, takes this incident in all seriousness, calling it "almost a parody of the situation in Herman Melville's 'Benito Cereno.'" "A Life of Charles Warren Stoddard," (Ph.D. diss., Duke University, 1939), pp. 4–5.

9. Stoddard to William Gilmore Sims, 28 July 1869 (Columbia University Library); quoted in Stroven, "A Life," p. 127.

10. Miller and Keeler are quoted in Stroven, "A Life," p. 128. See also Thomas Wentworth Higginson to Stoddard, 23 August 1869 (Collection of American Literature, Beinecke Rare Book and Manuscript Library, Yale University); Jay B. Hubbell, "George Henry Boker, Paul Hamilton Hayne, and Charles Warren Stoddard: Some Unpublished Letters," *American Literature* 5 (May 1933): 163, 165.

11. The story itself provoked at least one remarkable hate letter, which Stoddard attributed to the Reverend Dr. Lee, M.D., of New York: "I have read with the greatest possible disgust your stupid and assinine [*sic*] article. . . . It is so fearfully silly and stupid that I shall keep it to use as an emetic. Whenever I wish to disgust an enemy I have only to send him 'My South Sea Show.' Sir, you are an insensate hummox—the very worst writer I ever knew or heard of. Poh! you make me sick—go bag your head. Dolt and miscompoop avaunt!" See Mary Bell, "The Essayist of the West—Charles Warren Stoddard," *University of California Magazine* 2 (November 1896), 277.

12. Horace Traubel, *With Walt Whitman in Camden*, vol. 3 (Philadelphia: University of Pennsylvania Press, 1961), pp. 444–45.

13. *Walt Whitman; The Correspondence*, 2:97.

14. See Jonathan Katz, *Gay American History: Lesbians and Gay Men in the U.S.A.* (New York: Crowell, 1976), pp. 499–500.

15. Stoddard to Will Stuart, 15 December 1880 (HM 2981, The Huntington Library).

16. Bayard Taylor, *Joseph and His Friend: A Story of Pennsylvania* (New York: Putnam, 1870). See Roger Austen, *Playing the Game: The Homosexual Novel in America* (Indianapolis: Bobbs-Merrill, 1977), pp. 9–10.

17. *Exits and Entrances: A Book of Essays and Sketches* (Boston: Lothrop, 1903), p. 223. Henceforth *EE*.

18. Robert L. Gale, *Charles Warren Stoddard*, Western Writers Series, no. 30 (Boise, Id.: Boise State University Press, 1977), p. 14. In DeWitt Miller's copy of *South-Sea Idyls* (University of Hawaii at Manoa Library), Stoddard wrote in the

margin of "In a Transport": "Every word of this is true. The little Frenchmen were mighty good to me."

19. In DeWitt Miller's copy of the book, Stoddard wrote: "This chapter is absolutely true in every particular, *So help me God!*"

20. See John Horne Burns, *The Gallery* (1947; rpt. New York: Bantam, 1948), pp. 332–33.

21. See also Stoddard to George Sterling, 15 November 1907 (The Bancroft Library, University of California, Berkeley): "Once when I was starving in Tahiti . . . I would have joyfully have [*sic*] thrown myself upon the bosom of the Angel of Death, but—I knew not where to find him. Certainly the Sea invited me and its song was like a dirge; but I am afraid of the water as I can't swim." Quoted in Stroven, "A Life," p. 146.

CHAPTER 5

1. Albert Parry, *Garrets and Pretenders: A History of Bohemianism in America* (New York: Covici-Friede, 1933), pp. 213–14.

2. Kevin Starr, *Americans and the California Dream, 1850–1915* (New York: Oxford University Press, 1973), p. 242.

3. From a poem by Richard H. Savage, dated 14 June 1881, in Stoddard's autograph "Album" (HM 35075, The Huntington Library, San Marino, California).

4. Ambrose Bierce to Stoddard, 29 December 1872 (HM 10102, The Huntington Library).

5. George Wharton James, "Charles Warren Stoddard—An American Appreciation," *Ave Maria* 68 (22 May 1909), 655.

6. "Swallow Flights," *Daily Alta California*, 14 January 1872.

7. "In Old Bohemia," *Pacific Monthly* 18 (December 1907), 639.

8. Joaquin Miller to Stoddard, 24 March 1873 (The Huntington Library); quoted in Carl G. Stroven, "A Life of Charles Warren Stoddard," (Ph.D. diss., Duke University, 1939), p. 167.

9. Ibid., p. 323.

10. *Overland Monthly* 11 (December 1873), 577.

11. "Recent Literature," *Atlantic Monthly* 32 (December 1873), 740–46. Howells's review was unsigned. The generic vagueness (fiction or nonfiction) of *South-Sea Idyls* was another ploy by which Stoddard confounded the reader who might suspect some of his persona's libidinous activities. Although most of the tales were indeed based on fact, Stoddard could always claim, if the need arose, that he was making the whole thing up. Libraries tend to catalog the book under "travel" rather than "fiction."

12. *Nation* 17 (18 December 1873), 411.

13. Van Wyck Brooks, *The Times of Melville and Whitman* (New York: Dutton, 1947), p. 263.

14. Francis O'Neill, "Stoddard, Psalmist of the South Seas," *Catholic World* 105 (July 1917), 512.

15. Franklin Walker, *San Francisco's Literary Frontier* (New York: Knopf, 1939), p. 273.

16. Xavier Mayne, *The Intersexes: A History of Similisexualism as a Problem in Social Life* (1908; rpt. New York: Arno, 1975), p. 383.

CHAPTER 6

1. Ambrose Bierce to Stoddard, 28 September 1873 (The Huntington Library, San Marino, California); quoted in Carl G. Stroven, "A Life of Charles Warren Stoddard," (Ph.D. diss., Duke University, 1939), p. 172.

2. "A London Drawing Room," *Ave Maria* 41 (26 October 1895), 463.

3. To a California friend, Stoddard wrote: "We talked and talked and talked. He saw few people; he was nervous and ill and irritable, and no one suited him but me, and sometimes I didn't exactly suit. But we were together night and day, and we went deep into each other's lives—I deeper into his than he into mine, for he loved to talk and I to listen. Then there are so few who care to look into my case beyond the mere surface ripple." See George Wharton James, "Charles Warren Stoddard," *National Magazine* 34 (August 1911), 662.

4. *Mark Twain's Autobiography*, ed. Albert Bigelow Paine (New York: Harper, 1924), 1:140.

5. Fred W. Lorch, *The Trouble Begins at Eight: Mark Twain's Lecture Tours* (Ames: Iowa State University Press, 1968), p. 146.

6. Paul Fatout, *Mark Twain on the Lecture Circuit* (Bloomington: Indiana University Press, 1960), p. 184.

7. Stoddard to Sarah Makee, 22 December 1873; quoted in Mary Bell, "The Essayist of the West—Charles Warren Stoddard," *University of California Magazine* 2 (November 1896), 278.

8. W. D. Howells, "Editor's Easy Chair," *Harper's Monthly* 136 (December 1917), 149.

9. W. D. Howells, "Introductory Letter" to *South-Sea Idyls*, second edition (New York: Scribner's, 1892), p. vi.

10. Quoted in the catalog of the Swann Galleries, sale 89 (15 June 1944), lot 299. See also John W. Crowley, "Howells, Stoddard, and the Illustrations for *Summer Cruising in the South Seas*," *Gay Studies Newsletter* 13 (November 1986), 23–25.

11. Stroven, "A Life," p. 178, n. 32.

12. "A Friend in Need," *Ave Maria* 39 (28 July 1894), 93.

13. Joaquin Miller, "Charles Warren Stoddard," *Overland Monthly* n.s. 26 (October 1895), 380.

14. "Student Life in Rome," *Ave Maria* 26 (3 March 1888), 198.

15. Stoddard's letter in "Etc.," *Overland Monthly* 13 (July 1874), 92.

16. Stoddard to Jeanne Carr, 30 March 1874 (CA 167, The Huntington Library); quoted in Stroven, "A Life," p. 182.

17. "In the Days of Pio Nono," *Ave Maria* 39 (18 August 1894), 175–78.

18. "Traces of Travel," *Ave Maria* 39 (7 July–24 November 1894), *passim*.

19. Stoddard to Jeanne Carr, 30 March 1874 (CA 167, The Huntington Library); quoted in Stroven, "A Life," p. 182.

20. See "The Artist's Fete," *Ave Maria* 39 (22 September 1894), 315–17; "Artist Life in Rome," *Ave Maria* 39 (3 November 1894), 491–94; "The Carnival in Rome," *Ave Maria* 40 (23 February 1895), 206–9.

21. Stoddard to Sarah Freeman Stoddard, 12 April 1874 (Charles Warren Stoddard Collection [#8533], Clifton Waller Barrett Library, Manuscripts Division, Special Collections Department, University of Virginia Library).

22. Stoddard to Sarah Makee, 21 July 1874 (Clifton Waller Barrett Library).

23. Stoddard to Ambrose Bierce, 30 June 1874 (Collection of American Literature, Beinecke Rare Book and Manuscript Library, Yale University).

24. "A Fin de Siècle Friar," *National Magazine* 24 (June 1906), 257–64. Father John's last name, Kroeger, is mentioned in a letter from Stoddard to Mark Twain, 12 December 1874 (Mark Twain Papers, The Bancroft Library, University of California, Berkeley).

25. Stoddard to Sarah Makee, 21 July 1874 (Clifton Waller Barrett Library).

26. "A Modern Monte Cristo," *National Magazine* 24 (August 1906), 463.

27. Ibid.

28. "Crossing the Rubicon," *Ave Maria* 24 (15 January 1887), 54.

29. *San Francisco Chronicle*, 3 January–28 March 1875, *passim*.

30. "Florence," *Ave Maria* 24 (30 April 1887), 418.

31. The last phrase echoes the ending of Whitman's "When I Heard at the Close of the Day," which was Stoddard's favorite poem:

> *For the one I love most lay sleeping by me under the same cover in the cool night,*
> *In the stillness in the autumn moonbeams his face was inclined toward me,*
> *And his arm lay lightly around my breast—and that night I was happy.*

See *Leaves of Grass*, Comprehensive Reader's Edition, ed. Harold W. Blodgett and Sculley Bradley (New York: New York University Press, 1965), p. 123.

32. Frank Millet to Stoddard, 10 May 1875 (George Arents Research Library for Special Collections at Syracuse University).

33. "A Modern Monte Cristo," pp. 463–69.

34. "The Mediterranean," *San Francisco Chronicle*, 8 August 1875.

35. Frank Millet to Stoddard, 10 May 1875 (Arents Library).

36. Frank Millet to Stoddard, 15 August 1875 (Arents Library).

37. "Over a Wall," *National Magazine* 25 (March 1907), 547–53.

38. "An Adriatic Queen," *National Magazine* 25 (November 1906), 130.

39. Stoddard to Ambrose Bierce, 13 September 1875 (Beinecke Library).

40. "A Sea Syren," *San Francisco Chronicle*, 12 December 1875.

41. Ibid.

42. Frank Millet to Stoddard, 15 November 1875 (Arents Library).

43. "Gay Paris," *San Francisco Chronicle*, 9 April 1876. This passage was deleted from the version of this essay published in *Mashallah!.*

44. "A Modern Monte Cristo," p. 468.

45. *A Cruise Under the Crescent: From Suez to San Marco* (Chicago & New York: Rand McNally, 1898), p. 146. Henceforth *CUC*.

46. Frank Millet to Stoddard, 9 July 1876 (Arents Library).

47. Mark Twain to Stoddard, 20 September 1876 [*] (Rutherford B. Hayes Presidential Center, Fremont, Ohio).

48. See *Mark Twain—Howells Letters*, ed. Henry Nash Smith and William M. Gibson (Cambridge: Harvard University Press, 1960), 1:153–55.

49. Joe Strong to Stoddard, 22 September 1876 (HM 38023, The Huntington Library).

50. Frank Millet to Stoddard, 21 February 1877 (Arents Library).

51. Charles H. Webb to Stoddard, 21 March 1877 (location unknown).

52. Quoted in George Wharton James, "Charles Warren Stoddard," *National Magazine* 34 (August 1911), 661.

53. Frank Millet to Stoddard, 29 June 1877 (Arents Library).

Chapter 7

1. Stoddard to Jeanne Carr, 8 July 1874 (CA 168, The Huntington Library, San Marino, California).

2. William H. Rideing, "A Corner of Bohemia," *Bookman* 32 (February 1911), 623–24.

3. *Life and Letters of Edmund Clarence Stedman*, ed. Laura Stedman and George M. Gould (New York: Moffat, Yard, 1910), 2:318.

4. San Francisco *Alta California*, 2 April 1878, quoted in Carl G. Stroven, "A Life of Charles Warren Stoddard," (Ph.D. diss., Duke University, 1939), p. 201.

5. Stoddard to Sarah Freeman Stoddard, 27 March 1874 (Charles Warren Stoddard Collection [#8533], Clifton Waller Barrett Library, Manuscript Division, Special Collections Department, University of Virginia).

6. *Life and Letters of E. C. Stedman*, 2:339.

7. Monterey Diary, 6 October 1905 (Robert Louis Stevenson House, State of California, Department of Parks and Recreation, Monterey, California).

8. Burton Kline, obituary for Woodworth, *Boston Transcript*, 5 June 1912.

9. *The Annals of the Bohemian Club*, ed. Robert H. Fletcher, vol. 2 (San Francisco: The Bohemian Club, 1900), pp. 24–25.

10. Jerome A. Hart, *In Our Second Century: From an Editor's Notebook* (San Francisco: Pioneer Press, 1931), p. 187.

11. M. E. Grenander, "Ambrose Bierce and Charles Warren Stoddard: Some Unpublished Correspondence," *Huntington Library Quarterly* 23 (May 1960), 292.

12. *The Wrecker*, in *The Complete Works of Robert Louis Stevenson* (New York: Scribner's, 1919), 10:144–45.

13. Isobel Strong Field, *This Life I've Loved* (New York: Longmans, Green, 1937), p. 125.

14. San Francisco *Alta California*, 13 February 1879; quoted in Stroven, "A Life," p. 211. See also "Lecturing by Limelight," *National Magazine* 23 (March 1906), 597–606.

15. Stoddard to Daniel Hudson, 31 October 1879, 1 November 1880 (CHUD, University of Notre Dame Archives); quoted in Stroven, "A Life," p. 213.

16. Stoddard to Daniel Hudson, 10 February 1880 (CHUD, University of Notre Dame Archives); quoted in Stroven, "A Life," p. 214.

17. Stoddard to John Hay, 15 September 1881 (Brown University Library).

18. *San Jose Herald*, 28 April 1881 (Santa Clara University Archives).

19. Stoddard to W. D. Howells, 17 October 1881 (Houghton Library, Harvard University).

20. Edward B. Scott, *The Saga of the Sandwich Islands* (Lake Tahoe, Nev.: Sierra-Tahoe Publishing Company, 1968), p. 181.

21. "How the King Came Home," *Ave Maria* 37 (1 July 1893), 8.

22. Stroven, "A Life," p. 223.

23. Many of the originals of these editorials are to be found in the George Stewart Collection (California State Library, Sacramento).

24. Diaries for the period 1882 to 1883 are in the University of Hawaii at Manoa Library.

25. Theodore Dwight to Stoddard, 7 July 1882 (CSTO, University of Notre Dame Archives).

26. Stoddard to Daniel Hudson, 21 July 1880 (CHUD, University of Notre Dame Archives).

27. Stoddard to Will Stuart, 23 September 1882 (location unknown).

28. Stoddard to Daniel Hudson, 14 November 1883 (CHUD, University of Notre Dame Archives).

29. Isobel Strong Field to Stoddard, [? March] 1882 (HM 37963, The Huntington Library).

30. Albert Pierce Taylor, *Under Hawaiian Skies* (Honolulu: Advertiser Publishing Company, 1926), p. 425.

31. "Fetes and Furies," *Overland Monthly*, n.s. 4 (December 1884), 599.

32. This was Stoddard's last mention of Doyle in his diary.

33. "The Schism at St. Aidenn," *Overland Monthly*, n.s. 1 (April 1883), 345–46.

34. Although Stoddard's diary entries broke off at about this point (and resumed in March 1884), this event is documented in "My Hospitals, Hawaii," *Ave Maria* 57 (26 September 1903), 396–400.

35. Quotations in this paragraph and those following are also taken from D Mar.–May 1884 (CSTO, University of Notre Dame Archives), excerpts from which appear in Stroven, "A Life," pp. 346–76.

36. George N. Shuster, *The Catholic Spirit in Modern English Literature* (New York: Macmillan, 1922), p. 294. For an overview of anti-Catholic literature in this period, see Ray Allen Billington, *The Protestant Crusade 1800–1860: A Study of the Origins of American Nativism* (New York: Macmillan, 1938), pp. 345–79.

37. Stoddard to Daniel Hudson, 12 September 1884 (CHUD, University of Notre Dame Archives).

38. *The Lepers of Molokai* (Notre Dame, Ind.: *Ave Maria* Press, 1885). See also *Charles Warren Stoddard's Diary of a Visit to Molokai in 1884*, ed. Oscar Lewis (San Francisco: Book Club of California, 1933).

CHAPTER 8

1. Arthur J. Hope, *Notre Dame: One Hundred Years* (Notre Dame, Ind.: University of Notre Dame Press, 1943).

2. Diaries for the period February to April 1885 are in the University of Notre Dame Archives.

3. Father Damien, who read the proofs, objected to the original title, and it was changed to *The Lepers of Molokai* (Notre Dame, Ind.: *Ave Maria* Press, 1885).

4. Mark Twain to Stoddard, 1 June 1885 [*] (CSTO, University of Notre Dame Archives).

5. Stoddard's accounts of his Alaskan trek were published intermittently in the *San Francisco Chronicle* from May to December 1886, and later collected in *Over the Rocky Mountains to Alaska* (St. Louis: B. Herder, 1899).

6. Stoddard to Daniel Hudson, 1 August 1885 (CHUD, University of Notre Dame Archives).

7. Stoddard to Daniel Hudson, 31 December 1885 (CHUD, University of Notre Dame Archives).

8. Stoddard to Arthur Stedman, 23 December 1886 (The Huntington Library, San Marino, California); quoted in Carl G. Stroven, "A Life of Charles Warren Stoddard," (Ph.D. diss., Duke University, 1939), p. 243.

9. Hope, *Notre Dame*, p. 214.

10. Stroven, in fact, suggests that honors had been denied not to Cleary but to Charles Porter ("A Life," p. 243), but this conclusion seems to be based on a misidentification of Stoddard's "Cub" as Porter rather than Cleary.

11. It pleased Stoddard to think that the clerics at Notre Dame were hypocrites who forced hypocrisy on others—and thus provided him a kind of rationalization: "What a lovely two hours we [Stoddard and Cleary] had—with such sweet assurances as are ours alone. Very satisfactory all this! Later, walking around the Lake we met—but met as mere acquaintances. O, ye hypocrites—teaching *us* hypocrisy—out upon ye!" (D 23 May 1886).

12. Stoddard to Father Damien, 15 September 1886; quoted in Stroven, "A Life," p. 245n.

13. The inscription is quoted in Charles E. Goodspeed's 1909 sale catalog of Stoddard's library. Buchanan's views on American literature may be found in *The Coming Terror and Other Essays and Letters* (New York: United States Book Company, 1891). Stoddard described the letters he received from Buchanan as "lovely, loving, most heartfelt and honest" (D 13 Apr. 1886).

14. Stoddard to Daniel Hudson, 11 April 1888 (CHUD, University of Notre Dame Archives).

15. Fanny later caricatured Stoddard as Laurence Cathcart, an effete Catholic poet, in "The Half-White," *Scribner's Magazine* 9 (March 1891), 282–88. The author is grateful to Barry Menikoff for bringing this story to his attention.

16. Stoddard to Daniel Hudson, 20 October 1888 (CHUD, University of Notre Dame Archives).

17. About the gift slippers, Stoddard told Father Hudson on 9 August 1888:

"So you see I have stepped into Howells' shoes and must perforce become realistic" (CHUD, University of Notre Dame Archives); quoted in Stroven, "A Life," pp. 251–52.

18. Howells's reaction to the draft was negative. He wrote to Louise Imogen Guiney on 3 January 1896: "I never saw good material so slightly and inconclusively treated by so charming a master as in his story. There was the potentiality of three or four beautiful stories in his strange performance; but they seemed not to arrive at any common destination. . . . I felt, as you did, the pathetic nervelessness of it. . . . I doubt if the book ever finds a publisher, or if it does, a public." *Selected Letters of W. D. Howells*, ed. George Arms et al. (Boston: Twayne, 1979–83), 4:137–38.

19. Stoddard to W. D. Howells, 9 September 1888 (Houghton Library, Harvard University); Stoddard to Daniel Hudson, 14 December 1888 (CHUD, University of Notre Dame Archives).

20. About Father Regan, Stoddard wrote to Father Hudson on 8 July 1888: "I wish I could feel safe—with Regan about—but I cannot; and I never never shall. He is not one of Christ's folk!" A year later, on 9 July 1889, Stoddard was still brooding about the "accursed atmosphere" at Notre Dame: "O, my God! Will I never get the taste out of my mouth? the iron out of my soul? I wish I could forget it and everybody in it, save you alone" (CHUD, University of Notre Dame Archives).

21. Patrick Ahern, *The Catholic University of America, 1887–1896* (Washington, D.C.: Catholic University of America Press, 1948), pp. 3ff.

22. Stoddard to Daniel Hudson, 25 March 1889 (CHUD, University of Notre Dame Archives).

23. Frank Millet to Stoddard, [July 1889] (George Arents Research Library for Special Collections at Syracuse University).

24. Henry James, "Our Artists in Europe," *Harper's Monthly* 79 (June 1889), 50–66.

25. Stoddard to Daniel Hudson, 30 July 1889 (CHUD, University of Notre Dame Archives).

CHAPTER 9

1. The facts and quotations in this chapter are derived from a large body of material, including Stoddard's diaries, twenty-eight of his letters to Father Daniel Hudson, forty-five pieces of miscellaneous correspondence (much of it from Theodore Dwight), yearbooks for Catholic University, Stoddard's articles in the *National Magazine* and the *Ave Maria*. Exact sources will be cited only when quoted material is of extraordinary interest or length. Stoddard's diaries for the periods September 1892 to March 1893 and October to November 1895 are at the Catholic University of America.

2. See Patrick Ahern, *The Catholic University of America, 1887–1896* (Washington, D.C.: Catholic University of America Press, 1948), pp. 121–61.

3. Stoddard to Daniel Hudson, 28 November 1889 (CHUD, University of

Notre Dame Archives); quoted in Carl G. Stroven, "A Life of Charles Warren Stoddard," (Ph.D. diss., Duke University, 1939), p. 260.

4. Stroven, "A Life," p. 261.

5. The program for the Cyril Tyler concert was pasted into the Diary after the entry for 22 November 1892.

6. Harold Dean Cater, *Henry Adams and His Friends: A Collection of His Unpublished Letters* (Boston: Houghton Mifflin, 1947), p. lxxi.

7. "Mrs. Emma D. E. N. Southworth at Prospect Cottage," *National Magazine* 22 (May 1905), 188.

8. Quoted in Stoddard, "Kate Field, Cosmopolite," *National Magazine* 23 (January 1906), 370.

9. Theodore Dwight to Stoddard, 2 December 1890 (CSTO, University of Notre Dame Archives).

10. Theodore Dwight to Stoddard, 31 July 1892 (CSTO, University of Notre Dame Archives).

11. Quoted in Jonathan Katz, *Gay American History: Lesbians and Gay Men in the U.S.A.* (New York: Crowell, 1976), pp. 382–83.

12. In a letter to Carl Stroven, 24 May 1938, Charles E. Goodspeed, the famous dealer in Americana, recalled buying some of Stoddard's letters from his sister in 1911: "a lot from M[eredith] N[icholson] which as Mr. N. was still living, I returned to him."

13. Quoted in Marcus Dickey, *The Maturity of James Whitcomb Riley* (Indianapolis: Bobbs-Merrill, 1922), pp. 42–43.

14. Richard Crowder, *Those Innocent Years* (Indianapolis: Bobbs-Merrill, 1957), p. 130.

15. Stoddard to James Whitcomb Riley, 17 December 1890 (Lilly Library, Indiana University).

16. Stoddard to Riley, 28 December 1890 (Lilly Library). According to William Lyon Phelps, Riley "never could see anything in the poetry of Walt Whitman. Without raising his voice, he would purl along, 'Old Walt found the —— stuff he wrote wasn't worth a ——; so he mixed up a lot of —— nonsense, and fooled the whole —— world.'" Phelps also notes that Riley habitually kept up "a stream of profanity in conversation," which seemed more "lyrical" than "vulgar," spoken as it was "in that soft, gentle voice." *Autobiography with Letters* (New York: Oxford University Press, 1939), p. 407.

17. Riley to Stoddard, 19 January 1891 (HM 6240, The Huntington Library, San Marino, California).

18. Stoddard to Riley, 10 February, 28 January 1891 (Lilly Library, Indiana University).

19. Riley to Stoddard, 9 March 1891 (HM 6237, The Huntington Library).

20. Stoddard's autograph "Album" is in The Huntington Library (HM 35075).

21. Stoddard to Riley, 15 October 1893 (Lilly Library).

22. Stoddard to Thomas Russell Sullivan, 5 September 1892 (Thomas Russell Sullivan Papers, American Antiquarian Society, Worcester, Massachusetts).

23. *South-Sea Idyls* (New York: Scribner's, 1892). "The Last of a Great Navigator" (on Captain Cook) was dropped from this edition, but two other sketches were added: "A Tropical Sequence" and "Kahéle's Foreordination." Stoddard had apparently also considered deleting "In a Transport"—an idea that Theodore Dwight protested: "I love every line of In a Transport & have always loved it." Dwight to Stoddard, 7 August 1892 (CSTO, University of Notre Dame Archives); quoted in Stroven, "A Life," p. 272.

24. *Dial* 16 (October 1892), 245.

25. *Catholic World*, October 1892, 133.

26. Norton quoted in Stoddard to Daniel Hudson, 16 January 1893 (CHUD, University of Notre Dame Archives); quoted in Stroven, "A Life," p. 275.

27. Rudyard Kipling to Stoddard, 30 October 1892 (The Bancroft Library, University of California, Berkeley).

CHAPTER 10

1. Stoddard to Daniel Hudson, 4 December 1895 (CHUD, University of Notre Dame Archives); quoted in Carl G. Stroven, "A Life of Charles Warren Stoddard," (Ph.D. diss., Duke University, 1939), p. 283.

2. Stoddard to Daniel Hudson, 4 December 1895 (CHUD, University of Notre Dame Archives); quoted in Stroven, "A Life," p. 283.

3. Letter copied in Diary, 22 October 1895 (The Catholic University of America).

4. Stoddard to Daniel Hudson, 4 December 1895 (CHUD, University of Notre Dame Archives); quoted in Stroven, "A Life," p. 283.

5. Stoddard to Daniel Hudson, 9 December 1895 (CHUD, University of Notre Dame Archives).

6. Ethel Armes, "Aloha, Wela, Wela!," *National Magazine* 21 (December 1904), 315–16.

7. Hamlin Garland, *Roadside Meetings* (New York: Macmillan, 1931), pp. 366–67.

8. Quoted in Patrick Ahern, *The Catholic University of America, 1887–1896* (Washington, D.C.: Catholic University of America Press, 1948), p. 180.

9. Stoddard to Daniel Hudson, 12 November 1896, 7 October 1897 (CHUD, University of Notre Dame Archives).

10. Stoddard to Daniel Hudson, 6 March 1896 (CHUD, University of Notre Dame Archives); quoted in Stroven, "A Life," p. 284.

11. Egan was not unaware of Stoddard's achievements as a writer, which he praised in "Cameos: VII—Charles Warren Stoddard," *Ave Maria* 50 (3 February 1900), 149–51.

12. Stoddard to Daniel Hudson, 6 March 1896 (CHUD, University of Notre Dame Archives); quoted in Stroven, "A Life," p. 284.

13. Maurice Francis Egan, *Recollections of a Happy Life* (Murray Hill, N.Y.: George H. Doran, 1924), p. 187.

14. Dwight's interest in Italian boys was undiminished, however. From Rome, he sent Stoddard some pictures and an account of his visit to Pluschow's

studio: "Pluschow himself was not visible but I was given all the opportunities to see his collection, without, apparently, any expectation of [a] sale, by his German assistant. . . . While we were talking who should come in but a very handsome, black haired & mustachioed Italian, quite stout built, broad shouldered, perhaps 24 years old, who seemed anxious to be noticed & very much in command of the place; & presently I learned that he was Vincenzo Goldi, the subject of so many of our pictures. He posed for those in sitting posture on the wall, with a fillet round his head & with Edoardo, the more beautiful youth, in an infinite number of others. I told him that I knew him from the soles of his feet to the top of his head & he immediately became most talkative, showing me all his favorite attitudes. We established such friendly relations that I have now the privilege of making photos myself in the Pluschow studio & of his models." Theodore Dwight to Stoddard, 18 January 1896 (CSTO, University of Notre Dame Archives).

15. Stoddard to Daniel Hudson, 21 May 1897 (CHUD, University of Notre Dame Archives).

16. Stoddard to Daniel Hudson, 17 March 1897 (CHUD, University of Notre Dame Archives); quoted in Stroven, "A Life," p. 288.

17. The inscription is quoted in Charles E. Goodspeed's 1909 sale catalog of Stoddard's library.

18. Charles E. Goodspeed, *Yankee Bookseller* (Boston: Houghton Mifflin, 1937), pp. 91–92.

19. "Between Balestier and Kipling it was a case of camaraderie and of love, almost at first sight. Platonic, quite clearly. Both would have been terrified at any other suggestion." Leon Edel, *Stuff of Sleep and Dreams: Experiments in Literary Psychology* (New York: Harper & Row, 1982), p. 335.

20. "Rudyard Kipling at Naulakha," *National Magazine* 18 (June 1903), 268.

21. Ibid.

22. Thomas Russell Sullivan, *Passages from the Journal of Thomas Russell Sullivan, 1891–1903* (Boston: Houghton Mifflin, 1917), pp. 180–81.

23. Sydney Coffin, "Travel 6,000 Miles to Find Kin's Ashes," *Nantucket Light* 1 (2 October 1964), 10. See also John W. Crowley, "Eden Off Nantucket: W. S. Bigelow and 'Tuckanuck,'" *Essex Institute Historical Collections* 109 (January 1973), 3–8.

24. Stoddard's "Tuckernuck" ran in four installments: *Ave Maria* 58 (2 January–23 January 1904). See also "Nantucket Notes," *Ave Maria* 56 (3 January–31 January 1903).

25. Edith Wharton, "George Cabot Lodge," *Scribner's Magazine* 47 (February 1910), 236.

26. Cecil A. Spring-Rice, quoted in William Miller, *Henry Cabot Lodge: A Biography* (New York: Heineman, 1967), p. 17. See also John W. Crowley, *George Cabot Lodge* (Boston: Twayne, 1976).

27. Stoddard to George Cabot Lodge, 27 September 1900 (location unknown).

28. Yone Noguchi, "In the Bungalow with Charles Warren Stoddard," *National Magazine* 21 (December 1904), 307.

29. Stoddard to Daniel Hudson, 23 April 1898 (CHUD, University of Notre Dame Archives).

30. Stoddard to Daniel Hudson, 25 May 1898 (CHUD, University of Notre Dame Archives).

31. Stoddard to DeWitt Miller, 9 June 1898 (HM 38370, The Huntington Library, San Marino, California).

32. Stroven, "A Life," p. 293. Stoddard later wrote to Father Hudson, 8 February 1907: "When he [Kenneth] went to Cuba he seemed to have had his finer instincts blunted" (CHUD, University of Notre Dame Archives).

33. Stoddard to DeWitt Miller, 15 October 1901 (HM 38383, The Huntington Library).

34. Dr. Irving C. Rosse, quoted in Jonathan Katz, *Gay American History: Lesbians and Gay Men in the U.S.A.* (New York: Crowell, 1976), p. 42.

35. "A Life's Labyrinth," entry for 24 December 1901, 1 January 1902 (The Bancroft Library, University of California, Berkeley).

36. Stoddard to DeWitt Miller, 10 September 1907 (HM 38407, The Huntington Library).

37. "A Life's Labyrinth," entry for 13 November 1901 (Bancroft Library); quoted in Stroven, "A Life," pp. 291–92.

38. Stoddard to Daniel Hudson, 1 January 1902 (CHUD, University of Notre Dame Archives).

39. "A Life's Labyrinth," entry for 7 April 1903 (Bancroft Library).

40. Stoddard to Daniel Hudson, 1 August 1902 (CHUD, University of Notre Dame Archives).

41. Robert L. Gale, *Charles Warren Stoddard*, Western Writers Series, no. 30 (Boise, Id.: Boise State University Press, 1977), p. 42.

42. John Berryman, *Stephen Crane* (New York: William Sloan, 1950), p. 86.

43. "He [Stoddard] is misunderstood by many—as Kipling, one of his most sympathetic friends, predicted he was bound to be when he read 'For the Pleasure of His Company.'" Charles Phillips, "Charles Warren Stoddard," *Overland Monthly*, n.s. 51 (February 1908), 139.

44. William Morton Payne, *Dial* 35 (1 October 1903), 155. The reviewer for the *Sunset* excused the novel on the grounds that it was "the child not of his thought, but of his heart," and interpreted it as a possible sermon with this message: "Do not judge men solely by outward appearances; try to read into their souls and learn the true characters before you condemn." *Sunset* 13 (July 1903), 283–84.

45. *Overland Monthly*, n.s. 42 (October 1903), 365. The headline over the *Out West* review was "A Story Without a Plot."

46. Josephine DeWitt Rhodehamel and Raymund Francis Wood, *Ina Coolbrith, Librarian and Laureate of California* (Provo: Brigham Young University Press, 1973), p. 253. See Stoddard's comment on the novel in his Notebook: "It has perhaps made me some friends; has worried some old ones; has stirred the venom in the hearts of some enemies" (Bancroft Library).

47. Ibid., p. 440, n. 46. Stoddard nevertheless annotated George Wharton James's copy of the novel, providing him a key to its characters and events. See

George Wharton James, "Charles Warren Stoddard—An American Appreciation," *Ave Maria* 68 (22 May 1909), 650–56.

48. Stoddard to W. D. Howells, 21 July 1903 (Houghton Library, Harvard
University).

CHAPTER 11

1. Diaries for the period November 1901 to August 1903 are in the Bancroft
Library, University of California, Berkeley. On the first page of the diary that
covers the period from 6 April to 24 April 1903 was written: "The Resurrection
and the Life of Charles Warren Stoddard who descended into the Limbo of the
Catholic University and of Washington D.C., but who rose again from the dead
after fourteen grievous years on Monday of Passion Week, 1903." Quoted in
Carl G. Stroven "A Life of Charles Warren Stoddard," (Ph.D. diss., Duke
University, 1939), p. 297, n. 12.

2. Stoddard to Daniel Hudson, 16 June 1903 (CHUD, University of Notre
Dame Archives).

3. LaRose was a leader among those Harvard undergraduates in the 1890s
who had aped Oscar Wilde's "decadence" and who had founded a Bohemian
little magazine, *The Mahogany Tree*. See Shirley Johnson's fictional portrait of
this group in *The Cult of the Purple Rose* (Boston: Richard Badger, 1902).

4. Kenneth O'Connor also came to Stoddard's bedside. It was to be their last
meeting.

5. [Pierre Beringer], "Charles Warren Stoddard," *Overland Monthly*, n.s. 43
(April 1904), 346.

6. *Overland Monthly*, n.s. 44 (July 1904), 24.

7. Stoddard to Daniel Hudson, 28 October 1904 (CHUD, University of Notre
Dame Archives).

8. "A Summer Rest," *Ave Maria* 65 (6 July 1907), 4.

9. Henry James quoted in Leon Edel, *Henry James, The Master: 1901–1916*
(Philadelphia: Lippincott, 1972), p. 286.

10. Ibid., p. 285.

11. *The Annals of the Bohemian Club*, ed. Clay M. Greene, vol. 4 (San
Francisco: The Bohemian Club, 1930), pp. 214–15.

12. The events of the Bohemian Club dinner are reported in "Welcome to the
Author of *South-Sea Idyls*," the San Francisco *Call*, 14 April 1905, p. 1.

13. In *The Ambassadors* (New York: Harper, 1903). This famous remark was
James's version of something reportedly said by W. D. Howells to Jonathan
Sturges. See *The Notebooks of Henry James*, ed. F. O. Matthiessen and Ken-
neth B. Murdock (New York: Oxford University Press, 1947), pp. 225–28.

14. See Leon Edel, *Henry James, The Treacherous Years: 1895–1901* (Philadelphia: Lippincott, 1969), pp. 306–16; *Henry James, The Master: 1901–1916*,
pp. 181–91.

15. Diaries for early June 1905 are in the Stanford University Library. Diaries
for the period late June to October 1905 are in Robert Louis Stevenson House,
Monterey, California.

16. "From a Bay Window," *Ave Maria* 66 (7 March 1908).

17. Michael Orth, "A Biography of George Sterling" (M.A. Thesis, San Francisco State University, 1963), pp. 10–11.

18. George Sterling to Stoddard, 30 September 1907 (Bancroft Library). The poem is reprinted in Clark Ashton Smith, "George Sterling, An Appreciation," *Overland Monthly and Out West Magazine* 85 (March 1927), 79.

19. Quoted in M. E. Grenander, "Ambrose Bierce and Charles Warren Stoddard: Some Unpublished Correspondence," *Huntington Library Quarterly* 23 (May 1960), 290.

20. Ibid.

21. Andrew Sinclair, *Jack: A Biography of Jack London* (New York: Harper & Row, 1977), p. 24.

22. Ibid., p. 181.

23. *Letters From Jack London*, ed. King Hendricks and Irving Shephard (New York: Odyssey Press, 1965), pp. 354–55.

24. Ibid., p. 251.

25. Stoddard to Jack London, 13 August 1903; letter copied in Stoddard's Notebook (Bancroft Library).

26. Inscription quoted in Charles E. Goodspeed, *Yankee Bookseller* (Boston: Houghton Mifflin, 1937), p. 91.

27. Stoddard to Horace Traubel, 8 October 1906; letter copied in IH (Bancroft Library).

28. Monterey Diary, pp. 92, 97 (Department of Special Collections, The Stanford University Libraries).

29. M. M. Marberry, *Splendid Poseur: Joaquin Miller, American Poet* (New York: Crowell, 1953), p. 257.

30. Stoddard to Daniel Hudson, 13 May 1906 (CHUD, University of Notre Dame Archives).

31. "A Life's Labyrinth," p. 17 (Bancroft Library).

32. Ibid., p. 28.

33. Ibid., pp. 20–21.

34. Stoddard to Harry McKenzie, 3 August 1906; letter copied in Stoddard's Notebook (Bancroft Library).

35. Mary Austin quoted in Brian McGinty, "Charles Warren Stoddard: The Pleasure of His Company," *California Historical Quarterly* 52 (Summer 1973), 166.

36. Stoddard to Ina Coolbrith, 19 August 1907 (Bancroft Library).

37. George Wharton James, "Charles Warren Stoddard," *National Magazine* 34 (August 1911), 667.

38. Stoddard was also drafting his autobiography. A section on his youth, titled "Confessions of a Reformed Poet," was completed but never published; a section on his early childhood remained unfinished at his death.

39. Stoddard to Ina Coolbrith, 20 February 1907 (Donohue Rare Book Room, Gleeson Library, University of San Francisco) Robert Ballard to Stoddard, 19 March 1906 (Bancroft Library); Stoddard to Sarah Makee, 25 January 1906 (University of Hawaii at Manoa Library); Yone Noguchi quoted in Stroven, "A

Life"; Stoddard to Jack London (The Huntington Library, San Marino, California); Stoddard to Booth Tarkington, 26 August 1905 (location unknown).

40. Stoddard to Horace Traubel (Bancroft Library); Herbert Peet to Stoddard, 9 October 1907 (Bancroft Library); Corinne O'Connor to Stoddard, 10 August 1906 (Bancroft Library); Iza Hardy to Stoddard, 28 July 1905 (IC 349, The Huntington Library).

41. Stoddard to Daniel Hudson, 18 November 1905, 9 December 1906, 22 April 1908 (CHUD, University of Notre Dame Archives); Stoddard to DeWitt Miller, 10 September 1907 (HM 38407, The Huntington Library); Stoddard to Mark Twain, 27 May 1907 (Mark Twain Papers, Bancroft Library); Stoddard to Benton Gifford, 8 February 1907 (Robert Louis Stevenson House).

42. Stoddard to Ethel Armes (location unknown); Stoddard to Edwin McKenzie, 17 January 1906 (location unknown); Stoddard to George DeVoll, 15 March 1906 (Bancroft Library).

43. Stoddard to DeWitt Miller, 10 January 1907 (HM 38405, The Huntington Library).

44. See Roger Austen, *Playing the Game: The Homosexual Novel in America* (Indianapolis: Bobbs-Merrill, 1977), pp. 20–27.

45. Tan Notebook (Bancroft Library).

46. *The Poems of Charles Warren Stoddard*, ed. Ina Coolbrith and Thomas Walsh (New York: John Lane, 1917). One reviewer criticized the omissions from this "collected" edition, placing the blame for inept editing on Father Thomas Walsh, who had known Stoddard at Notre Dame. See Edward F. O'Day, "*The Poems of Charles Warren Stoddard*," *Town Talk* 30 (25 August 1918), 5–6.

47. See "Find Dying Poet Made Bonfire of Manuscripts of All of His Work," San Francisco *Bulletin*, 9 October 1909 (Ina Coolbrith Papers, Bancroft Library).

48. Xavier Mayne [Edward I. Prime-Stevenson], *Imre: A Memorandum* (Naples, Italy: The English Book Club: R. Rispoli, 1906), p. 188.

Index

Index